Clipper Studies in the Theatre
ISSN 0748-237X
Number Five

INK

from a

CIRCUS PRESS AGENT

An Anthology of Circus History
From the Pen of Charles H. Day

by

Charles H. Day

Edited and with a Circus Personnel Reference Roster
by William L. Slout

R. REGINALD
The Borgo Press
San Bernardino, California   MCMXCV

THE BORGO PRESS

Twentieth Anniversary, 1975-1995
Post Office Box 2845
San Bernardino, CA 92406
United States of America

*   *   *   *   *   *   *

Copyright © 1995 by William L. Slout

Library of Congress Cataloging-in-Publication Data

Day, Charles H., 1842-1907.
    Ink from a circus press agent : an anthology of circus history from the
pen of Charles H. Day / by Charles H. Day : edited and with a circus
personnel reference roster by William L. Slout.
    p. cm. — (Clipper studies in the theatre, ISSN 0748-237X ; no. 5)
    Includes index.
    ISBN 0-8095-0302-6 (cloth). — ISBN 0-8095-1302-1 (pbk.)
    1. Circus—History—19th century. I. Slout, William L. (William Law-
rence) II. Title. III. Series.
GV1801.D38 1995   94-28522
791.3'09'034—dc20   CIP

FIRST EDITION

CONTENTS

To my dear colleague,
HARRY CAULEY,
for thirty-five years of friendship

ACKNOWLEDGMENTS

I am indebted to Fred Dahlinger, Jr., Director of the Robert L. Parkinson Library and Research Center at the Circus Word Museum, Baraboo, Wisconsin, for the help and encouragement he has extended in the development of this anthology. I also want to express my appreciation to Leonor De La Vega and her staff at the Hertzberg Circus Collection and Museum, San Antonio, Texas, for hospitality shown me during my research there.

INTRODUCTION

At a time when most communities had little in the way of entertainment, the traveling circus, under its canvas pavilions, brought thrill, spectacle, and wonderment to a longing public. At a time when isolated audiences knew little about natural history, the circus introduced them to the zoo and museum---animals and oddities---experiences which they would not have otherwise had. The circus, at best, was a most marvelous entertainment, bringing momentary joy to millions and millions of people.

The growth of circus activity closely followed the growth of other aspects of American culture, beginning in the late 18th century and continuing until competing amusements and advancing technology made its mode of operation obsolete. This is most clearly illustrated in the areas of transportation and commercial growth. Circus history is interwoven with the history of waterways, roadways and railways as these facilities evolved from crude paths to complicated networks of steel. The transition from the use of a single wagon to multi-car rail transportation, from one-ring to three-ring spectacles, and from fifty-foot round-tops to huge tent cities, reflects the burgeoning of American industry and commerce during this same period.

The early equestrian troupes were housed in semi-permanent facilities within metropolitan areas. As early as 1795, Ricketts' Amphitheatre in New York City was thoroughly renovated to include "scenery, machinery, decorations, etc.," a move that marked the beginning in America of combining the equestrian arena and the dramatic stage into a single spectacle, forcing horsemen to become actors and actors to become horsemen. Early 19th century extravaganzas, such as "Timour the Tartar" and "The Cataract of the Ganges," were adapted for use in the ring, allowing the circus program to become more varied and more competitive with the regular theatres.

During the first three decades of the 19th century the conditions for land travel were irregular. Only the northern and eastern sections of the country and as far west as Pittsburgh offered favorable routes. When, during the War of 1812, the British cut off the sailing lanes for commerce between the northern and southern states, it forced increased activity in road building and more rapid improvements in land travel. Still, road development dates from the beginning of construction on the Cumberland route in 1808, a project designed to establish a permanent thoroughfare from the Atlantic Ocean to the Mississippi River. It took nine years for the workmen to reach Ohio but, until mid-century, the Cumberland Road was the chief artery from east to west.

Meanwhile, the urban circuses were hard pressed to operate profitably on a regular basis. Competing summer gardens, seaside resorts, athletic events, and more vigorous dramatic performances were usurping a share of the entertainment dollar. The combining of the ring and stage for horse dramas meant keeping two companies on the payroll---riders and actors---and laying out money for elaborate and expensive scenic effects to create greater spectacle. So, when travel became more feasible, when improved roads allowed them to move heavily loaded wagons with modest regularity, enterprising showmen left the cities and trouped their equestrian companies up and down the eastern seaboard and then inland, following the expanding frontier. Where halls and barns were not available, shows were performed behind canvas fencing, open to the whims of the elements.

It was soon determined that some sort of portable shelter was necessary to forestall costly lay-offs brought on by unpleasant weather. So the ring was placed under a canvas cover. What appears to be one of the earliest uses of a tent pavilion devoted to entertainments in America was constructed in 1823 at Chatham Garden, "a resort of beauty and fashion of New York." However, there is nothing to suggest that the structure was designed for portability and, since Chatham Garden was a place for summer gatherings, it is logical to assume that the sides of the pavilion were not enclosed.

The early circus tents were round-tops, measuring 50 feet or more in diameter, held up by a single pole in the center and by several smaller ones around the perimeter. Canvas sidewall protected the performances from those who might prefer to see the show without passing the ticket wagon. But by mid-century, competition was pushing circuses to provide greater spectacle, which forced them to enlarge their portable facilities. With the addition of a second ring and hippodrome track, the old round-top became an extended oval. Any number of "middle-pieces" could be added to the "round-ends," much like the leaves to a dining room table, to make the tent more spacious. Canvas pavilions grew even larger when, in 1871, P. T. Barnum opened his Great Traveling World's Fair. The show was equipped with "vast tents covering nearly three acres of ground." By 1881, the impresario boasted he had enlarged his "already immense tents three different times" to accommodate the crowds.

This kind of growth could not have continued without the establishment of a complex railroad system throughout the country. Although full development took the entire 19th century, once the locomotive problem was solved by the creation of Stephenson's Rocket in 1829, track mileage spread steadily. The 9,000 miles in 1850 increased within a ten year period to a national railway system of around 50,000 and by 1880 there was a total of 93,000.

Still, circuses were slow in making full use of rail transportation. There was a variance in gauge from one rail line to another that made train travel cumbersome. Circuses moving on cars designed to operate on one gauge had to unload and transfer equipment to cars compatible with the gauge of another line. And routing a show was restricted by limitations in track mileage, regardless of gauge. But by mid-century rail transportation began to take hold. In 1853, Charles H. Castle and H. M. Whitbeck originated a show out of Cincinnati "designed to travel by steamboat, canal and railroad." In 1856, Spalding & Rogers' New Railroad Circus went on the road with "the ring, marquee, seats, performers, horses, stables, and all the appurtenances being carried in railway cars built for the purpose and so constructed they can be used on any road." O. W. Hyatt's Great Railroad Circus was performing around Ohio in 1859. James M. Nixon's Railroad Circus was out in 1863. In 1864, Robinson & Howes announced they were traveling by rail in the mid-western part of the country. Haight & Chambers disposed of their baggage stock in Atlanta in 1866 and began to utilize rail travel. And, finally, with the completion of the transcontinental railroad, Dan Castello and his company made an historic tour to the Pacific coast, facilitated by the show's capability of traveling on country roads when the management wanted to play towns off the established lines.

The early uses of rail travel were exceptions rather than the rule. It wasn't until 1872, the second season of P. T. Barnum's Great Traveling Exposition and World's Fair, that a serious commitment to railroading occurred. The show toured sixteen states in an area as far west as Kansas. One of the proprietors, William C. Coup, can be given credit for innovations in the design of flat cars and for developing special techniques in the loading and unloading of them and for the intricate planning of railroad scheduling so that shows were able to make longer jumps between towns and carry more equipment and personnel.

With the transition to permanent rail travel, the American circus entered its golden age, featuring mammoth street parades, three rings of continuous performance, huge spreads of canvas, and a company comprised of literally hundreds of performers and working men. This was also an age of brutal competition, paralleling that of American industry and banking. Huge sums were spent on advertising, with billing crews covering the surrounding towns and countryside for a fifty mile radius. Press agent Welles Hawks paid this tribute to these indomitable workmen:

> ... But it is the billposter with the sack of small bills swung across his shoulder and with bucket and brush who does the work often most conspicuous. No smooth surface that will hold a bill ever misses his eye. The sign "Post No Bills" does not always terrorize him, for he has been known to post his bills over the warning.

The use of large lithographs for advertising purposes began in the mid-19th century, a technique pioneered by the American circus. These lithos, which depicted with splashes of color the exciting events within the circus program---horsemanship, trapeze flying, animals, etc.---were daubed on the sides of structures or on fences or wherever there was a flat surface within public viewng. Each "stand" included as much litho paper as the space allowed. A single sheet, 28 x 42 inches [which was as large as could be printed on the old presses], was called a one-sheet. It was not uncommon to see as much as a 100-sheet spread on the side of a large building.

By the latter part of the 19th century, there was a sizable billposting industry, enough to encourage the creation of a trade paper, *Billboard*, which was founded in 1893. Because many of the readers were people connected with outdoor amusements, by 1900 the paper was running news items relating to circuses, as will as carnivals, fairs, etc. Within ten years from its origin, the *Billboard* had changed its emphasis to become a show business weekly.

Once the railroads extended westward, cities and towns seemed to appear overnight, opening avenues for adventurous amusement enterprises. Touring companies of every variety proliferated this growing country, competing side by side, vying for the entertainment dollar. With newspapers operating on a continuing basis in almost every community in the country by mid-19th century, the industrious age of advertising began and the circus was in the forefront, puffing attractions through concoctions of word and picture.

The circus parade, symbolic of the events within the large, white tents, also served as a dynamic advertisement. In earliest times, the "mud shows" made a "grand entry" into town, after having halted on the outskirts to wash the wagons, don parade costumes, and bedeck the horses and equipment with fancy trappings. But, when shows expanded their capacity to transport an unlimited amount of paraphernalia by flat and stock car, the parade evolved into an immense processional of elaborately carved pageant and band wagons [featuring mythological and Biblical scenes], elephants, camels, elegantly comparisoned horses with plumed and bejeweled harnesses, and performers on foot in glittering costumes, all designed to enhance a moral and educational image of the circus. The parade, a moving pageant along the main streets of America, became an immense show in itself, always pro-portionately indicative of the attractions inside the tents. But when the modern circus eliminated it from the daily schedule, there was buried once and for all an important part of circus tradition.

Company titles reflected the circuses' aggressive promotional methods, as they emphasized in glowing promises the coming of the show. For examples, there were *Montgomery Queen's Great European Menagerie, Transatlantic Circus, Roman Hippodrome, and Troupe of Bedouin Arabs; VanAmburgh & Co.'s Great Golden Menagerie, Combination Circus, Roman and Egyptian Museum, Captain John Grimley's Great Australian Bird Show, etc;* and *L. B. Lent's Leviathan Universal Living Exposition, Metropolitan Museum, Mastodon Menagerie, Hemispheric Hippozoonomadon, Cosmographic Caravan, Equescurriculum, Great New York Circus,* and *Monster Musical Brigade.* These titles appear to be parodies but, seemingly, they were meant to be taken seriously, even though they were in all probability inspirations from the productive mind of a press agent or bill writer.

Perhaps the most colorful breed of men in circusdom was the press corps. H. E. "Punch" Wheeler, prominent as one of the profession, defined the circus press agent as "an umpire between the show and the newspapers, to see that neither one of them gets the worst of it too much." It was the agent's duties to "propound the myth of prosperity," to bolster the sagging coffers of their employers in the face of untold public apathy, to build an eminence through printed matter, sprightly and star-spangled, indelibly and eternally marking their circuses' greatness. The successful agent was endowed with a lively imagination. A constant flow of ideas was essential in keeping his client before the public. His mind was a dictionary of superlatives to fit any and all situations. His conscience was without moral impediments, which allowed him to freely advance unlimited, unsubstantiated claims. And, yes, he was a writer of some ability. [However, there is some disagreement on this point. Many successful agents were notoriously bad journalists.] Finally, he performed with a certain *savoir-faire* under fire, enabled him to boldly carry out a gigantic farce in the face of a dubious working press.

Exuberance of language---with dash, zest, and flair---was the press agent's tool. With it, he created a unique style of writing. Such phrases as "a congestion of amusement" and "a resonant tantara of merriment" were not uncommon. Words were pumped into copy as air into a balloon, tinseled, splashed, tandemmed, alliterated, creating "ballyhoo" through a most colorful language. The climate of competition between the big shows led to a war of words, as claims were made and countered about the stupendous wonders under the "big top." Press agents had free rein and their language was the language of joy.

With the merging of the two behemoths of the industry into the combined shows of Ringling Brothers and Barnum & Bailey, the need for big catch words disappeared. The "big show" really was big. It really was a "scintillating, kaleidoscopic, unparalleled, heterogeneous, aggregation of multiplied wonders." The sizzling pace of the 20th century, uncovering before our very eyes true marvels of the advancement of man, has created a condition that dwarfs all language. The press agent's big tool, his hyperbole, has been rendered impotent by our realization of real wonders, actual wonders that are more colossal than mere words.

Times have changed. Today there are far fewer circuses touring the country. The famed Ringling Brothers, Barnum & Bailey Circus---'The Greatest Show on Earth"---performs in indoor arenas with their two units. The new ownership reflects the state of the modern circus, run by a corps of business executives in "gray suits" who read complicated surveys and rely on the impersonal messages from computers. Gone are the old managers who figured by rule of thumb, who were there to batter the elements and lead the charge from town to town. Gone are the deep traditions of the circus wanderer. There is an appearance of youth about the Ringling show today, a new generation of performers, perhaps establishing new traditions. The circus acts are the same, only more elaborate---more like the Ziegfeld Follies than the old wagon show. The three rings are alive with action. The death defying acts still pack a thrill. The spectacle is as breathtaking as ever. And one can still smell the elephants from the fifteenth row. The circus hasn't disappeared. No! It is "bigger than ever." And it will remain that way until next year, when it "will be even bigger."

Charles H. Day, author of this anthology, was representative of the old school of "puffers." One of the leading press agents and bill writers of his time, he was most active in the circus business from 1872 to 1887, often working under the title of "Director of Publications," which usually appeared along with his name on the various booklets and bills he created. His first season of show life was with Sol Smith Russell and a small concert company. Early in his career, he was manager and agent for negro minstrel troupes, such as those of William Arlington, W. W. Newcomb, Sam Sharpley, and W. S. Cleveland.

Interest in writing was probably cultivated when as a youth he worked in his father's book exchange. As a free lance scribe, he published more than 100 pieces, contributing articles to the *New York Clipper, Billboard, New York Dramatic Mirror,* and the *Sporting and Theatrical Journal* over a thirty-five year period.

Day was noted for his originality of thought and expression, for his ability to put on paper that "which oft was thought but ne'er so well expressed." His couriers [advertising booklets] were always original, "surpassing in range of thought and vividness any published by circuses at that time." In writing opposition bills, he straightforwardly described the short-comings of rival shows in a frank and convincing manner. It might be added that Day's belief in the power of press agentry extended to his personal pursuits. He was unique in his particular profession by consistently publicizing himself through display advertising in the *New York Clipper.*

Considered by his colleagues to be "a man of energy and resource" [One called him "a spectacular figure in the amusement world."], he was a gentleman of the old school, a congenial, convivial companion. Grant Parish, in a portrait of Day for the Cincinnati *Sporting and Dramatic Journal* of March 21, 1885, wrote, "When he was born, he was a man---he never was a boy. When he first saw daylight, his head revolved with schemes and, ever since, his mind has been rattling away on new ideas to startle mankind." But Day's appearance belied his competitive nature. As one writer put it:

Physically Charlie has not much to boast of, and as an athlete, lion tamer or acrobat would be of no consequence whatever to the great aggregation with which he is connected, but mentally he is a giant, and measures fourteen inches to a foot and weighs seventeen ounces to a pound every time. He has by times crushed opposition with a few strokes of his fluent pen and paralyzed every traveling show that dared to compete with the great aggregation that has its winter quarters in the home where its renown proprietor was born and expects to die, too, when he is called upon to succumb to the inevitable. In fact, Charlie is the Warwick of the profession of showmen, and has both built up and pulled down those who have made a mistake in his caliber mentally because of his delicate construction physically.

In 1902, after his retirement, he married a young lady of only twenty-three years of age. [I have found no evidence of a previous marriage.] He died five years later, on October 3, 1907, in New Haven, CT, of erysipelas at the age of sixty-five.

In putting together this volume, I have purposely excluded Day's professional "puffery" and fiction writing in order to serve a greater interest in Day as a circus historian. Part One of the volume is comprised of selected articles taken from a variety of journals which follow this purpose. The pieces, having been written well over a period of thirty years, sometimes have moments of repetition. Occasionally, when these occur, I have made short deletions, always indicated with the standard elliptical marks.

Part Two features excerpts from Day's contributions as a weekly columnist for the Chicago and New York based *Sporting and Theatrical Journal* from 1884 to 1887. The paper was issued by the Adams & Corbett Publishing Co. At the outset, Charles C. Corbett was the editor. It was the claim of the publishers that the *Journal* contained more circus news than any other periodical in America. Day began writing under the column title of "Sawdust," with the first installment appearing in the November 22, 1884, issue. A title change to "Day-Light" occurred with the December 25, 1886 issue, because Day was not limiting his reportage to circus news alone but was looking into broader areas of the entertainment field. Or in his words, "The old, familiar 'Sawdust' confined my pen to the circus arena; but, hereafter, with the kind permission of Messrs. Adams and Miles, I shall have my say about matters and things in general." And, one may add, Day's voice was strongly opinionated.

The material in Part Two was compiled at the Hertzberg Circus Collection and Museum in San Antonio, TX, selected for its usefulness from a scrapbook with the cover description of "Circus Collection of Townsend Walsh. 791.084 circa 1885. SC-MISC #22." Here again, a large amount of anecdotal material has been culled to allow a greater focus on the items of factual value that lend insight to circus operation, circus personalities, and to Day's views regarding the showmanship of his time.

I have included a section of short biographical sketches of circus people mentioned in Day's text for the use of readers unfamiliar with the names of performers, cadre, and showmen of the period. The sketches are arranged alphabetically in a section under the heading, "Circus Personnel Reference Roster."

William L. Slout

THE DAY CHRONOLOGY

1842: Born in New York on the banks of the Mohawk but came to maturity in New Haven, CT., where his father ran a book exchange.

1868: On the road as agent with Billy Arlington and his Arlington Minstrels in and around the Chicago area.

1869-70: Agent with actress-manageress Laura Keene's company at the Chestnut Street Theatre, Philadelphia, opening September 20. The run was followed with a tour of the East and Midwest.

1870: Published his book *Fun in Black; or Sketches of Minstrel Life.*

1871: Agent for Newcomb & Arlington Minstrels, N.Y.C. Correspondent for *Sporting Times* and contributor to the *Sunday Mercury.*

1872: Published "Humors of Show Life," *New York Clipper,* February 10; "Wandering Showmen," *New York Clipper,* March 9; "The Fakir," *New York Clipper,* April 6; "Sawdust," *New York Clipper,* April 13; "Barnum on the Tented Field," *New York Clipper,* July 6; "With Tights and Spangles," *New York Clipper,* July 13; "In Winter Quarters," *New York Clipper,* August 10; "Showmen and Their Troubles," *New York Clipper,* August 31; "At the Dramatic Agency," *New York Clipper,* November 23; "Ancient and Modern Troubadours," *New York Clipper,* December 14; "On the Road," *New York Clipper,* December 28.

1873: Published "The One-Man Show," *New York Clipper,* January 25; "Seeing Tony Pastor," *New York Clipper,* March 22; "'Dried Up!' An Idyll of Oil Creek," *New York Clipper,* November 29.

1873-74: Spent the winter season composing press releases for Sharpley, Sheridan & Mack's Minstrels, N.Y.C.

1874: Published "Room No. 1, or A Night with the Circus Folks," *New York Clipper,* April 18.

1872-75: Was introduced to circus press agentry with a four season employment on the John H. Murray Circus, where he coined the phrase, "Refined Gold Needs No Gilding."

1875: Published "Sam Sharpley the Minstrel," *New York Clipper*, July 3.

1876: Agent with L. B. Lent's New York Circus. That year Day directed a rat bill at the Cooper & Bailey organization which declared, "Thirty scoundrels who feared the light of day had in the darkness of night and on the Sabbath Day circulated vile, slanderous and libelous literature, stating that the New York Circus had been quarantined on account of a small pox epidemic and would not exhibit as advertised."

1876: Published "Between The Acts in the Greenroom," *New York Clipper*, October 28.

1877: Director of Publications with John O'Brien's Six Separate Shows Consolidated.

1878: Agent with D. W. Stone's Grand Circus and Musical Brigade, which went to the barn early when the show failed to attract. Agent with W. C. Coup's Equescuricculum following the preceding engagement. One of Day's rat bills directed at an intruding rival sharply stated, "VanAmburgh Show Dissected! Post-Mortem of a Galvanized Corpse."

1879-81: Agent with Adam Forepaugh's Circus. Wrote every line of a 16 page newspaper, the *Adam Forepaugh Illustrated Feature Journal*, which included something of interest for every member of the household---helpful hints, poems, recipes, remedies for common ailments, and a children's section. Is credited with the idea for Forepaugh's $10,000 Beauty Contest and the pre-arranged selection of actress Louise Montague as the winner. First brought out for the season of 1881, her appearance with the show was profitable for Forepaugh. Day's street pageant, "Lalla Rookh's Departure from Delhi," with Miss Montague paraded atop the famous elephant, was a press agent's dream. Day was acknowledged for this contribution in a display ad within the December 17 *New York Clipper* of that year:

"HONOR TO WHOM HONOR IS DUE, THERE THE CREDIT BELONGS. To Managers, the Profession and the Public. During the summer of 1880, MR. CHARLES H. DAY of my staff suggested for an attraction for the season of 1881 the spectacular pageant of Lalla Rookh DEPARTING FROM DELHI with the HANDSOMEST WOMAN IN THE WORLD as the heroine. To that end I was induced by MR. DAY to advertise for The Loveliest Lady in the Land, offering a premium of $10,000 and inviting that photographs be submitted by contestants. The scheme was developed under MR. DAY'S personal direction, and in due time the award was made...... etc.

1879: Edited "A Clown's Log," *New York Clipper*, February 14, 21, 28. Published "Recollections and Reflections of a Retired Gymnast," *New York Clipper*, November 29.

1880: Published "The Eventful Career of Levi J. North," *New York Clipper*, March 6.

1882: Agent with Cooper & Jackson, Charles F. Cooper and Lyman A. Jackson, proprietors.

1883: Published "Bruce's Parlor Circus and Royal Melange, an Old-time Agent's First Managerial Experience," New *York Clipper*, March 17. Agent with Forepaugh & Adams' "Humpty Dumpty" Troupe, as announced in September.

1884: Agent with the Barnum & London Combined Shows, a merging of James A. Bailey's, and P. T. Barnum's circuses. Began his weekly column, "Sawdust," for the *Sporting and Theatrical Journal*. Published "The Lost Opera House," *New York Dramatic Mirror*, December 27.

1884-85: Wintered with Daniel Herzog's Museum, Washington, DC., resigning February 14, 1885.

1885: Is honored by Herzog's Museum, *New York Clipper*, February 28. Agent with VanAmburgh [Hyatt Frost], Charles Reiche & Brother. In a flyer announcing the shows 25-cent policy, Day added, "Blood on the face of the moon---war declared against VanAmburgh's Circus because it exhibits for 25 cents." Published "Circus Managers," Providence *Sunday Telegram*, May 17.

1886: Agent with Sells Bros.' Enormous Railroad Shows, which purported a "1st Trans-Continental Tour" and featured the clowning of Billy Burke and the equestrian feats of Willie Sells, William Gorman and Pauline Lee. His father, James B. Day, died on May 20, at his residence near Lake Whitney, Whitneyville, CT, where in late years he had been in the grocery and boat rental business. Following, Day went to New York to settle the estate as executor of the will.

1887: A return to Adam Forepaugh's Circus, with debut performances for Adam Forepaugh, Jr.'s "Blondin," the plank-walking horse, and the introduction of the sharp shooting act of Capt. A. H. Bogardus and Sons. Took an ad in the *New York Clipper*, July 2:

"UNMASKED! TO THE PRESS, MANAGERS AND BROTHER AGENTS. At my solicitation MR. ADAM FOREPAUGH gave temporary employment to one JOHN J. FOSTER, who at the end of the period for which he was engaged STABS ME IN THE BACK and assails MR. FOREPAUGH, proving himself unworthy of anyone's confidence."

Published a book in five chapters, advertised as "ready April 4," *Young Adam Forepaugh, Elephant Trainer*, selling for 25 cents (postal notes preferred, 1 and 2 cent stamps accepted).

1888: Began contributing to *The San Francisco Music and Drama*. Published "The Wild Man of Alaska," *New York Clipper*, January 7; "The Lion Tamer's Mother-in-Law, a Tragic Story in One Chapter," *New York Clipper*, January 21; "In the Minstrels' Dressing Room," *New York Clipper*, May 12; "Blood on the Face of the Moon!" *New York Clipper*, June 16; "Excommunicated," *New York Clipper*, July 7. Believed to have been agent for W. S. Cleveland's Magnificent, minstrel company, beginning in September.

1889: Published "C.O.D., $23.50, or An Advance Agent's Revenge," *New York Clipper*, June 15.

1892: Published "Concerning a Certain Circus Clem, Including a Romantic Relation," *New York Clipper*, November 5.

1897: Published "Cage 50," *New York Clipper*, December 4.

1898: Published "The Fat of the Land," *New York Clipper*, May 7.

1899: Published "Whoa, January," *New York Clipper*, July 8. Began a series of stories for *The Home Magazine* with "Tales of the Old Circus Man."

1900: Published "The Menagerie's Mascot," *New York Clipper*, January 6. Serialized a story for *Golden Hours*, "VanAmburgh, Elephant Performer and Lion Trainer."

1901: Published "The Invented Advertisement," *Billboard*, March 23; "The Elephant as an Advertisement," *Billboard*, March 23; "Taking One's Own Medicine," *Billboard*, April 6; "Shop Talk," *Billboard*, May 4; "Making Much of Music," *Billboard*, May 11; "Considering and Concerning the Children," *Billboard*, May 18. At 59 years of age, he married 23 year old Gertrude H. Garvey.

1903: Published "The Landlord Plays Santa Clause," *New York Clipper*, December 5.

1904: Published "Happy Days at the St. Charles," *Billboard*, November 5; "The Only Original Sam Johnson," *Billboard*, November 5.

1905: Published "The Press Agent's Antiquity," *New York Dramatic Mirror*, November 25.

1906: Contributed short biographies of circus notables to the Barnum & Bailey Annual Route Book. Published "History of American Circus and Tented Exhibitions," *Billboard*, December 29; January 5, 1907.

1907: Published "Fakirs, Freaks and Frauds," *Billboard*, May 11; "Charles Stowe, Circus Writer," *Billboard*, August 31; "Prominent Circus Managers," *Billboard*, September 7. Died of erysipelas at the hospital in New Haven, CT, October 3, age 65. He left a brother, William, residing in Whitneyville, CT. Published posthumously "The Intelligence of the Old-time Circus Manager," *Billboard*, November 9.

General Tom Thumb as Frederick the Great

Part One: Ballyhoo

The Charles H. Day Anthology

Prof. Richard Risley and His Children

THE PRESS AGENT'S ANTIQUITY

[*New York Dramatic Mirror*, November 25, 1905]

According to the misstatements of several recent magazine articles, the press agent in theatricals is a person of modern use and discovery, dating no further back than the days when Daniel Frohman secured a journalist to boom "Hazel Kirke."[1] The professional "writer," as he was called by the circus manager employing him, was so early appreciated that it tasks the memory and the records to state accurately when his career began, there being no evidence to prove that Noah took a purveyor of publicity into the Ark along with the menagerie. One of the first known scribes of the sawdust circle was a Mr. Cooke of the famous circus family of repute to this day in the United States and Great Britain. Mr. Cooke came to America to do the newspaper booming for an English importation.[2]

Spalding & Rogers and Spalding & Bidwell (their successors of circus and theatrical fame) employed a press agent, a very talented gentleman named Van Orden, the brother-in-law of Dr. Spalding. He is credited with having "made Dan Rice" with his pen.[3] This was certainly prior to the birth of the estimable Mr. Frohman.

P. T. Barnum, in his early days, was the bill writer and press agent of the New York Bowery Theatre and employed a press man in all his years of management of the American Museum; one of whom was credited with writing P. T.'s life, although Phineas, an ex-journalist, was perfectly capable of doing the job himself, as he undoubtedly did.[4]

With the origin of American stage negro minstrelsy, an outgrowth of the circus, several of the managers, circus bred, employed circus press agents to advertise their companies. Among these was Richard P. Jones, who was particularly successful in "working the papers." Even the use of "cuts" in the reading columns of newspapers is of no modern origin. The "first-part" scene, showing six people, was used as early as 1848 by Campbell's Minstrels and the letter press bears evidence of having been written by a professional adept.[5]

In placing Jenny Lind before the public, Barnum employed Charles G. Halpine, afterwards known as the soldier-poet Miles

O'Reilly, although the scribe passed as Barnum's "secretary." Scrapbooks in the possession of the writer prove that, between Barnum and Halpine, Jenny Lind secured a prodigious amount of publicity, unsurpassed in quantity and quality to this writing.[6]

Writing from personal knowledge, the title of press agent was used as long ago as 1868, at which time the undersigned joined the advance of the great Arlington Minstrels for the sole purpose of writing and securing the insertion of advance notices in the newspapers, Perry A. Waffle being the general agent.[7] On the distribution bill, the scribe was mentioned as "Director of Publications." At Troy, N.Y., the press agent met with his first rebuff in the office of the *Sunday Budget*, presided over by a blunt Scotsman named MacArthur. It was one of the few Sunday papers published in the country and was the amusement authority of the city (and ran a special department by Oscar Carpenter). The editor sat down on this press agent real hard, informed him that he and his staff did their own writing, reconsidered, and then blurted:

"Let's see what you can write!" pushing a pencil and paper within reach.

The notice was written and appeared, as did numerous others in after-years for a great variety of attractions; and many a hearty laugh did the scribe and the editor have over the former's warm reception on his first visit to the sanctum of the *Budget*.

In 1869, the writer joined Laura Keene at the Chestnut Street Theatre, Philadelphia, having been employed especially on account of his ability to write in addition to his other qualifications.[8] I performed all the duties of a press agent of today and also accompanied Miss Keene to Washington for a run of six weeks at Wall's Opera House. At the capital, I wrote the greater part of the advance notices for nearly all the daily and Sunday papers, as my veteran friends, John, Jack and Frank Mordaunt, will bear witness.

The following summer we went on tour in the West. Prior to the opening and during our two weeks' stay at the Opera House, St. Paul, I not only wrote all the advance notices but nearly every line of the criticisms, adapting my style to each daily and discreetly keeping my mouth shut. On this extended tour and that which followed through the South, I wrote also the advance notices, generally writing them in the offices and supplying no printed copy. Type-writing was of course unknown. How many others representing star attractions were doing the same thing I do not know.

*   *   *   *   *   *   *   *   *   *

In the winter of 1873-74, the same pen was called into requisition by Sam Sharpley, Sheridan & Mack at $40 per week and expenses, including "incidentals," a good off-season salary for a circus press agent.[9] Two other agents were employed, Tom Fitch and Jesse Kane.

Charles Gayler, the dramatist, author of Jack Emmett's first success, was an experienced circus press agent, for many years representing several of the largest tent shows. Like Mr. Pollock, he wrote his own plays and did his own press work to profitable purpose. Besides, he was his own manager and partner of the star. Mr. Gayler never laid any claim to being the first theatrical press agent.[10]

I will confess that, when I first sought editorial favor as a press agent, some of the powers were a little shy of "running your stuff" and even went so far as to copy it before sending it to the compositor. Lately, scribes have boldly advertised themselves as "promoters of publicity" without censure. But when I dubbed myself in the early '80's, in an advertisement for an engagement, as a "press manipulator," I got a warm jacketing from many newspapers that now welcome the press agent and his readable copy with the glad hand.

THE PRESS AGENTS OF WAY BACK
[*Billboard*, June 29, 1907]

The press agent of way back represented the circus. It was the circus manager who discovered the publicity promoter and the best use of advertising. It was related that at an early date a high-class English arenic organization appeared under cover in New York and that the exhibition was accompanied by a gentleman of literary gifts, of the famous Cooke family, who still hold prominent places in equestrian amusements on both sides of the Atlantic. Mr. Cooke's mission was to "look after the newspapers."

The press agent best known to fame was the original and impressive individual, Phineas Taylor Barnum. He was initiated into the business by the Turners, pioneer circus managers, who early in their career made Danbury, Conn., their headquarters and place of residence. Later, Barnum represented the Bowery Theatre, New York. Years afterward, while conducting the American Museum, he gave his personal attention and pen to booming his enterprise and was in close touch with the famous journalists, James Gordon Bennett, Horace Greeley, Henry J. Raymond, and Gen. Webb. During Barnum's entire career he was ever writing or suggesting and was particularly strong in cards, statements and proclamations. As to the work of his enlisted professional writers, he was an excellent judge and a severe critic. One season, when the big show was under the direct management of James A. Bailey, a great amount of copy for publication of distribution matter was prepared in New York by two of the best arenic scribes in the business and the entire mass of manuscript was forwarded to Bridgeport for the inspection of the head of the Greatest Show on Earth. The two writers had written without consultation, and each had cut loose with his best assortment of adjectives and assertions. The copy came back forthwith with the significant hint:

"Please lie with some sort of uniformity."

John Tryon, a printer, became a circus manager and his own press representative and bill writer, and he was one of the best bill writers that ever edited a program. (Some of the work of Seth B. Howes has never been surpassed.) For many years he boomed the arenic enterprises of James E. Kelley and associates, remaining in New York and preparing the advertising ammunition which was supplied the advance of the several enterprises. In event of opposition, Mr. Tryon appeared on the spot to thwart the enemy.

Dr. Richard P. Jones was in high repute with circus managers and, of a winter, he was in demand to boom the minstrels, the men in black being warm competitors. Jones was learned in many things and, being diminutive, was familiarly known as the "Little Doctor." It was he who invented the famous Adam Forepaugh trademark of "4-Paw," used by that showman to so much advantage.

Charles Gayler was a versatile man of commanding presence. He was educated for the law but got into the sawdust through writing for the "Flatfoots" for many years. Gayler was novelist, dramatist and journalist and made himself famous in fitting J. K. Emmett, the Dutch comedian, with several German plays.

Jabes Johnson was a humorist who wrote as U. B. Dam. He went out to California when the Golden State was new with Nixon & Castello.

William Adams was a fine writer---no better in the lot. Fortunately for himself, he joined the staff of the *New York Sun* and for years he was the right-hand man of Charles Dans. No proposal ever tempted him to again go with the red wagons. On his death, Mr. Dans paid him a particular tribute. He wrote of him as a journalist: "We have known as good, but none better."

Fred Lawrence was a writer of ancient memory, who for decades served the "Flatfoots" and was connected with Adam Forepaugh for many seasons. As good as they made them, Fred was a pessimist of direct type and was always filled with foreboding and a tale of woe. When he prophesied bad business, the show turned away people. His prognostications always amused Adam Forepaugh, if verbal. If written, he delegated a deputy to read the communications. One day Fred turned up with the show in an Ohio town and met the manager at the front door.

"What are the prospects?" asked Forepaugh.

"Bad. You can't get a plug of Gravely tobacco in town."

Chester Clarence Moore was a typesetter in Albany. He was credited with writing some red hot stuff for a scarifying sheet called *The Lash*. Dr. Spalding had a quarrel on with Dan Rice. The Doctor got Moore to write Rice down. Rice hired Moore to write up "Pills." And thus the war waged until the duplicity of Charles Clarence Moore was discovered. Moore was a practical joker, regardless of consequences. A delegation of Irishmen visited the New York Circus to hire the spotted horses for a Saint Patrick's Day parade. "Chet" impersonated Mr. Lent and promised them the horses. There was the deuce to pay when the party came after the calico steeds on Saint Patrick's Day in the morning.

George J. Guilford served the "Flatfoots" and "Old" John Robinson for many seasons. Guilford could write but was born tired and remained fatigued all his days. Peter Sells was wont to illustrate George's failings with an anecdote. Meeting him in Cincinnati one day, the scribe of the sawdust struck the arrival for the loan of a twenty. Peter was agreeable and produced the note. The lethargic Guilford did not clutch it with the anticipated avidity, he only drawled:

"Put it in my vest pocket, please."

William C. Crum was a cousin of Dan Rice and wore spinach on his chin the same as the Colonel. He attempted the role of performer while with Rice and was so popular in the company that they threw a pillow into the ring for him to alight on in somersaulting. He was a religious fanatic and while with Adam Forepaugh attempted to cut out the manager's Sunday advertising.

A. P. Newkirk was humorous and original and could keep his end up in a circus war. The VanAmburgh party thought highly of him.

Fred Hunt was one of the old guard. He wrote an extended biography of Dan Rice, the Colonel supplying the facts and footing the bill, but [it] never saw print.

Charles Stow, poet and epigramist, was at one time editor of Dan Rice's newspaper, the *Cosmopolite*, published at Girard, Pa. For years Stow was James A. Bailey's favorite bill writer.

William W. Durand, before he wrote circus literature, was city editor of the *Louisville Courier-Journal*, under the control of the talented George D. Prentiss. Durand was a close contractor for advertising space. One day he ran up against an unusually tough customer, who claimed [a] seven thousand circulation.

"What did you say was the name of your sheet?" William W. inquired.

"*Truth*," was the reply.

"Change it," exclaimed Durand.

John A. Wood wrote his circus literature with a view of attracting the attention of the farmer and was quite happy in the rural vein.

John H. Murray informed the writer that there was a Charles Day, press agent, in the business years before Charles H. came to the front.

This relation appertains to the ancient and honorable, only, and does not include even that lively young fellow, "Tody" Hamilton, who, with his brother Jack, appeared later on. The press agents of way back were a clever lot, although their thrifty employers looked upon them as [being] regardless of the value of money and disinclined to put aside a dollar for a rainy day and, as a class, so many grown up children with the literary gift.

The scribes rode over the pike with the route agent and principal contractor ahead of the "good old wagon show" and endured many hardships in fatiguing journeys in all sorts of weather. In the eastern and middle sections of the country the drives were not so long and were endurable; but, in the sparsely settled South and the new West, patience and fortitude were put to the test. The hotel accommodations of the day were primitive and the best of taverns was none too good.

The managers of the shows were ever hunting up new territory, the country was expanding westward, and the circus kept close on the heels of the tenderfoot. The red wagon was never far behind the prairie schooner of the pioneer and the newspaper man was prompt to get to the front and grow up with the country.

Winters, some of the shows went South and the press agents took a course of course hog and hominy instead of hibernating at Bartlett's Hotel in the New York Bowery or Sam Miller's Showman's Home in Philadelphia.

On tour, the first of the press agents encountered many dangers of the crude highways, especially when benighted in storm and stress of the elements. Little [did they] dream that there would come a day when the press agent of the tent show would glide along the rail in a palace advertising car instead of plugging over the road in a top buggy. The early scribes were fulfilling their mission in blazing the way that greater things might grow out of their earnest endeavors in behalf of the show they loved to extreme infatuation. As one of the enthusiasts exclaimed:

"I had rather advertise the circus than edit the *London Times*."

THE INTELLIGENCE OF THE OLD-TIME CIRCUS MANAGER
His Business Ability Was Way Above Par And, For Enterprise, He Was In Advance Of The Majority Of The Mercantile Community; In His Way, An Explorer And Pathfinder. [*Billboard*, November 9, 1907. Published a month after Day's death.]

The old-time circus managers were, as a whole, men of character and more than ordinary ability and conducted their business honorably and aboveboard. Their travels at home and abroad gave them an education not to be found in books. Exploiters and explorers, they assumed risks and profited thereby. They faced dangers on the seas and in the wilds and the Star of Empire never moved so far west that it failed to have a circus wagon hitched to it. And these same old-time circus managers showed the American flag on a center pole in about every inhabitable spot on earth and still pined for the showman's unrequited, insatiable desire---"new territory."

The old-time circus managers in this country, it may be said, discovered advertising. Who ever took any noticeable space in a newspaper until after the circus made the experiment and demonstrated the profit and the possibilities? Who appropriated the poster to his purpose and adopted it as almost solely his own? The old-time circus manager. Who first, last and all the while believed in printing ink, in the distribution of the handbill, not only locally but for miles and miles around the place of exhibition? The old-time circus manager. Who first employed men of literary ability to prepare their announcements and secure publicity in the newspaper? The old-time circus manager.

And while these same old-time circus managers were ever alert and venturesome, the representative merchants and men of commercial interests were a rather slow lot and not a bit ready to risk their dollars in enterprise or exploitation. In fact, the old-time merchant believed it was beneath his dignity to advertise; so he sat in his counting room and waited for customers to come, as his father and grandfather had done before him. The merchants were a half century behind the circus managers of the time in appreciating and appropriating the increasing methods of publicity discovered and developed by the showmen.

Even the theatrical managers were slow to learn or pattern after the tenters; and it was decades after before the slumbering directors of the drama woke up and realized that the world had moved and that they had not moved with it. The theatrical manager, in time, came to follow in the wake of the circus manager but his step was slow and he was ever very far behind in the promotion of publicity.

The cheapening of the process of poster printing by the discovery of the use of the pine block gave a general impetus to circus business and advertising. Joseph Morse, the inventor, had his hands full, as he was both artist and engraver.

And now, something of the manner of men who were the pioneers in the circus business in the United States and developed it as fortune favored and capital accrued. They were not an uncouth, ignorant lot, did not wear loud clothes, chew plug tobacco, and unloose an oath every other word as they have often been pictured in imaginative literature. They were men of affairs; and as for practical knowledge of the general condition of finance and trade throughout the country, they were the best posted people in the land. It would never do to take a circus into a section that was not prosperous; and the old-time circus manager rarely made any mistakes in the selection of profitable territory.

And now let some of these heroes of the sawdust arena of yore pass in review: Turner, who left the shoemaker's bench to become an innovator in the circus line and induct P. T. Barnum in the sawdust; Barnum, the writer, the humorist, lecturer, and most famous of showmen; Nat Howes, who put the top on the tent; Seth B. Howes, who sent out the first golden chariot drawn by twenty horses. This same Mr. Howes was always the prime mover in the organization of large enterprises and an extensive importer of wild animals. He was also instrumental in touring a magnificent American circus in England with the cream of the Yankee performers in the ring.

The first of the "Flatfoots," the progenitors of the later tribe who succeeded to the heritage, were financiers of great ability. They set out to monopolize the menagerie business and came well nigh doing it. They also aimed to syndicate the shows. June, Titus & Angevine and their associates were making good progress with the scheme when the panic of 1837 made the merging of interests impossible. And this was many years before the time of Rockefeller, Hill, Gould, and Harriman.

General Rufus Welch went in strong for expensive spectacles. In his tours, "the world was an oyster"; and he visited many lands and also made a venture in the importation of wild animals in opposition to the "Flatfoot" trust. Lewis B. Lent, a manager of culture, travel, and wide information, founded the famous "kid glove show," the New York Circus. Levi J. North accumulated a fortune in the ring and on the road, built an amphitheatre in Chicago in 1856, and became an alderman of that growing burgh. P. T. Barnum represented Bridgeport in the Connecticut legislature and also served his city as mayor. "Old" John Robinson ran for mayor of Cincinnati but failed of election.

Dr. Gilbert B. Spalding was one of the brightest of the old-timers. He invented the use of quarter poles, eleven tier seats and extra front seats; and with his associate, Charles J. Rogers, put a "Floating Palace" on the Mississippi River and also the water minstrel hall, called "The Banjo." Rogers, who was originally an equestrian, was a polished gentleman of the old school but not so aggressive as his pushing, demonstrative partner.

Isaac A. VanAmburgh, the Lion King, got his fill of glory at home and abroad. Stone, Rosston & Murray were managers of worth and gentlemen in all that word implies. Hyatt Frost was a sterling character, a wit, humorist, and versifier who could find lots of fun in an ink bottle. O. J. Ferguson, many years an associate with Mr. Frost and the VanAmburgh party, [was] a linguist and a show writer of no mean ability. Col. Dan Rice, the most popular clown, who, having no early advantage of education, under the inspiration of Van Orden, the press agent, took to the books and made good his deficiencies.

John J. Nathans, during his career as manager and performer, visited a good part of the world and for many years participated in many ventures in about every land under the sun. He was one of the latter day "Flatfoots," headed by Avery Smith, whose name was never used in connection with any show of which he was part owner. George Fox Bailey of Danbury, Conn., [must also be mentioned]. The Turners made Danbury a circus town and Mr. Bailey---not to be confounded with James A. Bailey, the great---was the son-in-law of a Turner. When the "Flatfoots" ran the Barnum show, George F. Bailey was the manager.

Many managers [who] have made the "last stand" and for whom the band has played "Home, Sweet Home"---for they are at rest--- might be classed as old managers. Adam Forepaugh, Ephriam, Allen and Peter Sells, W. C. Coup, several of the younger associates of P. T. Barnum, and even James A. Bailey are not to be included in this important reminder of those who actually created the American circus. The circus as it was born in a topless tent, without seats, and exhibiting but once a day, grew under the skillful directions of its managers to become the great popular amusement for decades, whose one ring was plenty. [Then], the prodigious innovations of millionaire managers had not been made to present at every performance, at enormous expense, an army of performers in the presence of a world of people.

Taking into consideration all the conditions, the original American circus managers, under the lead of the Turners, the Howes, Raymond & Waring, [and] the "Flatfoots," made rapid progress in the enlargement and the improvement of the tent show. At the outset, the population of the entire country was small. But few cities of any size existed; and New York, Boston, and Philadelphia were little better than large towns. The masses were not in possession of much "cash money"; barter was in vogue in many localities. The people were close fisted, being bred that way, and the larger majority of them puritanical and narrow minded. One might as well be frank about it and out with the truth. Pleasure and recreation was a sin and it was better to weep in woe than to rejoice and be glad.

"The entrance of the theatre is the gateway to hell," said the preacher who inveighed against amusements, "and the ring of the circus is the bottomless pit itself."

As to faces, they were worn long and the preachers and Pharisees set the fashion.

Occasionally a newspaper man was under the rays of the "blue light" and declined to advertise the circus; and then, full of Christian charity, preceded the appearance of the show with a venomous libel.

In estimating the ability of the first circus managers, it may be said that they succeeded for two reasons: (1) They were smarter than their fellow men then on earth. (2) They knew how to advertise and were about the only persons living who did. And when they were up against each other, as for instance the fierce wars of Dan Rice and Dr. Spalding, it was diamond cut diamond.

PROMINENT CIRCUS MANAGERS
Who Were Expert Advance Men---Something of Their Personalities and Methods. [*Billboard*, September 7, 1907]

Quite a number of circus managers of the past directed their individual efforts in advance of the show, believing the routing and advertising to be the great essential. Several of these were equally at home with the show as in advance of it, and in this category may be included George Fox Bailey of Danbury, Conn.; [who], after marrying a daughter of one of the Turners, a son of the original Aron (with the single "A") abandoned merchandising at his father-in-law's solicitation and connected himself with Turner's circus. In the course of time, Bailey attracted the attention of the "Flatfoot" party and became affiliated for the balance of his life with their interests. These veterans of the tent shows believed that their best interests were the better "subserved" with George in advance, spying out territory and directing details at the front. Mr. Bailey did enjoy considerable prestige ahead from the fact that he was the advertised head of the firm of George F. Bailey & Co. There is no doubt that George's presence in the van redounded to the benefit of all interested parties and, to employ a Hatterstown expression, this partner in advance was "as smart as a whip."

At a later day, when Mr. Bailey left the front and returned to the main body to take up the managerial reins at the desire of his associates, Lewis June, a "Flatfoot" by inheritance, looked after the advance business of this ancient and honorable combine of sterling managers. "Lew" June was a quiet, unassuming man, after the manner of his senior, George Fox Bailey, who did his business without fuss or feathers and passed on, avoiding publicity and exhibiting no desire for

14

professional distinction. That was a characteristic "Flatfoot" way of doing business. A "Flatfoot" advance man never beat a drum, sounded a trumpet, or cried aloud to make his presence known.

Lewis B. Lent, the grand old man, looked to his own interests in the advance of his circus, that kid clove affair from the Iron Building in New York. Mr. Lent was a well informed man and he knew his United States as well as if he had himself surveyed the map. He was arbitrary in his orders and they were to be obeyed to the letter without excuse. His commands were issued in black and white and there was no dodging the instructions. He was ready with the pen, a most entertaining correspondent and, as Uncle Charley Castle, the veteran circus agent, once remarked:

"Lew Lent would write you a letter if you both were in New York." And so he would.

The manager was of bulky build and did not get around much on his feet. Arriving at a principal point ahead of the show, Mr. Lent would establish his headquarters and keep in touch with his advance men, who were required to report their movements by wire daily. Methodical in everything, he kept within reach a time table showing the location of the general agent, the press agent, the paste brigade, and the program distributor on the day and date.

Although Mr. Lent was arbitrary in his commands and brooked neither discussion nor divergence, he was, aside from business, more a comrade than a domineering employer who must be obeyed. He was thoughtful of his agents' comforts; and one ordered to report to headquarters from the field would find that the manager had selected a room for him and on the way the representative was liable to receive a telegram on the train, reading: "Don't eat until you arrive."

Lewis B. Lent was an epicure; and if you dined with him, you certainly had your fill of the best that the market afforded. Gruff and blunt to an extreme, the manager, with a voice of rolling thunder, had a keen sense of the humorous and was a delightful conversationalist. But, in anger at the failure to perform a duty, he was a holy terror. It was not conducive to an employee's happiness to excite his ire. The old man was liable to smash the table with his fist and lift the roof off with his voice.

One season, when running the paste brigade, Mr. Lent put Charles F. Haskins in charge of one and John W. Abbott the other. Haskins was the local billposter in Providence and Abbott held forth in the same line at Binghamton. Both were capable men but Haskins had the superior address and, in consequence, was always assigned to the cities. This led Abbott to ask the manager:

"Mr. Lent, why is it that you always send Haskins to the cities and me to the jay towns?"

The manager looked over his glasses and answered seriously, "John, it takes a man with a head to make the jay towns."

In selecting territory for exhibition, Mr. Lent had a peculiar Sherlock Holmes method of deduction. He had his doubts about the advisability of playing St. Paul and went there to take in the situation. As he got off the train, a hackman called:

"Take you up town for a quarter."

The manager passed into the depot where he was solicited by a bootblack:

"Shine 'em up for five cents."

The famous showman gave a great grunt of disgust and, talking to himself, said:

"Hack a quarter! Shine five cents! Ugh! The New York Circus will not show in St. Paul this summer."

The Lent & French show was organized in Detroit in 1876. Several of the advance staff were attending upon the chief in his room when John W. Abbott came in and squatted on the Governor's sole leather trunk, remarking as he did so:

"Great town this, Mr. Lent, roast turkey ten cents."

The manager immediately returned, "Turkey ten cents? No money in the town." And then, discovering the seat that the boss of the paste brigade was occupying, he thundered, "Turkey ten cents. John Abbott, get off my trunk!"

Abbott jumped as if propelled by a catapult and the manager roared with laughter.

Mr. Lent was averse to unsought advice. He believed that he knew his own business best and always insisted on having his own way in conducting it. His programs were printed by Alexander Calhoun at Hartford. The printer dabbled largely in theatricals and minstrelsy. Lent and Calhoun were cronies but the printer so far forgot himself one day as to give the circus manager some pointers in regard to routing the circus. The advised expressed himself loudly:

"Alec Calhoun, you run your printing office and I will run the New York Circus."

With all his great capacity for handling a show at the front, it would have been better for the final finances of Lewis B. Lent if he had remained at the door of the New York Circus as the man behind the gun. The manager realized this when too late. The stable was not fastened until after the theft of the horse.

Andrew Haight preferred to be in advance of the show and there he was at his best, producing business and letting others look after the results of his resourceful energy. He could drive a close bargain and was never known to get the worst of a deal. John H. Murray once said:

"If there is any fault in Andy Haight, he is too close a contractor."

Peter Sells was the brightest of the Sells Brothers and Ephrian, Allen and Lewis were justly proud of him. Peter was a well-equipped advance man with a good business head and he could write as well as a professional press agent. He once remarked:

"My place is ahead of the show. I could not travel with it and put up with the turmoil and hurly burly of a fourth of July every week day all the season."

James A. Bailey, during his career with Cooper & Bailey, the Great London, and his early connection with the P. T. Barnum show, was very much in evidence in the advance and, having been an advance agent before he was a manager, he was experienced in the handling of a show. Mr. Bailey, with all his great ability as an advertiser, lacked one desirable qualification. He could not write, although he was a most excellent judge of circus literature.

For several seasons the great showman's favorite press agent was John W. Hamilton, a brother of "Tody"; and when there was trouble ahead, Jack accompanied the manager when he assumed command in the face of the enemy.

And there was and is Michael Coyle, who left the treasury and became an advance agent when John H. Murray and he were the sole owners of the Murray & Stone Circus. If Mike had a fault it was the reluctance to go to bed of a night. John H. Murray used to call on his partner of a morning at the Rule Head Hotel, New York, to find him in his room half dressed. One morning John H. asked an explanation:

"Mike, when I come here of a morning, are you retiring or getting up?"

Mike replied indefinitely, "It is either one or the other."

When the P. T. Barnum show, under different regimes was pressed by opposition, his partners would ring in a still alarm and the great showman would come to the front and add the weight and influence of his presence. His name alone was a tower of strength; and when he came to town himself, the editors opened their arms and columns in welcome. The showman's arrival was chronicled; he was interviewed and frequently editorialized during his stay. And what is the wonder? P. T. Barnum had preached and practiced advertising successfully all his life. The press of the country was under a lasting obligation to him and is unto this day. An enthusiastic admirer of the great showman exclaimed:

"P. T. Barnum is the father of advertising."

A bystander improved on the assertion by declaring:

"P. T. Barnum was the grandfather of advertising."

TAKING ONE'S OWN MEDICINE
[*Billboard*, April 6, 1901]

It is nothing nowadays to pick up a copy of the *Billboard*, or any of the papers devoted to amusement interests, and read the cards or wants of professionals. But it was not ever thus, as I well recall. Now you may read the personal address of John Drew and Jim Flake---good on either end---side by side, followed by the announcement of Maude Adams and Gertie Glue.

While with Newcomb & Arlington at their minstrel hall on Twenty-eighth Street near Broadway in 1871,[11] I became the New York correspondent of John Stetson's *Sporting Times*, writing on theatrical matters and incidentally looking after some of the Boston publisher-and-manager's other interests, considerably to my profit and a good deal more to my satisfaction.[12] Being so pleased with New York, I elected to remain in the large town and not accompany the black band on tour. As it resulted, I was the better off for it financially. But the "X a week" for the letter from Stetson would not permit one to hang on to Gotham except by the eyebrows. So, to add to my income, I contributed a series of humorous statistics to the *New York Sunday Mercury*, now extinct but then a powerful and highly profitable and successful newspaper. It also issued a country edition with the "Sunday" omitted and a large share of the extra issue devoted to amusements in an endeavor, a vain endeavor, to compete with the *New York Clipper*.[13]   And, by the way, I also wrote for the *Clipper*.

Fortunately, during the summer, John Stetson came to town and I made his acquaintance to considerable advantage, selling him a serial and getting thereafter many jobs that he was glad to put in my way and I was joyful to execute.   Stetson was coining money and paid liberally.   Although the ex-pedestrian was a terror to some of his employees, we never had a word and I was never more fairly treated by anyone for whom I shed ink.

Occasionally I was called upon for special writing or attention to some manager's or star's interests and I did not scramble for existence by any manner of means.   But I had to spread lots of ink on paper to foot my bills.   It cost a pretty penny to live in New York and keep up with the procession.

Some professional people were not loath to announce in the *Clipper* that they were "resting" or had "open time."   A good many, in fact, of the younger performers and actors and managers were also tooling their teams and trying to sell their claims.   That was what aroused the cupidity of the *Mercury* folks in seeking to trespass in the *Clipper's* field of tall grass.

The growth of amusement advertising in the *Clipper* was slow and it was some time before local managers used it as a medium or lent it any encouragement.   Laura Keene was the first to lead the way.   Being an Englishwoman, she, of course, was a reader and a believer in the class paper because she appreciated its value by the knowledge and use of the London *Era*.   And it may be remarked that the *Era* was originally modeled in the same type as the *Clipper* and was devoted to sporting matters and amusement interests as well.   Later, the *Era* dropped the sports.

Living at the St. Charles Hotel, 648 Broadway---the circus headquarters---I came in contact and acquaintance with many advance agents of the tent shows and was a welcome visitor to Room No. 1 where they gathered to exchange stories and boast of the triumphs of the past season.   A smart, sharp, jolly lot they were.   And I wrote them up in the circus number of the *Clipper* in a big spread entitled "Room No. 1, A Night with the Circus Folks."[14]

By the time my yarn was in print I was ready to follow off a red wagon and, being an advertiser, I took my own medicine and inserted the following card in the *Clipper*:

To Managers of First-Class
Circuses and Menageries
CHARLES H. DAY

New York Correspondent of the *Sporting Times*, Author of "Humors of Show Life," published in the *New York Mercury*; also "Alice Drayton," "Jersey Blues," "Actress and Minstrel," "Up Hill" and numerous other novelettes, can be secured as

WRITER

For the Tenting Season of '72 and '73 by any Responsible Management. Five years' experience as an Advertiser. Two years Agent and Business Manager with Miss Laura Keene. Address care St. Charles Hotel, 648 Broadway, N.Y.

When the announcement came out in print, I was called to account and "read out of meeting" by the sticklers, who looked upon advertising for an engagement as non-professional. And I believe that I would have been put under the ban and ostracized but for the fact that I was earning a dollar and could be touched to a limited extent. Even some of my circus friends shook their heads and remarked, "I would like to see you get into the business but that is not exactly the way to do it." Those who did not like me somehow just sniffed and turned up their noses and remarked: "Upstart!" "Mr. Fresh!" "Bran' new!" "Oh, what a gale!"

Well, being an advertiser, I did not feel guilty of any crime; and if I had disregarded the ethics of the profession, the matter was already past mending. I couldn't see why I should go barefooted because the shoemaker's wife did. And I knew that even doctors and lawyers had no objection to publicity without expense; so where was the greater sin if you paid for it? I did not cry over the adverse comments of my carping critics. Neither did I smile, I will admit. I was firm in the opinion that to ask for what you wanted was very proper. A personal experience satisfied me for I had proved the problem by replying to an advertisement by Laura Keene in the *Clipper* and securing the engagement invited therein. Certainly there could be no harm in the agent's advertising; the manager needed the service and the agent needed the situation. The newspaper column served as the means of communication. That was the way I looked at it. All the good things of the amusement press are not for the manager alone.

For all the warnings of the false prophets, my want was supplied; and through the *Clipper* announcement, added to the influence of Mike Coyle, I became director of publications for John H. Murray and remained in his employ for four years.[15] And I am quite sure that neither Murray nor Coyle thought any the less of me because I advertised.

After that, when I was "at liberty," I made haste to herald the fact and always successfully. In fact, I found such publicity better than direct application to a manager, circus, theatrical or minstrel. If a manager is much in need of you, he may wire in haste; but if you write, he begins with the shrewd palaver, "I think it might be possible to use you at a moderate salary. You see, etc., etc., &c., &c." Having time in correspondence, the applicant is held at arm's length and negotiated with. The advertisement of the agent or the performer opens competition to the advantage of the advertiser.

I am free to admit that up to a much later date in after years my occasional cards in the show sheets were a subject of sarcastic comment. In advertising to gain the object sought, I tried to make the announcement catchy, just as much so in my own interests as if I was penning it for an exacting manager. And why not, pray? I recall one of mine in the columns:

CHARLES H. DAY
AND
HIS PEN
CAN BE SECURED

Wasn't that cute? It got me an engagement. And I'll tell you the rest of it frankly; the very next week appeared an advertisement similar to this:

BILL ROCKS AND TWO PENS
can be secured for the concert of any circus that pays salaries and
does not feed the troupe on monkey bread.

I never knew the result but I will wager the fellow did not get lost in the shuffle.

WITH TIGHTS AND SPANGLES
[*New York Clipper*, July 13, 1872]

With the song of the thrush comes the circus with its glittering street pageant---golden chariots, gaily uniformed bands, and richly comparisoned blooded steeds---to amuse the people of town and country in our northern latitude. In the more congenial clime of the "Sunny

South," their tents are often spread in the winter months. It was during one of these campaigns, "way down in Dixie" in an obscure Georgia town, that I first met the individual to whom I'm about to refer. Cotton was "down," a general financial depression was felt throughout the Southland, and there was pretty close "cutting of cloth" all around among the managers and agents to "make both ends meet."

With Charles H. Hall, then the advance of Laura Keene's Comedy Company and formerly with Charles MacEvoy's Hibernicon, I called at the railroad office to negotiate reduced rates fare over the road. The railway official was in close communication with a clerical individual whom I at once took for the pastor of a local church arranging for a Sunday school excursion. He was dressed in solemn black, wore a vest buttoned to his throat, and displayed no jewelry, while meekness and piety seemed to ooze from every pore of his placid countenance. Judge of my surprise when the ministerial stranger recognized Hall and I was introduced to Andrew Haight, of whom I had often heard in connection with the firm of Haight & Chambers. Mr. Haight was at this time contracting agent for the Stone & Murray Circus and I frequently met him thereafter as we worked our way over the same lines of railroad Alabama-ward.[16]

Stone & Murray closed their season immediately after New Years and returned to New York to fit out their northern tour. But Andrew Haight remained and connected himself with G. G. Grady's Unprecedented Old Fashioned American Circus, until he met with P. B. Wooten at Atlanta, Georgia, and organized the Haight & Wooten Circus, with which he made a forty-six weeks' season. Before the termination of which, Wooten withdrew from the firm. The Haight & Wooten show started from Atlanta; but before the summer was spent, explored the provinces of Nova Scotia and New Brunswick and, traveling by rail, managed to avoid other parties in the main.[17]

At St. John, New Brunswick, manager Haight, who was in advance, called upon the mayor of the town, one Charles Reed, the son of a royal father in the mother country.

"Your honor," said the manager, bowing profoundly and sanctimoniously, "we are coming to be with you for a little while and I have called to consult you in regards to license."

"Not necessary, sir," interrupted the mayor, at once mistaking the showman for a clergyman. "You are at perfect liberty to preach without a license."

"But I don't want to preach," expostulated manager Haight.

"Pray then, what do you want?" interrogated the puzzled official.

"I want," smiled Mr. Haight benignly, "to secure a license for the Haight & Wooten Circus, who propose to exhibit here with your honor's kind permission."

The mayor waited to hear no more but broke forth with a hearty laugh at this ludicrous mistake. When the account of the interview was related to the company, it was a question of who laughed the loudest and longest---Durand, of the eloquent quill; Jacob Haight; or the great admirer of Byron's "Mazeppa," George W. DeHaven.

The season of 1871, Stone & Murray, Haight & Wooten, G. G. Grady, and some others sent up hot air balloons every day with some venturous passenger as an outside attraction to draw the crowd to "the lot." This species of ballooning was much like a display of fireworks, attractive enough for the second; but the moment it was over and the descent made, it was a disappointment to the beholders, who were wont to enjoy a little growl.

One afternoon with Stone & Murray, the balloon failed to travel miles into the blue ether and, after reaching a moderate height, made a rapid descent, much to the disgust of an Hiberian matron, who exclaimed:

"Fust, and it is going no fudder up than that?"

"Whist," said a sister of the old bog who stood at her side, "how far would you have it go up for nothing?"

Another day, an individual who had brought to the grounds with him a descriptive program in which the airship was represented in red ink complained that the balloon was not the same color as that on the bill.

Brilliant in color and capital in design are the mammoth posters spread upon the billboards to attract the eye by the various circus companies and menageries. During the season, it was the delight of Tom Barry[18] on Sunday in a rural burgh to take his position near a large stand of bills and listen to the remarks of the bystanders. If the performance had taken place on the preceding Saturday, he heard many a freely spoken comment upon the merits of himself and fellow performers. One day while eavesdropping, he heard a little group of citizens expressing themselves upon the performance and the performers. And with that they commenced to walk the length of the bulletin board, saying as they went:

"They did that and that and that, too."

The clown followed carelessly along unnoticed. Stone & Murray had in the stand [of paper], a "rebus bill"[19] somewhat difficult to decipher, before [which the burghers paused for some moments in silence], while a shadow grew perceptibly over the face of a hitherto confident youth, who reluctantly and audibly admitted:

"Well, I swow, they didn't do that!" an opinion [with] which everyone [agreed], while the clown stole away to enjoy a quiet laugh by himself.

If there ever existed a happy-go-lucky individual, he was embodied in Billy Burke, the clown. Ever the same genial fellow, it matters not to him whether the sun shines or is behind a cloud. After returning from his summer's tour with James Robinson, he played an exceedingly brief engagement with Dan Rice and afterwards appeared for a few weeks at Lent's in New York City. The balance of the winter he lived at his ease---where so many of the profession center---at the St. Charles Hotel.[20]

Among those who dropped in from day to day to chat with a friend or the managers who were coming and going was Ben Maginley, a famous jester and equestrian director of Joel E. Warner & Co.'s show.[21] The rotund humorist had a dog---a black, shaggy fellow that was always at his heels---who soon came to be on familiar terms with the waiters of the restaurant who fed him as regularly as he appeared. It came to pass that the wicked Burke conspired against the digestion of that there dorg and daily purloined from the table large quantities of rich cheese, [which he fed to the] purp without the knowledge of his master.

"How's your dog, Ben?" asked Burke from day to day.

"He ain't very well," replied the unsuspecting jester. "I think he eats too much."

When [Maginley's] back was turned, the dog was again crammed with cheese, while the head waiter could not understand how it was that the patrons of the restaurant all of a sudden ate so much cheese with their pie. What would have been the fate of the dog no one can tell; but fortunately springtime came and it became necessary for Burke to join "the show" at St. Louis. When he came to settle the winter's score, he found a discrepancy of three and a half dollars between his memorandum and the account on the hotel books.

"Let's run them over," suggested bookkeeper Warner.

Thereupon they commenced running over the items until they came to one in the bold hand of landlord Leland, which read: "Cheese for Ben Maginley's dog---$3.50."

The clown admitted the cheese as he laughingly explained:

"I wonder which got the worst of that, me or the dog?"

HAPPY DAYS AT THE ST. CHARLES
[*Billboard*, November 5, 1904.]

Leland was a magic name to conjure with in the hotel business when the nephew of his nationally famous uncle came from Ohio and began business at the St. Charles Hotel, 648 Broadway, just above Bleecker Street.[22] Unlike the other landlord Lelands, the young farmer was not able to begin at the top with a large house on the American plan but had to be content with a European hostelry with a restaurant as the main stay of profit. The only thing in favor of the venture was the location, the very center of the theatrical Rialto and the busy axis of day and night life in the metropolis. Nearby was the Olympic Theatre, Niblo's, the San Francisco Minstrels (afterward Tony Pastor's), and further down the street the Theatre Comique; up the street Lina Edwin's Theatre and the old church property of A. T. Stewart, transformed into a theatre and occupied by "Sandy" Spencer, Augustin Daly and others. Close by were the immense hotels in the heyday of their popularity and profit. The Metropolitan, conducted by the great Lelands and the resort of the Tweed Tammanyites; and the famous American Club, the St. Nicholas Hotel, the Grand Central, and the New York Hotel, patronized almost exclusively by Southerners and famous during the Civil War as headquarters of conspirators and agents of the Confederacy.[23]

Union Square was looked upon as "up town" and it was years before it became the Rialto.[24] New York life, red hot or at a white heat, glowed about the St. Charles' location and the rival Revere House at Houston Street, a block below. Frequenters of the St. Charles rarely visited the Revere except on business.

The "Flatfoot" party of circus managers long maintained a room [during] the resting season at the Revere; and there [they] could be found regularly---Avery Smith, John J. Nathans, Lew June, Elain Quick, George F. Bailey and such of their staff of representatives who happened to be wintering in New York or vicinity.[25] Avery Smith was the only "Flatfoot" who made a habit of visiting the St. Charles and he was as free in his intercourse with high and humble as he was generous in his distribution of cigars and liquid refreshments.

The St. Charles in Leland's day had no regular bar, only a caged-in sideboard to the left of the restaurant. The favorite resort for the foaming lager and stronger stimulants was at Harry and Billy Cunningham's at the sign of "Daddy Rice," 636 Broadway. This wooden figure was carved by the pioneer star minstrel and represented himself in his inimitable character of "Jim Crow."

The Cunninghams were famous professionals. Harry had been with the Barnum Museum stock. He was also a member of a Bowery company and was a "heavy" man of considerable ability. Billy had been a clog dancer. Neither drank a drop of liquor and were absolute teetotalers, although their business card advertised them as "Dealers in Poison." Through their former connections, the brothers' place became the Broadway resort of the Bowery actors, the sojourning players and the resting Thespians.

Charlie Collins had the cafe of the Olympic Theatre and enjoyed a liberal patronage. The De Sotto was around the corner on Bleecker Street. It was an English chop house largely visited by the plainclothes men and headquarter officers of the police department. Harry Hill was coining money on Houston Street, and Broadway was lined with free concert saloons, down in the cellars and upstairs for blocks.[26] That section of the city was the hottest spot on earth with the low life but held well in check by the commander of the precinct, Captain Byrnes, afterward the best superintendent of police New York ever had.[27]

How Leland managed to popularize the St. Charles and make it the headquarters of the circus people and folks engaged in other lines of the amusement business is not so readily explained. About everything except the location was against the success of the project. The building had been condemned and was an unsafe, ramshackle affair that threatened to fall down at any time from its own weight and weakness. Illy furnished, it was not attractive. The attraction was the landlord and the society of the patrons. And you certainly met goodly company, day and night, at the old St. Charles in the hey-day of its popularity.[28]

Perhaps E. D. Colvin was responsible to some extent in attracting the circus patronage held by Leland. Colvin toured with circuses summers and acted as cashier in the St. Charles restaurant winters. It could be truly said that he knew everybody in the business, all the managers, performers, working bosses and show printers. Besides, Colvin had the correct idea about life; and when the reckless and careless sons of the sawdust were paying a meal check or having it charged up, he read a little homily about the advisability of putting by something for a rainy day. E. Darwin practiced what he preached. He was always employed, saved and saved, only to lose and lose with every investment until he was quite advanced in life. Then he began to gather coin which stuck by him, a final reward of industry and perseverance.

Leland was an early and late worker. At three o'clock every morning except Sunday he was up and off to the markets to buy the supplies and provisions for the restaurant, selecting every article in person and paying spot cash for the same.

Coley was granted the title of steward because he drove the horse and also relieved the day clerk for meals or held the office down for an afternoon. Coley was a clever fellow with Saratoga and prided himself on his resemblance to Col. Jim Fiske; but the second edition was a miniature, [although] as loudly dressed.

Once during the Leland regime, the St. Charles came near closing its doors. Coley resigned. And the shock of the resignation almost shook the foundations of the unstable structure. Wily Coley! A petition was at once framed and circulated for signatures, begging that the resignation be withdrawn. No one refused to sign the plea and the hotel was saved. So was the landlord, who smiled without remark. Coley did retire at a later period and embarked in the restaurant business.

Room No. 1 of the hotel was on the office floor, next to the clerk's cage and opposite the parlor. It was held sacred for the use of the great lights of the sawdust ring in management, [as well as] their business and literary representatives. Whoever registered for it always kept open house to all comers in the business and jollity and good nature reigned supreme. Even if some of the parties had been antagonized during the heat and passions of the summer's campaigns, they forgot the wounds and bruises of battle [and] made no exhibition of scars; but, [rather], rang the bell (there was no button to touch) and summoned John Keegan, the porter, from time to time as the night sped, to keep the wellspring of joy from running dry. Room No. 1 and other ones remunerated Keegan with tips to the extent that he [too] became a restaurant owner in due season.

It was an education for a young circus manager or agent to listen to the relation of the many experiences of the seniors. Two of the most entertaining characters were Captain Francis M. Kelsh of Philadelphia and Charles H. Castle of Syracuse, known to their friends as "The Two Orphans" and between whom existed a lifelong friendship of genuine Damon and Pythias sincerity. Castle possessed a most wonderful vocabulary and an eloquence of description that was remarkable. When he began to talk he began to walk and [he] held the floor and his audiences. It was Castle who named Martinho Lowande "The Hurricane Horseman," a most apt application. The veteran who had piloted Col. Dan Rice in the days of his greatest favor expressed himself quaintly. He spoke of himself invariably as Rucker. Syracuse was Salt Point and his home Piety Ridge. The manager who employed him was Master. For years he was the advance manager for John O'Brien and dubbed the show he heralded "The Irish Brigade." John O'Brien, by the way, always lodged at the St. Charles when in town but he did not register. He slept on a sofa and thereby saved a dollar. Mr. O'Brien was never known to ring for Keegan under any circumstances.

The story of many memorable nights in Room No. 1 would fill a big book. While Kelley, Hyatt Frost, Henry Barnum, O. J. Ferguson and other tent showmen of Putnam County affected the Putnam House on Fourth Avenue near the old 27th Street depot, after the exclusive manner of the "Flatfoots" at the Revere, the majority of the owners of shows and privileges turned up at Room No. 1 and, where the Master centered, came the talent and the understrappers.

As Room No. 1 got the benefit of the din from the kitchen of the restaurant, there was a rattling of dishes of the heavy and unbreakable sort that forbade easy slumber, except to the unusually fatigued. And one morning, in coming down to breakfast, the man from Piety Ridge, Salt Point, was greeted by the landlord with the query:

"Well, Mr. Castle, how did you rest last night?"

"Rest! Sleep!" exclaimed Rucker, "George, how can a man sleep when they wash dishes with a crowbar?"

In spite of all its disadvantages, there might have been seen of a winter's night in the star chamber such representative leaders in the circus world and its contributory callings, exchanging views and swapping experiences, as Adam Forepaugh, Doctor Spalding, W. W. Cole, Burr Robbins, Joel E. Warner, Andy Springer, Andrew Haight, George W. DeHaven, John B. Doris, George Batcheller, James Melville, Ben Maginley, James Cooke (the clown), Col. Joe Cushing, John H. Murray, Den Stone, Lewis B. Lent, Frank Gardner, Levi J. North, Piclo Russell, Bob Morgan and the ever-present too-numerous-to-be-mentioned.

When George S. Leland first came to New York, the prosperous uncles did not wish to greet the enterprising nephew. On the other hand, when they had occasion to go up Broadway, they passed on the other side to escape the odor of the St. Charles' hash. But the small concern coined money and was a mill that ground to the good, night and day, year in and year out. The St. Charles was alive nights. As Billy Burke, the clown, remarked:

"What a dreadful thing it would be if the St. Charles caught fire in the daytime."

There was too much fun going in the St. Charles by gaslight for the regulars to retire until after breakfast. While the mighty men of the circus select circle discussed the arenic affairs of the past and prognosticated the future with interludes of reminiscence and anecdote, a merry party held a session in the front office and pursued the clock points with stories until the arrival of Warner, the day clerk. Wicked wags they proved when a new visitor or stranger dropped in and was "reminded" [of a story] and attempted to relate [it]. If he made a mess of a good yarn badly told, the throng dropped to their knees in silent prayer and remained at their devotion until the unsatisfactory tale teller abandoned the subject.

One night in the front office was Ghost Night. Apparition after apparition was invoked until the midnight hour arrived. At that unseemly time a "stranger in the midst" opened out with a blood curdler of depth and length, a perfect horror of a yarn. Harry Stanwood, the banjoist and Ethiopian comedian,[29] stole to his room and returned wearing a fright wig and seated himself directly opposite the spook-spelling last registered. The man invoking the shade was a master at the art of yarn-spinning and his audience was rapt with attention and eye-extending interest. As the awful tale approached its climax, Stanwood removed his hat and gave the wig a gentle lift. Horrible and more horrible grew the story and the more the hair on Stanwood's head lifted. The relater of the adventure of departed spirits arrived at the climax and way up went the fright wig as the comedian shrieked with assured terror and rushed upstairs as if pursued by all the demons let loose from the bottomless pit.

"You've scared the man to death," screamed Dick Fitzgerald. "He will commit suicide sure!"

Dick pursued the escaping Stanwood and the man who told the ghost story slid downstairs and disappeared, never to return.

Great big, generous-hearted, pernicious, fearless Richard Fitzgerald, "The Irish Lord," was at one time associated with Tom Riggs, the comedian, in conducting a variety agency. The business between partners was transacted upon a perfectly equitable basis. The first man in the office in the morning opened the mail and appropriated the receipts. If Dick was the first man in, he did not return while the money lasted, thereby giving Tom an opportunity to even up. In the long run, both partners got their own. In the course of time, Fitzgerald put in a winter as night clerk of the St. Charles and it is a matter of fact that during the hours that Richard was on duty he never had to call on anyone to assist in preserving order. If you heard anyone bumping and thumping downstairs and made inquiry in regard to the noise, you were certain to be informed:

"That's only Dick firing a fellow for getting too gay."

Many of the roomers at the St. Charles were not professionals and the list included several unique characters. Among them [was] a tea-taster who was never busy except when the ships were in. The husband of one of New York's favorite actresses who had gone before and for whom there was no forgetting stalked the house, a pathetic figure of woebegone misery. There was a bevy of elderly beaux who sought favor in the eyes of the lady guests and never secured and never despaired. Also, there was Captain Geer of Col. Fiske's line of Sound steamers. He wore a uniform which would have become Admiral Dewey. Harry Stanwood always called Fiske's officer "Captain Jeer" because his official duties never extended beyond the pier.

The St. Charles also boasted of its chaplain, a retired Scotch clergyman and royal good man who married couples while they waited in the parlor. The preacher was highly esteemed by the boys and although they played pranks on his reverence at times he rather enjoyed than condemned the skylarking. The Reverend Doctor, who on occasion filled a pulpit, had an excellent library and was a man of deep learning and was often [the] deciding arbitrator in settling knotty questions of office discussion. Dick Fitzgerald suggested that the Doctor put up a sign in the office announcing: OFF-HAND FUNERALS AND SUDDEN MARRIAGES A SPECIALTY.

Generally, the divine spent his leisure hours in his room with his books but one night a newly registered was describing a wonderful machine for opening oysters. The Doctor paused at the office while getting his key and became interested. The gang tried to freeze the relater but the stranger was both fly and fluent, to the discomfiture of the madcaps and the enjoyment of the chaplain.

One of the permanent women residents was the forewoman of a factory, to whom, without affront, was given the title of "Corsets" by Harry Stanwood. During the estimable woman's stay, she proved an angel to the sick. But one day Dick carried her away and she became Mrs. Fitzgerald.

One winter this writer and Harry Stanwood roomed on Landlord's Row of the office floor. Harry Stanwood would bring his banjo into No. 1. Proprietor Leland would join in the festivities and help along the fun by ringing up Keegan. Of a night, other instrumentalists and vocalists would join in the free concert for the edification of the man who kept the place. As everybody that inhabited the St. Charles kept hours from choice, no one was disturbed to complain except the housekeeper, who reported to the head of the house, "I don't like the noise in No. 1."

"I do," responded the man who went to market at three o'clock in the morning.

One night, in going to his room, Leland met with a surprise; and so did the man who was in it and, also, inside the landlord's overcoat. George S. rang for Keegan, the porter, whom he sent on the run for a policemen; and, until the officer arrived, Leland drummed the thief good and hard.

Leland was a sturdy man and an admirer of Jim Mace, the Gypsy pugilist, who was so clever with his hands. On the other hand, he detested Joe Coburn, who was a low-bred ruffian [and] who for years made himself a terror in public places. When Mace and Coburn met in the ring, Leland hoped that the brutal bully would get a good drubbing. But, as "one was afraid and the other dassent," the pugilists fought the air to the disgust of their backers. Before the fight, Jim Mace was a welcome caller at the St. Charles but the first time he turned up after the fiasco Leland gave him the icy stare and cold shoulder of unconcealed contempt.[30]

From the time that William W. Durand came to New York, accompanying Andrew Haight and George W. DeHaven after their remarkable season with the Great Eastern Circus and Menagerie, he ever afterward quartered at Bleecker and Broadway. The circus ship, Great Eastern, was practically launched on wind for lack of capital and sailed to success on a light I.O.U. It was one of the most audacious ventures ever attempted by a management.[31] And much of its astonishing prosperity was freely attributed to the writer and newspaper advertiser, Bill Durand, the typical Southerner, who smoked like a chimney and chewed plug tobacco and wrote with the sledgehammer of conviction. His was a forceful and original pen.

George J. Guilford, another scribe, wintered at the St. Charles and breakfasted late. When the delegate from Cincinnati [sat] at the table, he always found himself in hot water and soap and suds because the floor-scrubber received the paid tip to "drown Guilford out."

32

ON THE ROAD

[New York Clipper, December 28, 1872]

Hoop la! Springtime has come for the benefit of gentle Annie and the public at large. The winter snow has melted and the roads are knee deep with the mud. Those gentlemen who have been watching for "sleepers" all winter about the faro table, uniformed in a fur collar and a linen duster, group where the genial rays of the sun shine warmest and return thanks that they have survived and pray that they may continue to exist until straw hats are again generally worn.

Roll out the bill wagon and the paste wagon in the glory of their new paint. Load in the glorious posters, the wordy programs, handsome lithographs and illuminated cards. Supply the agents with abundance of contract blanks. Give the press agent his cuts and instruct him to make the columns of the newspapers as flowery as the hillsides in the coming May and as gorgeous as the tinted heavens of an autumnal sunset. Fit the new paste brushes to their handles. Lay in a stock of starch and tacks and don't charge the manager a cent of profit thereon. Fetch out the horses and hitch up. I am anxious to see the first stand of bills for the season posted. Slap on the paste with a will. Blister your hands. All together, boys, "This is the best show on the road and we are the bosses in the business."

Opposition stand aside and clear the track. The grandest combination of the universe is on wheels. Never was the little old man who directs the posting more in his element [as] he sits upon his bill wagon shouting his orders like a colonel of militia in a sham fight. How the paste flies over the heads of the men, into the faces of the on-lookers. You never saw the Splinter? Why, he is a sight worth seeing. He is built on the plan of a clothespin and is as graceful as a turkey walking on a hot gridiron. His arms flap in the spring gale and he throws his brush with the skill of a veteran. What a Bardolph he would make. It would require no further reddening of the nose; the color there is permanent. Such a fellow as he would have shown well in the train of the fat and lying knight.[32]

This is the first season for Salts of Syracuse; and at the outset he pokes the handle of his brush into the stomach of Friday (much to the discomfiture of that individual), who says Nova Scotia, the province of his birth, is a very fine country---when it don't rain. Jersey, the ostler, who is now commencing his travels, conveys the impression to the small boys about the paste wagon that he is an "old showman" and wonders if the young lady who is viewing the picture of Mlle. Rosina on horseback does not imagine that he is the manager. He discovers during the evening that the mysterious maiden is a dishwasher at the hotel; and from the day he leaves Newark, New Jersey, until he terminates his engagement at Calais, Maine, the revenue of the postal department is increased and the national debt materially lessened by the bulk of their correspondence.

Tintype portraits in sixteen distinct positions are exchanged and midnight oil consumed in the indicting of love missives. John Garth, the program juggler, gives the workers the value of his experience and advice. The contracting agent is badgering a stupid Dutchman who deals in lager and bologna, speaks but little English and that very much mixed. The director of publications is annoying the managing editor. In short, the advance corps are all at work once more "on the road."

Wait until the day's work is finished and set yourself down with the boys in the comfortable warmth given out by the stove in the hotel office. The contractor is looking over the contracts he has made during the day. The man of the pen is thinking up the copy for a three-sheet poster. The paste brigade are indulging in reminiscences. The little old man is full of them and stretches the truth to an alarming extent. Jersey tells the most inane of stories, to the disgust of Salts. Friday and John Garth learnedly discuss the proper method of programming a show. And the Splinter at length secures the attention of all by relating his travels with Forepaugh, O'Brien, and Haight & Wooten. As a preliminary, he ties his long legs in a knot and proceeds by furnishing a recipe to keep paste from spoiling.

"You don't know Steve Young, do you?" said the Splinter. "He always travels with the show that Charlie Castle goes with. Bob Armstrong, who used to be ahead of J. M. French, told me this story. Last time I saw Bob he was a clerk in a hotel up in Rutland, Vermont. Dr. Jones, the writer, told me so. The doctor said that Steve's memory was not very good. So one day, that he mightn't forget the name of the next stand, he writ it on the foot board of the bill wagon with a piece of chalk. Ridin' over the country it got worn off, you know, by the rubbing of his feet; and when Steve came to a crossroads and wanted to ask the right road to take, he couldn't make out his memorandum and he sat there, scratching his head and trying to think of the name.

"After a minute or two he gave it up and sung out to a man who was workin' in the field close by.

"'I say, mister, can you tell me the name of a town near here which sounds sunthing like peck?'

"In course the farmer didn't know what peck meant, for he had never traveled with a show; but he commenced to name the towns and, by-me-by, sez he:

"'Eaton.'

"'That's so,' says Steve. 'Eating, Eaton, Eating, that's it! Get up.' And away he went before the countryman had half finished telling him the way."

Early to bed, for the paste brigade must be on the road before daylight. The stands are all for one day and there is no time to be lost.

"Breakfast at four, landlord. Good night, good night."

The trouble has not yet commenced. Wait until opposing companies strike our route, then the paper will fly. The little old man puts on his overalls and slings paste as if his existence were at stake; the contractor "jumps ahead" and secures billboards and posting places; the writer dips his pen in wormwood and the battle rages. Telegrams from the managerial commander-in-chief in the rear flash along the lines. The action has become general, the armor is buckled on and the cry is "War!"

The strength of the road stock is tested to the utmost, as the drives are long and man and horse begin to wear under the strain. Rains set in and the roads become almost impassable. The agents hunt lots and licenses wading in the slush. The newspaper man tells no more funny stories to local editors but is uglier and bitterer than his writings. Jersey wishes himself in Newark once more and loses his much needed rest in writing letters to the fair dishwasher. Friday is the only happy man in the crowd; the weeping heavens and the muddy streets remind him so much of the land of Longfellow's "Evangeline."

A mob of boys run howling after the two teams that are dragged through the street at a furious rate, considering the depth of the mud. The enemy have arrived. The paste brigade of the other show is here. "Now look out for a clash and a quarrel," you say? No, there is where you make a mistake. The representatives of the rival circuses greet each other in the most cordial manner, with many a hearty clasp of the hand and inquiry as to each other's health and prosperity. In an incredible short space of time the newcomers are at work. The ringing echo of the carpenter's hammer tells of the rising of the mammoth billboards. Like chivalrous soldiers, they fight for the flag of their employer, leaving no duty undone that shall tend to bring him success. But when the day's labors are over they will gather about the stove in the hotel office and revive pleasant recollections of the past and discuss the merits of their respective shows.

In the fall of the year you will find them resplendent with new suits, laden with jewelry and brilliant with diamonds, their pockets distorted with immense wads of small notes, finding a welcome wherever they go---as long as the money lasts. There may be a perceptible difference in the texture of the cloth which the Splinter wears and the stunning pin on his breast may be an "Alaska," but what of that? He feels just as big in his new suit as any man who has been ON THE ROAD.

CONSIDERING AND CONCERNING THE CHILDREN
[*Billboard*, May 18, 1901]

It is a saying, trite and true, that if you can catch the women you can draw the men. Charles White, in establishing located-minstrelsy at his Melodeon in the Bowery, New York, laid the foundation of public favor by getting the fair sex to attend upon invitation, until going to the minstrels came to be looked upon as a very proper caper. At a late date, Tony Pastor, in the same Bowery, admitted of a Friday night for a considerable time, free of charge, all ladies accompanied by paying escorts. Women were rather shy of the vaudeville, and Antonio, like White, was educating a new class of patrons and removing the prejudices that existed against the varieties in the minds of a great number of people who had put one of the most entertaining forms of amusement under the ban.[33]

To be sure, under the missionary plan of Messrs. White and Pastor, it frequently required two ladies to guide one gentleman to the performance. The shrewd inciters of public appreciation were not aggrieved thereat---only the more rejoiced.

The American newspaper humorists have made lots of fun for themselves, the show folks, and the general reader by dwelling on the number of adults it required to guide a child to and from the circus with safety. On the average, from a large front door experience, I should say three to one. Now, as the child seems both the magnet and an advertiser, it stands [that] the tent show manager, even if he has a menagerie, [needs] to reach the young folks and interest them in his coming. The child is not a hypocrite like many of the elders. [He] loves the show with a full heart and does not sneak out to the show grounds like a culprit with a mouthful of silly and untruthful excuses: "I didn't care to come myself but the children insisted." "If it hadn't been for the zoological collection, I shouldn't have been here." "Of course they are all alike and I have seen everything but the youngsters must be satisfied." And so on and so on.

The pictorial on the billboards bring the children around as thickly as flies gather at the bung of a molasses hogshead on a wharf. Facing the many-colored display, no feature is lost to view or discussion. It has been noted and the fact commented on that the most incorrigible children begin a period of good behavior and model conduct upon the billing of a circus and extending up to the show's performance. In many households, the hair brush and the slipper entirely disappear as weapons of correction and castigation. The only warning being needed on a rising infraction [is], "If you don't behave, you can't go to the circus." What boy or girl ever failed to come to time, facing so terrible an alternative?

Also, please to observe the great moral influence of the circus. Still, Sunday school superintendents and pastors of flocks have been known to get up picnics on circus day and have lured the youth away from the sawdust, the clowns and the elephant to the woods, cold victuals and the stomach ache.

All bright children of the present day read the newspapers and are thoroughly posted as to the important local details of the circus advertisement---the date of appearance, location of lot, scale of prices, opening of performances, hour of parade and route of procession. Even the smallest boy never bothers the ticket seller at the red wagon with a string of questions. He has received all the necessary information from the press or the small bills.

The child being an advertiser as well as an attendant, the youth's influence should be counted. I was of that opinion at my start in the circus line. Murray had a series of small cards in colors, advertising features of the show; and these were put in the hands of the little men and women at the coming out hours at the schoolhouses. These cards were issued with great care and, the work being faithfully done, it counted to advantage along with the other media of publicity. To be sure, there was nothing new in the idea but the picture cards were attractive. All were carried home and none were destroyed or wasted and each bore a well-worded announcement of the show.

One season I prepared for the show a small four-page affair especially for the juveniles and called it "The Sunbeam." It contained a single story that incorporated in the narrative the grand glories of the show. I also planned the insertion of single column stories for boys and girls in the newspapers, running them in regular reading matter, at small expense, in connection with the regular display advertising. Whether that last scheme paid I had no means of knowing but I believe that it did.

After a while it became impossible to distribute any printed or pictured matter at or in the vicinity of the schoolhouses, under the orders of the boards of education and the penalty of arrest. In spite of this, it was found to be an easy matter to reach the children promptly and efficiently.

For two seasons at least and perhaps more I prepared a special boys' and girls' publication for Adam Forepaugh; and the distribution was made from the first advertising car under the supervision of Mike Coyle, who described it a most excellent advertising medium and perhaps the best used by the show. From the moment the advertising car reached town and was sidetracked, genial Mike saw that every youthful visitor got a copy of the *Boys and Girls.* And the more he gave away the more they came, until the local edition was exhausted. Being sought for instead of distributed, they were all the more valuable as an advertisement and ever so much more appreciated. The procession, as "an exhibition of the resources of the establishment," has a powerful pull and determines many as to their attendance; but the little ones have known their fate and arrived at their conclusions before the fixed date.

The circus is an institution for the family, for young and old. And it is a clean amusement and that is more than can be said of some kinds of stage performances (I will not say entertainments.). Being conducted decently, the managers of American tent shows have been and are being patronized by the best people; whereas, in some of the first-class theatres, it is quite the necessary thing for a man to explore in advance, to learn for himself whether or not it would be the proper thing to invite a woman---wife, sweetheart, or sister---to the "reigning sensation of three capitals."

To return to our mutton, in one instance at least I know that my circus literature for juveniles was perused by an adult. Charles A. Potter, many years a circus agent and postmaster of Danielson, Conn., was distributing "The Sunbeam" in advance of the Murray show when he was accosted by a clerical individual with the inquiry:

"Is the gentleman who wrote that charming little story connected with the circus?"

"He is our director of publications---that is, newspaper man and writer," responded Potter. Then the good man threw up both hands and exclaimed

"What a wicked waste of talent!"

"Guess he thought you ought to be writing tracts," remarked Potter on reporting the conversation to me.

I am not the only person who has, perhaps, missed his calling; but as wicked an old wretch as I ever knew wrote yellow matter for publication with the same hands that he dashed off pious and goody-goody tracts. It is my belief that the writer who induces persons to enjoy themselves has a commendable mission and has the credit of creating happiness.

I have spoken of the value of pictorial advertising cards as a means of reaching children and that recalls the fact that the Sells Brothers got out the best, most elaborate and expensive series that I ever saw used in advance of a show. Like a certain cigar, "they were generously" large, and artistic as well. On the reverse [side was a place for] reliable information [about] zoology. The set was enclosed in a stout manila envelope and labeled as issued by the educational department of Sells Brothers' Shows. These really desirable pictures were given away in sets and not singly and were much sought after.

Sam Joseph and this writer went into Chicago to boom the show under the personal direction of that master of the advance, Peter Sells. While I gave particular attention to the newspapers, Samuel took to the educational department and proceeded to arrange for the distribution of the extra fine picture cards. Sam Joseph always was and is an enthusiast and he spread himself on the preliminaries. And I was only too willing to have the literary bureau push along the educational department.

Sam had arranged that the free-for-all gift distribution should begin at the music store of Lyon & Healy at a certain hour on a certain day. And Sam was on hand at the appointed time to do the giving.

Agreeable to the request, I had announced the presentations in all the newspapers; and, although I did not see the rush, I take Sam's word for it, supported by Peter Sells' statement, that all of Cook County surrounded and invaded Lyon & Healy's, overwhelming and overrunning Sam and the entire establishment of proprietors and clerks. The mob rioted in their struggles to secure the publications of the educational department of Sells Bros.' Shows and it was not until the police came to rescue in force and fought their way in that anything like order was secured.

Luckily, the police rescued Sam before he was torn to pieces or trampled under foot. [They] locked all the doors except an exit escape, which they controlled by force of arms. During the hubbub, pickpockets plied their fingers and the wails of the losers were added to the tumult and a good many musical instruments got out of tune or suffered material damage. Altogether, it was the most exciting day ever experienced by the educational department of Sells Bros.' Shows.

When the "free distribution of the works of art" was over, Sam, limp and weary, reached the Continental Hotel and dropped into a chair in my room. The eyes of Joseph always were a prominent feature of his face but on this occasion they protruded beyond all previous precedent and he talked so fast that he did not have time to lisp. As Joseph related his thrilling adventure and narrow escape from annihilation, he forgot his fatigue and soared in graphic language, although sore in body. Sam's eloquence was amazing and his language alarming and still I don't think he exaggerated the scenes at Lyon & Healy's a little bit. After all, Sam declared that the educational department of Sells Bros.' Shows was an unqualified success.

I was much interested in the attracting of the children to the circus but I did not think it was judicious to go around to Lyon & Healy's and learn their views. The musical firm was quite too busy straightening up things in the store, while a force of men were putting in new glass in the doors and windows. Peter Sells agreed with me that the time was highly inopportune. So neither of us pursued our investigations in that direction. Perhaps if any circus advertiser is in need of a branch of the educational department in Chicago, it would be as well not to invite the musical firm mentioned to interest themselves in the movement.

Herr Amidi Neuporte, Dutch Equilibrist, 1846

SHOP TALK
[*Billboard*, May 4, 1901]

Last season Burly Bluff, the manager and owner of one of the largest circuses and menageries, made an extraordinary season, playing to vast numbers of delighted people and adding enormously to his already substantial bank account. His season's proceeds being beyond all precedent, it naturally came to the notice and discussion of the Turn Over Club at its several conventions at the office of the *Billboard*. The receipts of the show were so large that they were a matter of much comment. But at one particular gathering, inspired by the editor of the *Billboard*, the representative experts present expressed themselves, not to the enlightenment of the head of the sanctum but to his entire mystification. To his inquiry as to whom the credit was due for Burly Bluff's unparalleled success, the several gentlemen present responded as below stated.

Mr. John Ringling, no novice in the matter of selecting territory for a show, freely expressed himself:

"Burly Bluff made money because his show was put out in the right towns. I don't think that from spring till fall there was a quisby or a doubtful stand. No show, Bluff's or anybody else's, can make money under unfavorable conditions. No amount of advertising or any quantity or quality of merit or vastness of dimensions can supply the advantage of spotting the right spots."

All the members looked at each other, some with nods of acquiescence; and then a general desire was expressed to hear Mr. Peter Sells. Being nothing loath, that past master of the art of announcement went on to say:

"There is much force in what our friend Ringling has said but, admitting that Burly Bluff's country was selected with rare judgment, no one will dispute that his outdoor advertising in every variety was something stupendous. To be frank, I never saw better and I concede and opine that Bluff caught the coin by the paper on the wall."

Will Donaldson did not have to be asked to address the astute assembly.[34] He took his cue from and agreed with Peter Sells:

"That's just where you are right. The paper was all lithographed, every sheet of it, and the window work was simply out of sight."

"Yes," put in Hennegan, "you should have seen my giant dates."

And then Dick Ball had an oar to put in in behalf of the contractor

"Bluff's man made mighty good contracts. I never knew of better and I am something of a close figurer myself."

"I should smile," William Henry Gardner remarked.

"I should rise to remark," Mike Coyle added.

"In the single, all important item of lots," Richard resumed, "Bluff was never left. His contractor always got him the best and most centrally located at the lowest price. How could he help but succeed with a man of such judgment and economy in front of him?"

J. M. Kane was not convinced and, having a mind of his own, was not slow in stating the case as he saw it from where he sat:

"Oh, fudge! And I don't so remark out of any feeling of disrespect for the opinions of my seniors. As a looker-on in Vienna the past season, I came to the conclusion that Burly Bluff's great year came entirely from the newspapers. He put no curb or limit on his director of publications and the result, gentlemen, you know it."

By this time the enthusiast was on his feet and gesticulating in his ardor. With warmth, he added:

"Every newspaper column poured dollars and dollars into Bluff's red wagon."

Just as Kane sat down, Captain F. B. Wilson was able to rise and express himself. He spoke with some feeling and marked emphasis:

"You are forgetting the press representative with the show. That fellow was a hummer. His mill ran all the while and he fed the newspapers ahead of the show with all kinds of sensations and write-ups. The greatest inventive genius that I know of in this line. He would get up the most impossible yarn and believe it himself by the time the ink was dry. You couldn't deny anything he put in print. And it all went, every line, and you couldn't pick up an exchange in a newspaper office without seeing something of his copied. Fact! I know what I'm talking about."

William Porter, a retiring, sturdy sort of a person who had been listening attentively in the back room, gained confidence enough in his self-evident modesty to come in and say his say:

"I was with Bluff's advance and I am satisfied that it was the country work that did the business. That is just what it was."

As Porter was a man of few words, he had no more to say. After a spell of solemn silence, Bob Stickney had the floor (as much as he wanted of it) to remark:

"Burly Bluff always gave a good ring performance. And last season he outdid himself and did the business of his life on the strength of his entertainment."

As Stickney, Jr., came to an anchor, the editor of the *Billboard* remarked that he had jabbed the mucilage brush into the ink bottle. And, looking from one to the other who had unburdened themselves as to the foundation of Burly Bluff's fortunate tour, he remarked with a rather amused air:

"Many men, many minds."

None of the previous speakers taking umbrage at the sally, he addressed the Sage of Geneva:

"What has Mr. Colvin to say on so interesting a topic? Certainly a man who served so many years under the banner of George F. Bailey & Co., Adam Forepaugh, Montgomery Queen, and W. C. Coup must be able to communicate without talking through his hat."

"Burly Bluff had a very complete menagerie," the doctor responded.

"Say, look here, Darwin," cried Louis E. Cooke, "spiels in the interest of Hagenbeck don't go."

Everybody laughed and Colvin's cheeks reddened to the color of a ripe apple off his New York State farm. For a moment the doctor hesitated but after a bit he resumed:

"As I was about to say when I was interrupted by the hotel keeper from Newark, Burly Bluff had a very complete menagerie and kept every cage full the entire season. Like my old master, Adam Forepaugh the First, he never allowed that department to deteriorate."

A chorus of large "Oh's!" from all around the room did not dismay the determined doctor.

"The menagerie," he resumed, "is the greatest drawing factor with the show. I have kept tabs on it during my entire career and, as the Dutchman said, 'I have long time in dot pizness pen.'"

"Did Hagenbeck say that?" joshed Si Semon, who, being baldheaded, is not able to wear long hair like Major Burke, also in advance of Buffalo Bill.

"You are not in the Wild West, Mr. Semon!" sharply returned the doctor, "and the gentlemen present have not become uncivilized by contact with savages."

Si sighed. Not at the retort, but laughed with the rest. The editor of the *Billboard* recovered the mucilage brush out of the ink bottle and said something. After the explosion and the resumption of calm, the veteran Colvin returned to the subject uppermost.

"You may jibe and you may josh but there isn't a one of you but will admit, if he cares to adhere to the truth and be frank about it, that the animals draw and are the great cards. Out of my own experience and from personal knowledge I can vouch for great profits from the menageries. How much did the 'Flatfoots' owe to the exhibition of the first hippopotamus in America? Didn't Adam Forepaugh make a power of money out of the elephant Romeo? Do you recall VanAmburgh, Herr Driesbach, Prof. Langworthy, and Crockett in the lion's den?"

"No, doctor," said the provoking Sam Joseph, "we are all too young to be acquainted with the ancient history of the American menagerie."

After all heads had chuckled at Sam's drive at the doctor, the editor of the *Billboard* remarked:

"What are you getting at, Mr. Colvin?"

"Getting at the drawing power of the menagerie, even a single animal in some instances, and to substantiate my claim that Burly Bluff's great big business last year came from the menagerie. It was the menagerie that did the trade, nothing else and nobody else. That's my opinion for what it is worth."

A great pause came after Colvin's confession of conviction. After a while, who should come from a corner where he had been sitting with the intention of writing but only as a forced listener? None other than Burly Bluff in person. He did not wait to be seated but, in some heat, delivered himself.

"As you gentlemen seem to know it all, with no two of you being agreed, it might be superfluous for me, an interested party, to express an opinion. But I am going to tell you all, and all the same, that Burly Bluff made a pot of money last season because---because Burly Bluff managed the show. That was the very reason, the sole and only reason, and Burly Bluff was alone responsible for the success."

Everybody in the sanctum came pretty near not breathing at the boldness of the egotistical statement. The assertive and indignant manager took the center of the room and struck a pose that Sam Joseph declared would do in the ring as a feature for "Ajax Defying the Lightning Rod Agent" or "The Roman Gladiator on the Way to Watertown." Sam always was up in the classics and at one time was credited in Cincinnati with being the author of the books of Josephus.

As the assembly neither contradicted nor sustained Burly Bluff, he turned on his heels and left the sanctum as mad as a hornet. The editor of the *Billboard* remarked not but he wrote on a piece of copy paper:

"MORAL: It all depends upon the point of view."

RECOLLECTIONS AND REFLECTIONS OF A RETIRED GYMNAST
[*New York Clipper*, November 29, 1879]

"Out of the business now," said the speaker, "although I have turned my hand to almost every branch of it in my time."

A wicked press agent, one Harry Cordova, who had come from the malarial-plagued spot of Missouri, crippled up like a scarred veteran at the end of a war campaign, made a casual allusion to 1492, a date well recollected in connection with the history of this country. Frank Donaldson made a good natured retort about "the natural effect of bile and circus bill writing" and then went on:

"I've got a record in the circus business that I'm not ashamed of and I have been a good deal in pantomime and burnt cork and my wife was one of the first, if not the very first, to give a dramatic performance in Texas. I will tell you all about it sometime. What is the business coming to?" asked the ancient gymnast, just as the critic of today prates of the decline of the drama.

No one seemed ready with a satisfactory answer to the conundrum, whereupon he renewed:

"The big fish have eaten up the little ones and the public are no longer satisfied unless they can see acres of canvas and a procession a mile long. The tent shows have grown in size but the performer has been ignored. Performers! Are we going to have any more, any more American performers?"

Charley Noyes, forgetting for the moment the twinges of his rheumatism, exclaimed:

"Yes, with your meddlesome Society for the Prevention of Cruelty to Children, so called. Ask my apprentices today if they do not thank me ten thousand times for teaching them the business. Ask Wooda Cook which he had rather do, measure tape at ten dollars a week behind a dry goods counter or somersault on the back of a horse as he does at one hundred?"

The profoundness of Mr. Noyes' argument was substantiated by the old-time gymnast, who brushed the somewhat disturbed nap of his tile and waxed eloquent:

"Look at the Robinsons, the Melvilles, Stickneys and Carrolls. The idea that Robert Stickney cannot teach his own son the calling his father taught him! Many's the man who envies Bob his two hundred dollars or more a week and a fat bank account in Cincinnati. If there had existed such a society in Bob Stickney's boyhood, Sir Robert might today be engaged in the lowest but humble vocation of opening oysters or sawing wood. Why don't the society expend its energies in putting shoes on barefooted newsboys and line their stomachs with warm meals instead of making raids that give them a little notoriety in the newspapers?

"Speaking about 1492, there's plenty of old timers yet living that could spin some very interesting yarns, such men as 'Old' John Robinson, Doctor Spalding, Rogers, Levi North, Lent, Dan Gardner and Barney Carroll. They could tell you some mighty interesting facts in regard to ring performances in America; for while the stage and minstrelsy have their historians, but very little has been done in the way of chronicling the rise and progress of arenic amusements on this continent. Although, on the other side of the 'pond', they have got it down as fine as silk, from Astley up to Hengler and Sanger."

At the earnest solicitation of a number of circus folk present, Mr. Donaldson turned back in memory the pages of his life book and, while all listened with great interest, said:

"The first circus I ever saw was in 1838. It was Rockwell's company. And I became enamored with the business. And from that moment my highest ambition was to become a circus performer, a desire I was not able to gratify until 1842 when I met Aaron Turner in Cherryville, Pennsylvania, and entered his employ as a posturer at twelve dollars a week. I well recollect giving him a sample of my abilities in a barn. Jim Myers, who is now a successful manager abroad, Mike Lipman, still living in Cincinnati, and Tom Withe were apprentices with the show. Tim Turner was riding a principal act; Nat Turner, four horses; and Jim Myers was doing the slack rope and just beginning to play clown.

"It was about a forty-horse show and our menagerie consisted of one elephant and something like six cages of animals. The prices of admission were twenty-five and twelve and a half cents and the canvas [was] a one hundred foot round-top. The sideshows, as well as dressing rooms, are quite that size nowadays. Hotel rates were thirty-seven and a half cents a day and it was no uncommon thing to see liquors placed upon the table free of charge and the performers, upon leaving the table, presented by the landlord with a 'choice Principee' two-for-a-cent, and good cigars they were, too.

"I was sorry to read the other day of the death of one of the Carlo Brothers. I recollect their father well, Felix Carlo, as pantomimist and gymnast. About '55, he lived in Forsyth Street and there projected and practiced an act for which he secured an opening at Frank Rivers' Varieties.[35] He constructed a revolving globe of huge proportions on which he was to do a brother act with two of his boys. Well, you know how the globes are made, common boards sawed out in a circular form, glued and nailed together and then covered with cloth and fancifully painted. Carlo worked away like a beaver on the act and it promised to be a big thing. But he made no attempt to move the globe to the theatre till the Monday he was to open. Imagine his chagrin when he found that there was no means of getting the globe out of the house. It could be got through neither window nor door. And the engagement was lost.

"I have in my time been either the originator of several acts or the first to perform them in this country or participate in their production jointly with others. The first double-perch was done in Cincinnati with Wesley Barmore's circus, exhibiting on Vine Street where the Palace Varieties afterwards stood. This was in 1853. For the first two days, E. L. Libby held the perch and the mounters were George Dunbar and Frank Donaldson. For the balance of the season, Dunbar held the perch and Oliver Dodge and myself did the mounting. It was afterwards long performed by Henry Magilton, Dunbar and myself. And I am glad to say all this trio are living today.

"In June, 1854, I was traveling with Spalding & Rogers. The VanAmburgh party was running two shows that season and we played against their English show, an importation, at Greenville, Indiana. There, George Dunbar held the perch and for the first time, I believe anywhere, there were four mounters: Henry Magilton, Nat Rogers, Charles Crosby, and Frank Donaldson. I shall never forget the expression of surprise of our English cousins who had come into the canvas to see the 'blarsted American performers,' as one after the other of the quartet of mounters took position. 'By jove! The bloody Yankee is going to take up the whole company!'

"By the way, my old partners and comrades in the ring, Henry Magilton and George Dunbar, were the first in America to do 'The Two Comics, or Motley Brothers.' Magilton and Mons. LaThorne afterwards did the act. The ladder perch was the first time performed about '56 at L. B. Lent's circus, Philadelphia, [with] Dunbar holding and Magilton and Donaldson performing.

"The winter of the exhibition of the Crystal Palace in New York,[36] Henry Magilton and myself did a double trapeze act at VanEpps Amphitheatre, Mobile, being the first to perform the act. Francois Siegrist, the same season at Franconi's Hippodrome, New York, performed a single-trapeze.

"Yes, I have done 'Pete Jenkins' to oblige a manager but there has been only one 'Pete Jenkins' and that was poor Charley Sherwood. Speaking of him, did you ever know the origin of the phrase 'red hot'? In '59, Uncle John Tryon put a circus into Purdy's National Theatre in Chatham Street. Sherwood was a member of the company and 'Pete Jenkins' was in the bill. I don't know whether you know it or not but Sherwood, in the early days of negro minstrelsy, was known as Master Champion and was a rattling good jig dancer. And many's the jig I have danced in public myself as well. Sherwood had given the b'hoys a touch of the jig and every night they would call on 'Pete' for a jig. And Sherwood would step it right lively on the boards between the footlights of the stage and the curb of the ring, never failing to receive as a reward a shower of pennies. One night some wretch heated a large, old-fashioned copper cent in a gas jet by the aid of a crotched stick and threw it to the interpreter of the rural and obfuscated 'Jenkins.' No sooner had the copper struck the stage than Sherwood pounced upon it and, almost at the same instant, dropped it as he exclaimed, 'Red hot!'

"From that day to this, 'red hot' has been a popular expression and the phrase was used over and over again by Sherwood until it became a saying of the day.

"That was a pretty good spec of Charley's picking up the shower of pennies and, as salaries were not forthcoming, the 'Original

Pete Jenkins' was the only man in the company who had spending money. But, as an insurance against 'red hot' coppers, Sherwood used to go on every night with gloved hands and pick up the heated coppers 'mid cries from his admirers of 'Red hot! red hot!'

"I recollect the coming to this country of the Siegrist Brothers, Francois and Auguste. They were the first to do 'Mons. and Madame Dennie'. This was in '53 in Levi North's circus in Philadelphia, where the Continental Hotel now stands. But the act was too Frenchified and did not take. I Americanized it and it made a hit. George Dunbar in the amended version played Mons. Dennie; Charles Brown, since deceased, was the Madame; and I acted the Servant.

"The first double-ladders in this country were performed while I was with Levi North in Philadelphia by Dunbar, Magilton, Hankins and Donaldson. We first learned of the act from the Siegrists, who explained it to Dunbar and wanted him to practice it for six weeks and then produce it in public. Our four went to work immediately upon it and, after three or four days of work, to the amazement of the Siegrists and the management as well, successfully performed the feat in public. This goes to show how ready is American wit and energy to 'pick up' business supposed by foreign artists to require a prolonged apprenticeship or arduous practice. The double-ladders were afterwards performed in England with Howes & Cushing's United States Circus under the title of 'The Rocky Mountain Wonders.' George Ware, who has since visited this country as a vocalist and has some considerable reputation as a song writer, wrote up a bill wherein he described 'The Rocky Mountain Wonders leaping from tree to tree in the barren sands of the great American desert.' That was a great bill. And it created a big laugh among the American performers, as John Murray and Burnell Runnells will tell you to this day. And I'll warrant you that Col. Joseph Cushing, the hale and hearty farmer 'way down in Dover, New Hampshire,' has not forgotten it himself.

"Yes, sir, the boys were not slow those days in picking up an act. When Hiram Franklin did the first double-somersault at Niblo's Garden on a Saturday night, Buck Gardner, the following Monday, duplicated the feat in the Bowery.[37]

"I have seen a heap of the world since I joined Turner in '42 and many is the thousands of miles I have traveled by roadway, rail and sea. I have had seasons of prosperity and reverse. But, in looking back, [I] can recall the triumphs of my profession and [I can] let its struggles, hardships and annoyances sink out of sight. There is many a comical incident to recall or laughable adventure to refer to. And that which was at the time the most provoking of occurrences has since come to be an amusing affair.

"I recollect that in '57 in Philadelphia with Lent I was in the pantomime of 'The Magic Banjo,' in which Joe Pentland appeared as the clown. As the curtain fell I was left in the tableau, almost up to the flies. And in this instance I was left without any means of getting down, to say nothing of escaping from the theatre. No sooner was the show out than douse went the gas and everyone raced out of the building. At last, after bellowing myself hoarse, I was released by the night watchman, who chanced to hear my cries. After that, I provided myself with a rope and [thus] managed to get to the stage about as soon as the curtain roll.

"It is getting late and is about time for me to go. I had no idea of remaining half the time but when one runs back to 1842 it takes time. One more and I'm off. In 1845 there was a little English clown playing with Welsh, Mann & Delevan. Jack Wells was his name and I presume many of you have heard of him. He used to do an act called 'The Magic Ladder.' He would, once at the top, dispose of one upright and the rounds and balance himself on his head on the sole remaining upright and, in that reverse position, drink a glass of brandy. That is, the genuine brandy was supposed to finish the act and Jack would not accept a substitute. When a colored liquid was provided, Jack dashed it aside and stoically remained upside down without apparent inconvenience, vowing his intention of 'hanging up there all night' unless the genuine cognac was brought. Many is the night Jack remained aloft, refusing to come down till a property man ran 'round the corner to the nearest saloon and got a glass of brandy."

BARNUM ON THE TENTED FIELD
[*New York Clipper*, July 6, 1872]

With every spring commences a vigorous campaign in the tented field. In this instance the invading army is on a mission of peace and is heartily welcomed everywhere by the people who pay tribute to the stranger without a murmur. The march of a circus company through the land with its host [of people] and the moving of baggage vans from town to town is similar to the progress of an army. No conqueror ever entered a city half so welcome or [was] greeted by so many smiling faces as the glittering pageant threads its way to the inspiring strains of martial music.

Adam Forepaugh made an innovation when he exhibited his aggregation under two tents for one price of admission, where those who had been brought up in a straight-lace school could contemplate the wonders of the animal kingdom without contaminating themselves with the tights and spangles of the arena.[38]

When P. T. Barnum and manager Coup placed their Mastodon on the road, the jovial Dan Castello and his circus were given the principal tent, a second being used for the menagerie, and a third for a museum of living and inanimate curiosities.[39] The success of the great showman's latest venture was without parallel. The seating capacity of the tents was again increased and still found to be inadequate. Wherever they went, the populace turned out *en masse* and every train and by-road running into the cities added their contributions by the thousands. A greater portion of the season, three performances were given daily, causing the fat woman and the giant to lose flesh and the living skeleton, if possible, to grow thinner than ever.

Phineas was ubiquitous, "here, there and everywhere," now ahead of the company, giving gratuitous lectures on "How to Make Money," not forgetting to always say a good word for the "greatest show on earth," to which he would hasten back to publicly present some faithful employee with a gold badge, medal, or other valuable gift as a token of his regard and esteem, an extra attraction that would cram the three canvases to overflowing.

While "way down east," it is reported that a bit of sharp practice was put up on the great showman. A party in Barnum's employ groomed with extra care a pair of P. T.'s own noble blacks, drove them up to where Barnum and Coup were overseeing the erection of the triple tents, and exhibited them as a bargain which he could buy at a reasonable figure. Barnum and Coup examined them critically and instructed their employee to make the purchase at the stated sum, while Genin, the treasurer, counted out the money; after which, the horses were returned to the stable [with] Barnum little aware that he had been duped worse than he ever humbugged the public, by buying at a good price a pair of his own horses. May the hale old fellow be spared these many days. And when the man of enterprise again seeks rest, I hope he will add a few chapters to his autobiography and, besides telling us how he bought the horses, enlighten us as to how he carried the news of the coming of his show upon the rostrum and in the Sunday school.

In Barnum's museum tent, I saw nothing of the club with which Captain Cook was killed. Probably George Wood could not spare it. But there was the sleeping beauty that would have made an elegant sign for a hair dresser, the automaton bell ringers that caused Ned Kendall to burn with jealousy when an attempt was made to persuade him that they were superior to the Berger family. In front of the Cardiff giant at every performance there gathered a group of the curious believers and unbelievers. While some saw in its huge proportions a quaint work of art, others pronounced it the figure of a giant turned from flesh to stone. A tiller of the soil, who had left the field and the plow to see Barnum's last "tarnal humbug," one day expressed an opinion. For half an hour he stood driven to the spot, regardless of the attraction of the happy family or the wart hog. At last, turning to the crowd who pressed closely about, he expressed his views:

"No man ever sculpted that thing out of stone in the world. It couldn't be done. That figure is a putrefied man."

Evidently the old gentleman knew more about farming than he did about Webster's unabridged.

A feature in the museum department was "The Last Supper." The figures were wax-faced and ghastly to contemplate, awakening in the beholder anything but feelings solemn or respectful. When the show reached Providence, Rhode Island, "The Last Supper" was left behind, the management probably arriving at the conclusion that it was rather sacrilegious than otherwise. The members of the company, noticing the absence after leaving Providence, were conjecturing the reasons among themselves, when Gus Lee, the clown, exclaimed:

"They've never heard of the twelve apostles east of Providence and they wouldn't draw a cent, so Barnum told Coup to leave them here." [This was] an explanation which was eminently satisfactory.

Wherever celebrities go in the show world there are many who seek to interview them and wherever Barnum and the "greatest show on earth in three tents" went he was bored by the intrusive, who wished to shake by the hand or have a conversation with the veritable man who had given us Jenny Lind and the "What Is It?" and [who] so many years directed the wonderful temple of amusement, the American Museum. P.T. Barnum is a genial man, easy to approach and happy when meeting the people but at times, being absent from the company, the curiosity of the admirers of Barnum was not satisfied.

In a down east town one day, while members of the company were enjoying a few moments' leisure sitting about the hotel, there entered a venerable old fellow who inquired of the clerk for Mr. Barnum. And [he] was referred to Billy Dutton, the equestrian, who sat near by [and] who in turn pointed to Gus Lee, the clown, deep in reading of the morning paper. (Gus is a blonde that never dyes. In fact, his hair is so light that it is nearer white than any color.)

"Good morning, Mr. Barnum," said the antiquarian, presenting himself to the clown; who, peering over his paper, saw the twinkling eyes of Billy Dutton dancing in suppressed mirth, while Miaco, the gymnast, or the "Boy with the Giant Head," was passing the cue to the rest of the boys.

The stranger had read the life of Barnum and was very much pleased thereat and enthusiastically declared that if he was to begin life again he would embark in the show business, as he always had had a sort of hankering for the life of an exhibitor ever since one of his cows gave birth to a three-legged calf. Unfortunately, or perhaps fortunately, the old gentleman was spared from being a showman.

The clown was pressed with numerous inquiries by the ardent admirer of Barnum for a full hour, to his discomfiture and the great amusement of the professionals. At length, Lee excused himself and the old gentleman reluctantly retired to visit the show, remarking to Billy Dutton as he passed out:

"Well, my young friend, I am very much pleased with my talk with Barnum. He's as chipper as a youngster yet. But one thing kind of surprised me; I didn't think he'd show his years quite so much as he does. Why he's as gray as a rat."

A hearty laugh from all the circus folks greeted the old gentleman; the reason whereof, he was entirely ignorant. And he went away delighted with his interview with P. T. Barnum.

CHARLES STOW, CIRCUS WRITER
[*Billboard*, August 31, 1907]

The title "circus writer," adopted by the circus managers who first employed literary representatives, best applies to Charles Stow, who died in Whitestone, New York, August 16. Mr. Stow was always reticent about his affairs and during his circus career avoided any personal publicity. He was twice married. His father was an Erie County, Pennsylvania, judge, and the son was expected to follow in the father's footsteps in a career at the bar. Col. Dan Rice, the famous circus clown, was the most prominent citizen of Girard and occupied a palatial residence. Rice evidently influenced Stow more than Blackstone. And, having the literary gift, the embryo attorney occupied the editorial chair of the Colonel's newspaper, the *Cosmopolite*, and as a matter of course wrote bills and puffs for the jester of national repute.

While some press agents, through personal magnetism and diplomacy, might have been able to accomplish more than Charles Stow, there was not one during his long career who wrote more effectively and with less effort. His jingles, rhymes and block verse were telling; and embellished his couriers and pamphlets, giving them a pleasing variety.

Mr. Stow was never by his consent mentioned as a director of publicity or press agent. His private card always read, "Charles Stow, Editor."

Mr. Stow possessed oratorical gifts and participated in political campaigns and was quite as strenuous in his way as Roosevelt of Washington. He wrote and delivered a lecture in verse entitled "The Cussedness of Inanimate Things." The circus writer had views about himself and others and expressed them freely because he had a superb opinion of his own unquestioned ability and believed in himself. He once calmly remarked in the office of a show printing house, in the presence of several scribes of established reputations:

"Mr. Durand and I are the only circus writers in the business."

The silence that ensued was felt with both hands by some of the literary lights of the arena; and that wretch, Bill Durand, smiled his approval, while Dr. Reilly at his desk was dumbfounded.

Some of the best work from Stow's pencil was written on behalf of the two shows of the Sells Brothers. He was in no way hampered and wrote and prepared all kinds of copy with perfect freedom of action. The writer was always at his best when having his own way. Peter Sells was himself a first-class writer and advertiser and equal to any of the scribes in peace or war; moreover, the junior member of the firm was a comrade as well as an employer. The elder brothers were appreciative, although Lewis was free to confess that he could readily find fault, but he could find none with Charles Stow.

James A. Bailey had a high opinion of Stow as a writer and held Durand in like esteem. But Bailey and Stow both had red in the hair and at times there was friction when the flint and steel came together. One summer Stow and Charles Sivals, representing different shows, met in St. Louis where they discovered that a variety theatre was on the market for a mere song. They bought out the place as a speculation with no idea of holding it. But Bailey called Stow down and informed him [that] no agent of Barnum, Bailey & Hutchinson Shows was permitted to engage in private business.

Regardless of consequences, Stow exploded and informed Bailey that he would engage in any form of business that he saw fit, that what he did with his money was his own affair, and B. B. & H., individually and collectively, could "go to." A split in the party followed, Bailey and Stow both being too stubborn to relent. Bailey was in a dilemma. He was short-handed for a writer. He invited Fred Lawrence to bear a hand. Lawrence declined. [He] then was proffered a season's engagement and, as a matter of principle, [he] refused to fill Stow's place. Ready circus writers have always been few in number and few arena scribes of caliber [could] suit the exacting James A. Bailey. The men with red in the hirsute got together again, to flare up at the first friction.

As contractors of newspaper space, Damon and Pythias, the only two on earth, Stow and Durand, differed in policy. Stow believed in a spirit of liberality in dealing with the press; at the same time not submitting to extortion. Durand, on the other hand, took a fiendish delight in making a grinding contract that left the publisher in no way disposed toward the show. Charles Stow's policy of equity proved a winner. Often in collision of opposition with a rival show, he would turn over his contracting to one of the other press men and go to the front and hustle all along the line in the interest of the Barnum show; [in so doing, he was] welcomed and boosted in every newspaper office.

Stow was peculiar in the desire not to be known as being connected with a circus and had strange ideas in regard to his personal stature. On his visit to San Francisco, en route to Australia in advance of the Sells Brothers' Shows, he was accompanied by his bride, the second Mrs. Stow. As if possessed of a dual personality, he said to the associate editor of music and drama:

"Please do not mention my marriage in your columns, for you know that I am not in the profession."

Charles Stow, himself to the contrary, was very much in the profession and an honor to it.

While Mr. Stow, the individual, depreciated any publicity as to his connection with the circus, he wrote with actual enthusiasm and his pen shed the flowers of a rich imagination. The writer controlled a wonderful vocabulary and every line was a lure to follow to the culminating climax of adjectives and amazing alliterations. Stow must have been inspired in his youth by the night told tales rehearsed in the winter quarters of the beloved Dan Rice's Show in Girard, even though he attempted to keep his identification with the show a secret.

Stow's assertiveness, aggressiveness and tremendous self-esteem expressed itself in his production in New York of a play from his pen. The verdict was unfavorable, but, in spite of the critics and the frank opinions of two true friends, he avowed that it was as good as anything that Shakespeare ever wrote; and [he] declared that he had been sacrificed by Barnum, Bailey & Hutchinson in a conspiracy to retain his services. He not only said it but believed it. And, in consequence, there was another break and "split" in the party.

In the passing away of Charles Stow, circus writer, another one of the members of the old guard has joined the majority, leaving but few behind to sound the praises of a member who, all in all, was a good fellow and a master at his calling.

THE INVENTED ADVERTISEMENT
[*Billboard*, March 23, 1901]

"Necessity, the mother of invention," is responsible for many a good thing in science, art, mechanics, medicine and advertising; and Farquar expressed the truism in the play of "The Twin Rivals" quite as well as I could have done it myself. How many a fair star owes her first column interview to the loss of her diamonds which she never had, or has wept over jewels held by her uncle instead of the feather-fingered or the burglar? How many, many times has the same old story, the josh of the jewels, found its way into print? The tale comes under the heading of "too numerous to mention." And still, without scarce a variation, it long served its purpose. In one particular version, I recall an exceedingly clever departure from the routine, and truth may have added the zest.

Fanny Davenport's diamonds were purloined at an inn in St. Paul [when] the star was out. And now comes the romantic twist to the tale. The priceless jewels were appropriated by a clerk of the inn and the clerk was possessed of a small wife and a large and interesting family. Being caught, the misguided husband and parent confessed and sued for mercy at the Court of Beauty and he got it.

"I forgive you. Go and sin no more."

Truly, I have no doubt that the event ... occurred and, in fact, I don't care two-plus whether it did [or] not. As an advertisement it was A-1 and the comments of the press would have enriched a clipping bureau had any been in vogue at the time.

It is "no fool of a job" to invent a pure fabrication that will enlist the attention of the press and the public; for it is just as important to interest the editor as it is to excite the citizen. I will admit that in these latter days, since the columns of the yellow journals are so readily open to anything sensational about the profession, be it good, bad, indifferent, false or true, it is an easier matter to float a story than it was in the first years of the seventies. And, then again, in those days a showman was not quite so ready to deceive the newspapers as he was to fool the people.

Previous to the advent of William C. Coup in the East, in company with his Wisconsin partner, Dan Castello, the popular one-ring circuses of L. B. Lent and John H. Murray held their own undaunted. The reintroduction of P. T. Barnum into the sawdust arena at once put a new aspect on affairs. Lent's New York Circus, by reason of its metropolitan reputation and excellent entertainment, covered a wide area during each vacation tour, extending its operation to the big cities of the far West. John H. Murray's Circus, fully as well conducted as Lent's, had grown out of an exhibition, the original owners of which were Den Stone, Frank Rosston, John H. Murray, and one Hutchinson (an athlete and working partner of Murray's), and my very good friend, Mike Coyle....

In 1873 Murray put out his show on the rail, using the company cars and, as usual, visited his favorite Down East stamping grounds, including New Jersey, New England, the lower provinces [of] Canada, New York, and Pennsylvania, touching nothing west of Buffalo.

Prior to P. T. Barnum's World's Fair on Wheels,[40] Lent and Murray had considered the combination of the circus and menagerie as an alarming competition. Neither the Great European, a show too large for its day, or the several shows of George F. Bailey & Co. and VanAmburgh & Co. had been strong enough to overbalance the universally admitted excellence of the highly artistic performance furnished by these two conscientious and experienced legitimate circus managers.

Although the Barnum show, from its birth, swept the country like a cyclone, it being necessary to give three performances a day, there was still a vast number of people who preferred their circus straight, with no cats and in one ring. But with the big Barnum boom there was a foreshadowing of danger ahead. The amount of money distributed by the Barnumites was something enormous and in keeping with the prodigious receipts. As a result, lots, licenses and billboards took an upward tendency, to the disadvantage of the owner of the one-ring show. And, if possible, a still worse feature of the situation was that the single-circle fellow looked very small indeed with his little ad in the newspaper counting room.

Again, P. T. Barnum and company were well nigh monopolizing all the native circus talent and that is, as always was, a limited quantity. Besides, the Barnum party did not halt for a dollar if they wanted anyone and they wanted all the performers in sight. The condition of affairs sent Murray to Europe in the winter of 1872-73; and he returned with a number of artists, including John Henry Cooke, the equestrian of style and finish, already favorably known in this country. To strengthen his reputation in the land of frugality and beans and carry conviction everywhere in the circulation zone of the Boston dailies, Murray resolved to appear at the Hub and risk the stake. P. T. Barnum & Co. and George F. Bailey & Co. had like intention and Murray's only safety depended on the excellence of the performance and anticipating his rivals. W. C. "Bill" Coup, as they used to call him out of Indiana, looked with contempt upon the invasion of George Fox Danbury Bailey, even at 25 cents a card; and the appearance of John H. Murray's Railroad Circus was altogether the best joke of the season.

For years the Stone & Murray Circus and the shows out of which it had sprung had exhibited annually in all the Boston suburbs. So John H. Murray was no stranger to the surroundings. Still, to look back upon the venture, it was an audacious one for Murray, [traveling] with one tent and one ring, to beard the lion, P. T. Barnum and the rest of his menagerie in many dens and in many tents.

John Henry Cooke was riding the now famous act of "Bounding Jockey," leaping from the horse to the ground and from the ground to the horse. And, it must be understood, the equestrian was riding the heralded new act for all it was worth, with almost unfailing precision and certainty and, to the amazement of the audience, "wearing his boots" as promised in the announcements. I want to say right here that the act was not a new one but I thought that it was when I enthusiastically advertised it. Some time afterward I read of it as a former feature before I was born. Thus does the circus act, as well as history, repeat itself.

As I had distaste to directly pulling the leg of newspapers, I [took] recourse to the advertising columns of the *Herald, Globe* and *Journal* and published in their amusement columns the following entirely fictitious correspondence:

$1,000 CHALLENGE

Boston Hotel, May 31, 1873

To the "Great John Henry Cooke:"

Having arrived in America, and desiring to ascertain how far your greatness extends, I hereby challenge you to ride me, for $1,000, three acts: 1. Your "Bounding Jockey" and carrying act with child. 2. Juggling and backward riding. 3. Hurdle, or six-horse act, as may please you best. As Murray's Circus, with which you are connected, is shortly to appear in Boston, there will be an excellent opportunity to test our respective merits.

WILLIAM DOUGLASS
Late of Astley's Amphitheatre, London
Champion Equestrian of All England

Murray replied to Douglass' challenge:

Webster, Mass., June 2, 1873

William Douglass, Esq.:

Dear Sir—In reply to your challenge I beg to say it is not my desire to enter into any newspaper controversy in merits of yourself or Mr. Cooke, which would serve to give you notoriety, which is quite evident by your preposterous cartel, as it is a well known fact that in England you have never been considered better than a TOLER-ABLY FAIR equestrian. I am opposed to all betting arrangements whatever, if from one reason more than another that you could ill afford the loss of your $1,000. If you wish to try your skill in the ring with Mr. Cooke during our stay in Boston, you can have the opportunity under the following conditions: Both are to ride the same horse, and in event of competent judges pronouncing you Mr. Cooke's superior, I will make you a present of the ENTIRE RECEIPTS OF THE DAY. Furthermore, Mr. Cooke wishes me to say that he will ride IN HIS BOOTS, while you can take the advantage of his voluntary impediment and appear free of any such encumbrance. If this should meet your views, you can arrange preliminaries with M. Coyle, Esq., my general agent who is now in Boston. Respectfully,

JOHN H. MURRAY

At this distance the illusion may appear rather thin but to the press and public it looked like and read like the real thing. Boston knew John Henry Cooke and believed in him and when the gentlemen, who resided in the outlying districts and did business in Boston, saw Cooke doing the "Bounding Jockey" with his boots on, they all agreed: "John Henry Cooke is getting ready to meet the vaunted English champion, William Douglass, in Boston." So said the circus-loving suburbans to their city friends. And by the time the Murray circus pitched its one tent and built its one ring in the center of the Modern Athens, the merits of Cooke and Douglass were being discussed along with the latest literary topics of the time.

Along with this, Billy Irving, Murray's boss billposter, in all the glory of a velvet coat purchased in Nova Scotia the previous summer, spent his evenings in touring Boston and impersonating William Douglass, champion equestrian of all England. Irving was possessed of a ready wit, an unparalleled gall, and was as handy a prevaricator as ever distorted the truth, as Mike Coyle, a friend and admirer of the qualification of the deceased in the direction of the distortion of the facts, will bear me witness. As the bogus Douglass, Irving was as good a walking advertisement as a perambulating billboard drawn by four horses to the music of a fife and drum.

The opening night, the still incredulous W. C. Coup came out to see the little circus under one tent. To his surprise it was closed, closed because no more could or would be admitted. Also and likewise came others high up in the councils of the circus: George F. Bailey, Charles W. Fuller, L. B. Lent, Col. Joe Cushing; and they, with one accord, expressed surprise and pleasure. But probably only one of the managerial party attributed any measure of the success to the invented advertisement. Lewis B. Lent was too old and shrewd an advertiser to have overlooked so important a factor. As he took his seat or rather, by reason of his bulk, two seats, he called the writer to his side and asked with a wink, "Can you inform me, Squire, at what hour the contest begins between John Henry Cooke, the great, and William Douglass, champion of all England?"

MAKING MUCH OF MUSIC
[*Billboard*, May 11, 1901]

So long as a one-ring circus was a drawing card, L. B. Lent enjoyed a prestige and advantage. The New York Circus had a metropolitan reputation and, furthermore, the manager was enabled to control the services of sterling performers all the year around. Such artists as the Melvilles, Robert Stickney, William Dutton and others of the same ilk continued season after season and aided in sustaining the show's great fame as a gilt-edged, kid-gloved affair. It is safe to say that every person who entered L. B. Lent's arena wore silk next to the skin and could find their way off the lot at night by the light of their diamonds.

In the winter season, it was the New York Circus as a whole that drew, the complete excellence of the entertainment pulling the people. But two out of all the great individual features caused any appreciable effect on the receipts and these were admitted by Mr. Lent to be Carlotta de Berg (Mrs. James E. Cooke) and a big monk billed as the "bynocephalus."

L. B. Lent, as a circus manager, in the language of the song, believed "it all depends upon the style in which it's done." On the road he drew the cream of the community and his outfit was always the pink of perfection. Added to a clean bill, every number was worthy of the reputation of the management. The music was a feature, although the noise was less than the bands of most rival tent exhibitions.

Late one season, when the show was almost home, it met with a railroad accident in which the capable manager, Harry Whitbeck, was killed and the band wagon, quite an elaborate affair, was destroyed.[41] Fisk and Gould were at the head of the Erie road. It might be well to reverse the order of the names, but the loud Colonel Jim was posing in the front rank and in such an important matter did his own squaring. Fielding was ordered to turn out a chariot to "beat the band" and produced a magnificent monster affair, by far excelling anything of the kind in the country, either for size or gorgeous display of carving and gilding.

The next spring the New York Circus took the road with a band that woke the echoes of newspaper and popular praise. The spielers not only made music that was music but they made money for L. B. Lent, who ingeniously, by poster, program and press, heralded the band! the band! the band!

The way the band drummed up recruits was a caution. And "everybody that was anybody" went to the show to get more of the band. As an advertising card, the big band was a large winner for several seasons. As the people used to say, "The band alone is worth the price."

During the winter of 1877-78, Den Stone, George R. Bronson, and Frank Hyatt combined to enter circus management and called to their council Frances M. Kelsh. Dennison W. Stone had been in management for a good part of the time from 1842 and had enjoyed much popularity as a clown. George R. Bronson had piloted many shows on land and western waters and stood high as a router. Frank Hyatt, who had invested his entire pile (and the only one that did), has for many years been the superintendent of the Barnum & Bailey Shows under several regimes.

When the three managers and Kelsh put their heads together, they all seemed to be of one mind or were readily brought to be. Frank had a most eloquent gift of convincing gab and, having been educated in the school of Col. Rufus Welch and L. B. Lent, succeeding Whitbeck as manager of the New York Circus, all his prejudices and predictions were in favor of a straight, one-ring, legitimate circus. Den Stone, bred to one ring and the good old way, readily acquiesced in the suggestion that the head of so high order of affair should not play clown. Bronson and Hyatt fell in line and a first-class, one-ring circus was determined on, with "no cats" (and this in 1878, after the people had been dosed with big Barnum shows and all the other managers were swelling to burst to increase their dimensions, both on the billboards and on the lot).

The head and front of D. W. Stone's Grand Circus and Musical Brigade argued that a very large number of persons did not care for the newfangled several ring affairs and a very large number of persons said so who would only go to a show with a large street display after all. Some folks telephoned through their tiles then as now.

A most excellent [and] phenomenal company was engaged: Caroline Rolland, Mollie Brown, the Lawrence Sisters, Emma Stickney, Robert Stickney, Rudolph Mette, Charles Lowrie, "Lewis" the colored rider, William F. Burke,[42] William Conrad and his dogs, Frederick F.

Levantine (F. L. Proctor), Shed LeClair, the Three Duval Brothers, James Campbell, Charles S. Burrows, Nicholas Lawrence, Adolph Livingston and Thomas Murray. Robert Stickney led the leaps and LeClair, Lowrie and Campbell appeared in the revival of "The Trampolins," the show concluding with "A Horse to Let." A feature of all announcements was, "Smoking in the tent not tolerated and most positively prohibited. A corps of uniformed ushers in attendance."

Yours truly joined out to do the bill writing and act as press agent with the show. My complementaries were headed with the quotation from Hamlet, "Report me and my cause aright." And the request was complied with. The newspapers praised the show without stint. But I will not anticipate.

With the success of Lent's big band in mind, Kelsh was instrumental---that's good!---in inciting the management to have a big band, also a fife and drum corps. But to save expenses and as a novelty the band should foot it and not ride in a golden chariot. Argumentative Kelsh figured that the fife and drum corps would wake them up to be entranced by the music of the band. To further entice music lovers, the advance man made a free distribution of sheet music, composed by the bandmaster.

The musical brigade of twenty-five pieces was led by J. A. Emidy, a most competent conductor, both as a manager of men and as a musician. And it is a fact worth mentioning that Mr. Emidy was a Negro, a fact which did not in any way interfere with his efficiency, either as a musician or director. His brother was also a member of the organization I believe. William Rolland was star B-flat cornet soloist and William E. Marsh, trombone soloist, performed on a solid silver instrument. The uniforms were as gorgeous as any I have seen.

Frank Kelsh, besides his ideas in regard to the show, had his views in regard to advertising. A 3-sheet in colors was prepared for each performer, who was also heralded by lithographic portrait in black. In consequence, the bills on the boards looked like those of a hall show and nothing circusy was to be seen in the windows.

The show opened at Mott Haven, then "next to nowhere" but now in the very heart of greater New York, and it was thought best to head the parade by a mounted man in uniform. I was offered the opportunity to display my horsemanship but declined; and Frank Whittaker, the sentorian announcer who had joined the forces, led the march.

He hadn't moved a block before I heard a son of the sod remark:

"D'ye mond, they've only one boss."

Until we left Boston we suffered many discomforts, having no sleeper and business at no point [being] remunerative. I was on my old New England stamping ground where I enjoyed a large newspaper acquaintance. The newspapers were kind but I felt that I was out of place and more needed in the advance. Those who did attend the show admitted that it was A-1 but they did not follow the big band in sufficient numbers, because the salary list was a large one.

In Boston the beaners found out what a good show we had when we jumped to Albany. But all the while the Boston press praised and they heeded not until it was too late and then they added their regrets to ours.

Again of the musical brigade, it was the most accommodating, best natured musical organization I ever met with and that is saying a good deal. No amount of work daunted either Emidy or his men. One night, at my request, they, after a performance, serenaded every newspaper office in Boston, playing several selections at each stop, Mr. Stone and myself climbing to the sanctums "to the music of the band."

As soon as it could be managed, a reform in the billing was instituted. Large, regulation circus posters were interspersed with the individual 3-sheets. But no remedy was attempted in the way of window work.

The show made a bee line for Chicago and I recall the fact that I headed the procession in an open barouche "at the request of management." Being reminded of the fact by a small boy's request to be passed into the show on the lake front.

"Why?" I asked.

"Because the feller what driv your carriage run over me today." And so he did. Of course the gamin went in free.

The Chicago newspapers were agreed as to the super-excellence of the circus. It was all circus and a good one but (and but again), but the paying people did not come, and the band stopped playing.

No vast amount of money was lent and it was just as well that more was not pooled in. The public was looking for quantity, and quality if they could get it; and if the quantity was there the great majority were not able to judge of the quality. Like the Irishman purchasing the boots, they were looking for the most for the money---size, not a fit.

At the collapse, when it would have been in keeping for conductor Emidy to have either directed a dirge on "Up in a Balloon, Boys," the prophets all chorused, "I told you so." And really, that was the prophecy of almost the entire managerial fraternity and their respective staffs. Indeed, I felt quite satisfied with myself when I put under the picture of the band on the program the quotation, also from Hamlet: "It will discourse most excellent music." A cynical friend read it and remarked, "But it won't draw the dollars." And it didn't to a sufficient extent to prove profitable or prevent the lithographer and printer from "paying the piper."

D. W. Stone made much of the music, booming the big band; but L. B. Lent's great success, with the prestige of the New York Circus to his credit and aid, was not to be repeated at so late a date as 1878. As a last resort, Mr. Stone donned the motley but the day of the clown as a drawing card had perished with the decline of Dan Rice and the disappearance from the arena of Wallet, Pentland, Nat Austin and Herbert Williams.

D. W. Stone, I believe, made the best attempt of any consequence to revive the glories of the one-ring, legitimate circus and [then] he himself resumed touring with the cat caravans. And my good friend Kelsh, Captain Francis, became united to the idols with the conglomerate shows of Batcheller & Doris and later guided the "Swift and Sure" of John B. Doris. As for the writer, he touched one wire to the home plate for fifty dollars and another to W. C. Coup, who was touring in Pennsylvania, where I immediately joined him.

I honestly believe that the splendid bands of Lent and Stone had an inspiring effect on other circus managers, even if the effect was not immediate. At any rate, year by year, circus bands, the main bands, grew better and better. Noise and small salaries gave way to merit and decent pay. And all the big shows took to having a pride in the music and the leaders were ambitious to please and excel.

Managers still make much of the music. And it is nothing unusual with a big show to see in line: big bands, little bands, fife and drum corps, martial bands, negro bands, cowboy bands, and even the ladies of the trumpet, not overlooking the jubilee shouters, the giant organ, the chime bells, or that ear-splitting, horse-scaring machine of torture, the calliope, sometimes described by the bill writer as the "steam piano." Not only do managers make much of music but so do their patrons, who are not stingy with their applause of the men with brass in the face. The dressing rooms no longer furnish the whole of the show, because the band has become an important factor in filling the programs.

THE ELEPHANT AS AN ADVERTISEMENT
[*Billboard*, March 23, 1901]

The first exhibitors of elephants gathering in sixpences and shillings were, for good reasons, chary of free peeps at the big beasts and the early menagerie managers stole their elephant exhibits across the country when most of the Reubens were slumbering, although the mountain of flesh was made the principal feature of the public parade.

James Raymond, an American showman and a man of most estimable character was one of the first to appreciate the elephant at its first value as an advertisement. He had experienced a rather unsuccessful venture at St. Petersburg with Carter, a famous wild beast performer of his day, and returned to New York in the autumn of 1842, resolved on recovering his losses by a bold, startling and expensive innovation. Already the owner of the famous elephants Columbus and Hannibal, he acquired Siam and Virginius and the mammoth quartet drew the band wagon in parade. And Raymond's next season was the most prosperous in the country, the show being called "Herr Driesbach's Menagerie," with Jacob Driesbach in the lions' den.

The "Big Four" of the elephant team were monster trickers and their weights were respectively: Virginius, 8,600 lbs.; Hannibal, 9,000 lbs.; Columbus, 9,300 lbs.; Siam, 9,500 lbs. Albert Thompson, at this writing living in Putnam County, New York State, is enthusiastic over these animals and he has seen all the large ones since both Oliver and Jumbo. Of Siam, the veteran keeper and trainer says:

"He was the finest built and most intelligent elephant I ever saw. Evidently, he was better bred, showing as much difference as exists between the thoroughbred and the dunghill."

During Raymond's continuance in the tent show business, both in exploiting circuses and menageries, he and his after-partner, Waring, believed in the drawing power of the elephant, whether attached to the band wagon or going it alone.

The desire to see the elephant, even after dark in a great city, has always been one supplied by purveyors of amusement and excitement. In 1852 and 1853, the late Lewis B. Lent, of New York circus fame, was partner and manager of P. T. Barnum's American Museum and Menagerie, exhibiting, among other curiosities, General Tom Thumb and the elephants. This show drew, according to Mr. Lent's veracious account, with "ten elephant power." As Lewis B. Lent began his circus career in 1834 and was himself a proprietor at the time of the great financial success of James Raymond's elephant band team, he was following in the footsteps of an illustrious predecessor. From my earliest acquaintance with Mr. Lent, he regaled me with many details of the triumphs of the ten elephant show and frequently reiterated his faith in the enticement of the elephant as an advertisement. Having suffered reverse of fortune, he was without capital to carry out his pet scheme and it was not until he engaged with Adam Forepaugh for the season of 1879 that he found an employer with the required herd of elephants.

Lewis B. Lent was a well-read man, a practical advertiser and one particularly capable of judging the value of an attraction on its merits as an advertisement. In the preparation of advertisements, press notices, couriers and small bills, he was adept and no manager or agent excelled him in the design of small newspaper cuts. Lent spared neither expense nor pains in the literary and artistic features of these announcements where he had the election and his taste and judgment are reflected to this day in the small bills by reproduction of the familiar cuts, representing such historical subjects as "James Robinson somersaulting on horseback," "James Melville performing his carrying act," "Carlotta de Berg leaping through the big balloon," "Robert Stickney leading the leaps," and others that would illustrate an era.

At the time that Lewis B. Lent and the writer "joined out" with Adam Forepaugh's Great Show, the official letterhead and envelope boasted that it was the "Largest Zoological and Arenic Aggregation in the World." It was a sizable show and, as its owner proudly remarked on repeated but justifiable occasions, "belongs to one man."

Forepaugh returned from a wintering in California [to his winter quarters] in the exposition buildings at Louisville. Hon. Joel E. Warner, ex-mayor of Lansing, Mich., was secured as general agent; W. W. Durand, director of publications; Lewis B. Lent, advance manager and railroad contractor and router; and "a fellow about my size" was to do the literary with the local press.[43]

Long before going to Louisville, I was commanded to appear in New York and hold converse with the veteran Lent and exchange views with him as to the best method of building a boom, with twelve elephants to help you. I write twelve elephants with some degree of uncertainty. The street bill of the day, a very poor affair printed at St. Louis, read "12" in numerals and in repeated print. Somehow I have faint recollection that the governor remarked with a chuckle, as he displayed a proof of the wood cut:

"Adam, the first man, is only shy two, and ten for twelve is as much as the public ought to expect from any showman."

Advance manager Lent enlarged on his theme, if it is practical to enlarge on "twelve elephants"; and, in his enthusiasm, I became quite as ardent. I was no tyro in amusement advertising and [I was] a long time admirer of the abilities and qualities of my versatile old friend. Of course Mr. Lent revived the marvelous ten elephant seasons of 1852 and 1853 and we were both quite agreed that the "aggregation" had a brilliant prospect before it. Four elephants had drawn a band wagon in the early forties, also amazing audiences. Ten elephants had pulled everything alive to the tents of Phineas T. Barnum and Lewis B. Lent in the young fifties. And was it too much to expect that twelve elephants, "count them," should fill the bill and the treasury? Besides, Adam Forepaugh had consented that the first "gun" of the season should be a splurge---a full-page advertisement in the *New York Clipper* and the "Showman's Bible" was a bed blanket sheet in those days.... Besides, again, Mr. Lent had prepared a 3-sheet and a large poster depicting, after the same design, one dozen elephants in line.[44]

As before remarked, Adam Forepaugh had a show of considerable size. And it might also be added that when it appeared in the streets it had a brass band at each end of it. Aside from the elephants, the parade had no distinguishing features. The horses were of course good or they would not have belonged to that sturdy judge of horse flesh. The menagerie was complete, including a giraffe, and the cages were ornately carved and gilded. The ring performance was fair, heralding Robert Stickney (Senior), Wooda Cook, Annie Carroll, Jeanette Burdeau, Millie Turnour, Pauline Lee and Lottie Miranda. "Bill" Monroe was equestrian director and---well, never mind, "Bill" was "Bill" and quite in keeping with the polish to be found at headquarters at that period.

Any alert advertiser would have jumped to the conclusion that the elephants were the thing to "bear down on hard" but somehow Durand either did not cotton to the idea or received a tip on the side from the old man about expenses. Be that as it may, arriving in Louisville, I found Mr. Lent very much perturbed. The sixteen-page courier had not materialized and there was little prospect of it ever seeing pen, pencil or print. Still, Lewis B. Lent, the large, had confidence in the drawing power of a dozen elephants. If there was ever a cold, miserable spring, A.D. 1879 was one and it will live as such in my memory. I recall a season of frigidity and heat connected with the opening in Louisville. I had not been on duty as press agent for five minutes when "danger" and the "literary bureau" collided. The proprietor had his peculiar methods of doing business but transactions in my province were somewhat different. I had never before been in the employ of a manager who failed to recognize the correspondence of the amusement journals or questioned my authority as to the "passing" of a local member of the press.

Adam Forepaugh was a very large man and his language was, well, say terse. He sat on me vocally, verbally and voluminously; but, if I say it myself, he, to the astonishment of nephew John and Bill Monroe, did not scare me a little bit. And I spoke my piece fearlessly and with excellent effect. The showman looked at my flaming face for a moment and took in my rapid remarks with astonishment as I informed him that I would not permit him or any attaché to dispute my authority in my office ... and if he did not like my style I would not be beholden to him for a return ticket to the land where nutmegs grow on pine trees.

It is diverging to say---while twelve elephants wait---that "Danger" saw the point and appreciated the moral deduced: that it was folly to spend large sums of money on advertising and then lose a great share of the effect on account of the finishing touches of courtesy at the door.

It [was] unsatisfactory as [well as] an unprofitable sequel that the boom of twelve elephants blasted at birth. That, unfortunately, was one of the seasons in which the manager did not "lay up a cent" and there were not many [others that did]. Perhaps the miscarriage of so flattering a scheme needs no recalling, save to prove the old adage of "the best laid plans of men and mice" and to demonstrate that in inciting public interest in an enterprise, on centering attention to an alluring attraction, the conditions as well as the proposition must be favorable.

A few years afterward, Adam Forepaugh, not at all mindful of the failure of a dozen elephants to draw, bought every elephant in sight in the home and foreign market and put "a-quarter-of-a-hundred on the street" as well as in the bills. P. T. Barnum & Company had fully as many and, if I recall correctly, Forepaugh at one time owned over thirty, renting a number to other showmen. I also remember Adam Forepaugh's coming into his office in Philadelphia one evening and asking in earnest inquiry:

"Say, look here, how many elephants do I own, anyhow?"

He had been up at the winter quarters and had missed a trunk in the herd.

I might come down to modern date and tell of the elephant as an advertisement in a political procession as well as in a circus parade but my lamented friend, William H. Harris of the Nickle Plate Shows, was familiar with the subject. Setting aside the elephant as a trade mark of the G.O.P., I expect at no distant date to return to so engaging a subject as the elephant as an advertisement.

THE EVENTFUL CAREER OF LEVI J. NORTH
[*New York Clipper*, March 6, 1880]

Levi James North was born in the township of Newtown, Long Island, June 16, 1814. In 1826, there was a circus playing under canvas in Brooklyn in the Military Garden where the courthouse now stands. The stock was sold and came into the possession of Quick & Mead. Young North apprenticed himself to Isaac Quick of that firm. They also had an interest in a small menagerie exhibiting in the South under the immediate management of Jerry Fogg and Ebenetiz Howes. Quick & Mead shipped direct from New York to Richmond, Virginia, by schooner, making the trip in nine days.

The performers in the company were Samuel P. Stickney, Major DeGroot, Chris Hughes, clown; William Lawson, ringmaster, and who also played Billy Button and sang comic songs; James Raymond (an apprentice boy often confounded in reminiscences of the arena with J. R. Raymond, the manager), and Walter Raymond, brother of James, a vaulter. There was no lady rider in the company.

The advertiser was a man by the name of French who traveled on horseback and kept his stock of printing in two saddlebags. The bills in size were square quarter-sheets, illuminated by two cuts at the head, one depicting an equestrian act, the other a performer balancing his body above an overturned chair, his hands clasping a rung thereof. Major Winn, a versatile musician, who boasted of the double accomplishment of being a manipulator of the violin and of the hurdy-gurdy, was sent on to the menagerie. Music for the circus was supplied by a Dutchman named Saunders, who played the hurdy-gurdy, and the performers took turns beating the bass drum. On the occasion of Saunders' benefit, he appeared as a musical moke in an act similar to that of the late Swaine Buckley and occasionally performed by street musicians.[45] On the bills, the hurdy-gurdy was called "King David's Cymbals."

The ring stock consisted of Romeo, a trick horse; Juliet was skewbald and matched Romeo; Fanny was the Billy Button mare; Lilly, a sorrel mare on which young Levi learned to ride; Lady, a cream colored mare; Arab, a small but powerful Kannuck horse ridden by S. P. Stickney; a horse called Doctor, used on the wagon; and Bob, a pony afterwards broken to do Billy Button.

The canvas was about fifty feet across, permitting of but little seating accommodations. In after years, Mr. Stickney informed Mr. North that the expenses averaged only about thirty-five to forty dollars per day. They carried side poles but a new center pole was ordered at every stand. The canvas was put up by the band and performers. One two-horse wagon carried everything except the curb. The performers traveled on horseback, riding the stock through the routes. [When it] arrived in town, the covered wagon was used as a dressing room. Performers dressed at the hotel for the parade. S. P. Stickney, being a star, was distinguished from the stock by an ostrich plume which he wore in his hat. Saunders led the procession, playing a keyless bugle. The parade brought up at the canvas and the show began as soon as the people were in. The paraders remained mounted and rode in for the entree. Except in the larger places, the performances were given only in the afternoon. Mr. Stickney was the only person who wore tights. The other performers wore shirts and loose fitting pants. No tights were to be purchased in the country. When the circus did not exhibit in the afternoon, the managers permitted the performers to give a room show for their own benefit.

Mr. North first stood on a horse's back in practice at Raleigh, North Carolina. In those days there was no Stokes' "mechanic" to inspire confidence in the pupil and save him from a tumble.[46] The novice held onto a rawhide, while the tutor ran at the horse's side. After five or six days' practice, Master North made his first appearance before an audience as an equestrian at Camden, South Carolina. James Raymond was riding bareback. It was the rule that apprentices should get all the properties, such as coffee for Billy Button, and snuff box, make the balloons, etc. Jim Raymond did not have his rosin ready, [so] the ringmaster forbade his going into the ring. And thus it was that young Levi was thrust before the public. He rode on a saddle, jumped his whip, and finished with the waving of flags.

Some of the feats that were a feature at the time are worthy of mention. One was leaping over a dining table set with crockery and glassware for dinner, [with] the horse running under. Mr. Stickney jumped through double balloons, which were supposed to represent an English mail coach. He accomplished the feat successfully and alighted upon his horse without difficulty. Levi became a favorite of the ringmaster and, after his debut, used to ride from town to town with that important functionary.

At Columbia, South Carolina, the managers erected an amphitheatre with board sides. At that time there was only one street in the town. The menagerie came up and the two shows were combined. They had the original elephant, Columbus, performed by a Negro called Bill. [They had] a lion, a tiger, and a performing pony and a monkey. The monkey rode the pony and was introduced by Bill, the Negro aforesaid. The menagerie brought with them three performers, George Nichols (a clown and fine tumbler), William Kelly (who excelled in tumbling), and Paddy Welch (a vocalist, whose favorite song was "Tippity Witchitt"). The united bands now consisted of a hurdy-gurdy, a violin and a bass drum. Mr. North believes [the elephant] Columbus died about 1828 at Snyder's Hotel on Second Street, Philadelphia.

There was quite a somersault mania among the performers, who somersaulted off a table blindfolded and with their hands tied. Master North was ambitious and determined to do all that others did and, if possible, excel them. He was daily somersaulting off a running horse.

The two shows next moved to Augusta, Georgia, but opened in opposition to each other. The circus exhibited in a building which had previously been erected for the purpose. They remained all winter. Lawson was discharged and John Rogers joined the company with his son, Charles J., now in retirement. Master Charley Rogers danced the

"Highland Fling" and his father played ringmaster. Dan Minnich, a slack rope vaulter who also did feats of strength, was added to the company.

When they started out in the spring [of 1827], a man named Aaron Barker was hired to transport the curb. They toured through Georgia. Barker at length seceded, taking with him Nichols, Kelly and Major DeGroot with the intention of starting a circus. He engaged James Hunter, said to be the first bareback rider that ever came to America, but who was past his prime. Major DeGroot returned to Fogg & Quick on account of salaries not being paid. Hunter struck for his wages, exciting the ire of Barker, who exclaimed:

"I'll kill you, anyhow!"

It is stated that Barker was a desperate man and had both the ability and the disposition to put his threat into execution. Hunter sought safety in flight. On the site of the city of Columbus stood a solitary house. Fording the river, Hunter entered an Indian cabin to seek shelter. It appeared deserted at first but as redskin after redskin began to put in an appearance the equestrian scooted.

The company cut their way through the Cherokee reservation, felling trees and clearing away undergrowth as they moved. In Montgomery, Alabama, was one small, frame hotel [where] they had to cut away trees and brush to make a lot to exhibit on....

Returning to Columbia, they met Asa Smith and Ben Brown and the shows were united under the name of the Washington Circus. Asa Smith was the husband of Mrs. Yeaman, the female rider. Appearing in Savannah [on] Christmas night, Master North took a benefit, [with the acts of the night's bill printed on] a pink satin program which he still preserves. He was announced thereon as "The Young American Prodigy." A Mr. Creighton sang a song. Of him, Mr. North says:

"He was a Baltimorian, a perfect gentleman, and a facsimile of Sam Long. He had a peculiarity---he could never go into the ring without a whip in his hand."

On this occasion, Master Raymond played ringmaster to his boy comrade's principal act, which was concluded by throwing a wonderful back somersault off his horse, his horse going at full speed. Master Rogers (Charles J.) played clown. "The Lilliputian Clown" (Rogers) rode an act and Master North officiated as ringmaster. The beneficiary also appeared in "Metamorphose of the Sack" on two horses.

In this act, North was placed in a sack and, after by-play between the clown and the ringmaster resulting in a wager, rode three times around the ring and, freeing himself from the bag, appeared in skirts. There were plenty of vocalists in the program. Ricardo, the Israelite, sang a song and Stickney sang "The Water Man." "Billy Button" concluded the entertainment under the title "The Lilliputian Hunted Tailor, or Young Mr. Button's Unfortunate Journey to Brentford" in which Masters North, Rogers and Raymond appeared.

The engagement in Savannah was in a building. And when the company moved to Charleston they found two buildings which had been especially erected for arenic exhibitions.

In the fall of 1828, the managers built the Washington Circus on the Old York Road, Northern Liberties, Philadelphia. There, Mr. North first met Richau, the scenic rider, who did "The Death of the Moor;" [and] John Whittaker (brother of Frank Whittaker, clown and middle man), who rode bareback. Jim Hunter, before alluded to, was also a member of the company and rode bareback and danced the tight-rope. Ben Stickney, brother of Sam and uncle of Robert Stickney (our present well known equestrian), was a rider and appeared in the horse dramas. During the winter they produced a succession of equestrian plays. In spring they traveled in Pennsylvania. At this time, Sam Stickney had accomplished the hitherto unparalleled feat of throwing eleven somersaults. Frequently, days were lost in moving to a place of exhibition but, [having] arrived in a town such as Harrisburg, Pennsylvania, it was not unusual for the show to remain a fortnight.

One of the features of the performance was a stilt dance, six or eight participating therein. Sometimes two of the performers, made up as an old man and an old woman, would walk out on stilts, impersonating "The Cobbler and His Wife" as an advertisement.

Fourth of July was a lively day in Harrisburg and there was an abundance of amusements. In addition to the circus, there came to town a hall show consisting of three people and, on top of all, a menagerie. The circus parade showed up eight horses. The menagerie sent out a monkey on horseback. To cap the climax, the hall show then paraded its forces. Two of the performers appeared in character, wearing their best stage clothes. The third wore the motley of a clown. The first actor played the violin as he led the way and the clown threw an occasional handspring to the delight of the gaping crowd. Here, also, a quarter race came off between Shad, the quarter horse of the circus, and the "dark horse" belonging to the menagerie. The menagerie folks imagined that they had a walk-over, as their animal was supposed to be a "fiver" and was kept on purpose for quarter racing. The race was run without the knowledge of the circus proprietor, Shad being taken from the stable on the sly. The course determined on was a road that ran alongside the canal. The distance was marked out and young North was selected to mount Shad. Mr. North relates that it was fortunate that the horse ran towards home, else there is no knowing where he would have stopped. As it was, he ran so fast that his rider could not see and he only stopped when he brought up at the stable, the winner of the stakes with plenty of time and distance to spare. The amount of the stakes was three dollars.

The salaries were not munificent. Ricardo (clown), John Whittaker, S. P. Stickney, Richau, James Raymond, Charles J. Rogers, and Dan Minnich were paid from eleven to twelve dollars per week. All the rest [earned] six dollars. The apprentices occasionally received a roll of twenty-five big coppers. If the show took [in] one hundred and twenty-five to one hundred and fifty dollars, the managers wrote to their friends in Philadelphia in regard to the big business. The expenses averaged about fifty dollars a day.

In the winter, the show returned to Philadelphia. This was the termination of Mr. North's apprenticeship. He then engaged with Handy & Welch to go to Cuba. Charles Laforrest, the very famous bareback rider of the day, was secured. A juggler by the name of Thompson was also a member of the company. His performance of the "rings," the familiar feat of magicians, was considered marvelous.

The expedition sailed from New York in a Baltimore clipper for Havana. Handy & Welch had exhibited in Cuba the previous season but, prior to that, no circus had exhibited there in twelve years. That one was owned by Pepin & Breschard. Handy & Welch played only on Sundays and the afternoons of holidays, which were numerous. The condition of affairs on the island at this time may be judged when it is stated that the circus exhibited outside the city and that it was dangerous for people to be out in that locality after sundown. The desperadoes [did not] hesitate to rob the patrons of the circus and [went] so far as to pull the earrings out of the ladies' ears.

Having exhausted the patronage of Havana, the managers decided on visiting Mantanzas and secured as a guide the notorious Roboyer,[47] a land and sea pirate. He had secured his freedom by fighting the most vicious beast in the bull pen for the edification of the populace and the officials. Roboyer, after his liberty and escape from death, took up residence in Havana, having apparently reformed.

Before the circus company set out on their journey under the pilotage of the ex-pirate, they received a sealed letter with the mysterious request that it should not be opened until the party were well on their journey. Yankee curiosity led to the opening of the letter before their departure and they were well-nigh frightened out of their wits to find that it contained a warning of impending danger. It went on to say that they would be led into a trap by the Spanish robber and probably never be heard of again. The letter came from the proprietor of the bull pen. The pirate's rage was terrible when he came to hear of the epistle. After he was over his burst of passion and had expressed himself freely to the man of the bull pen, he drew himself proudly up and exclaimed with a tragic air that meant every word he said:

"Rather than one drop of the Americans' blood should be shed or harm come to a hair of their heads, I would die!"

Thus reassured, the circus company set out for Mantanzas. As they moved through the country, they found the name of their leader a terror. The mention of his dreaded name secured immediate attention at both inn and plantation. Occasionally, he met his old pals, who treated him with deference and [who] extended civilities to the travelers on account of the presence of their old chieftain.

One night North was riding in the rear of the column when two horsemen appeared to him from a cross path. He related that in his eyes their horses loomed up mountain high. Whatever was their purpose, a stentorian, "What do you want?" and a string of Spanish oaths from Roboyer sent them on their way.

Halfway in their journey, while moving along a mountain path, the robber announced that he had lost his way and ordered a halt while he made a reconnaissance of the situation. Roboyer disappeared in the gloom and, after a patient waiting for his return, the awful impression fell upon the Americans that the pirate had led them to their death---that they were in ambush and on the eve of being robbed and murdered. A series of whistles that rang through the death-like stillness of the night confirmed their fears. Roboyer, the robber, was signaling to his pals! When they were worked up to their highest pitch of excitement and were one and all in a cold sweat, the pirate returned, singing an old Spanish air and making the woods ring again with his vocalists. He had found the path and Mantanzas was reached in safety. Roboyer, the robber, had kept his pledge.

While in Mantanzas, a Yankee schooner arrived from Maine, having been ninety days on the way. The managers of the circus chartered her. They were forty-seven days making St. Thomas. The charter was twenty-five dollars per day, the company providing their own food. They experienced a rough voyage, the performers taking turns in watching the horses. Laforrest was cook. During the heavy storm they could see the seams open in the sides of the vessel. The performers took the dangers and the discomfiture as cheerily as possible and, when they passed water and corn to the stock, they sang the merry chorus of the slaves, which they had learned "way down South in Dixie."

They put into Savannah River for water and, [as] North described, the singing of the birds as they neared land [was] the most grateful music he ever heard. In the meantime, Handy had given up the company for lost. It having been reported that they were all murdered by pirates, at the time of their arrival Handy was about to take his departure for the United States.

Before reaching their destination, they were put up on short allowance, the last remaining biscuits being divided. When affairs were at this stage, North, DeGroot, and Walter Howard arose in the night and, purloining the "chocks" from under the water casks, the store of wood being exhausted, stole some flour and made some biscuits that were more doughy than palatable. Two days thereafter, they arrived in St. Thomas.

At St. Thomas they visited the two ancient castles of the famous buccaneers, Blue Beard and Black Beard. Here the company was reinforced by Ned Derious (now in retirement), Gen. Eaton, John J. Nathans (now director of the Barnum show), Sol Lipman and Alf Johnson, two-horse rider. Eaton had been to the Windward Islands with his apprentice, Nathans. The rest of the season was made up in the West Indies.

North relates an anecdote of Gen. Eaton. He was a good-sized man, while North was a small figure. By accident, the General, who was just recovering from a fever, got hold of one of North's shirts instead of his own and without noticing his mistake was making frantic efforts to encase himself therein.

"Good God!" he exclaimed, "have I swelled?"

On the contrary, he was emaciated by his illness, a fact which gives additional point to the joke.

At San Diego, Cuba, the company opened in a building. Seats in the boxes were two dollars apiece and all were sold before the opening. North was amused at the Negro method of working, toting the heaviest of burthens on their heads with apparent ease.

A physician related his experience with a black laborer. To facilitate work, he sent to Philadelphia and got a wheelbarrow. The Negroes' method of using it was novel, if not labor-saving. They filled it with dirt and then carried it on their heads.

North was astonished to see priests dealing monte in the streets. Some Yankee faro dealers had come to the island and they received an official recognition, the Alcalde placing a guard at their doors.

At Jamaica, Mrs. John Drew, now manageress of the Arch Street Theatre, Philadelphia, but then a little girl, was playing at the theatre. Forbes was the leading man. He gave North a sword with which to do "The Death of the Moor." There were also in the company: Keene, a singer; Kelsey, light comedian; and Jones, an elderly man. Simpson was the manager.

From Jamaica, the circus shipped to Carthegenia, South America. Gen. Eaton went in advance but on arrival could find only one person who had ever seen or knew what a circus was. That individual was a priest who had seen a circus in Spain. By permission of the priest, they played in the courtyard of an old convent. Carthegenia was a walled city but had to surrender to about fifty men serving under the banner of Bolivia.... North, declining a tour of the interior, embarked with Gen. Eaton, John J. Nathans and Ned Derious for New York on the schooner Dennis McCobb and arrived home August 31. As a matter of record, we will state that during the season in the West Indies and South America, North's salary was thirty dollars a month.

[After arriving] in New York, Nathans engaged to travel with a wax figure show that was exhibiting in the Bowery. North and Derious engaged to Purdy Brown. Brown, having an amphitheatre in Cincinnati, sent Derious to [the] West Indies and North to Cincinnati. Brown ran a double company, giving a ring show and producing spectacles. He also carried a stage with him when he traveled in the summer season. North went to St. Louis in the fall of 1832 but did not play on account of the prevalence of the cholera. He continued with Purdy Brown until 1836.

Up to 1835, North was receiving from manager Brown fourteen dollars a week. When Weeks & Waring, who were on their way to New Orleans, offered him a bonus of five hundred dollars and a salary of twenty-five dollars per week, North declined to break his engagement. And Purdy Brown raised his salary to twenty-five dollars a week. In 1836, Purdy Brown died. Oscar Brown ran the circus for a while and it was then united with Fogg & Stickney's Show. L. B. Lent afterwards became a partner in the concern.

In 1837, North join in a combination of performers for the purpose of conducting a circus on the commonwealth plan. Frank Whittaker was a member of the company. They were located in Louisville....

As soon as the river broke up, North went to New Orleans and there joined Waring's Circus and Menagerie. Barney Carroll, who is still living, was a member of the company. There, Mr. North met Joe Blackburn, a favorite clown, who also juggled on horseback. Blackburn was a man of considerable literary ability, as is evidenced in his diary of a tour to England with North, and published in the *Clipper* under the title of "A Clown's Log."[48] He was known far and near as "Gentleman Joe" on account of his affability. While abroad he wrote communications to the Baltimore and Western press, which were widely copied.

During this engagement, the visit to England was planned. Cony and Blanchard, who achieved some fame in dramas in which trained dogs enacted important roles, resolved to join them in the voyage.[49] Before departing from the country, North and his new found friend played a short engagement with Bacon---appearing in Washington, Fredericksburg, Richmond and some of the smaller Virginia towns.

Arrived in London, North and Blackburn secured an opening at Astley's Amphitheatre, then under the management of the renowned Andrew Ducrow and William West, Jr., son of the James West who was the pioneer in spectacular horse pieces in America. At this time (1838), Price was the best vaulter in England. But, in spite of his fame, he was obliged to succumb to the little Yankee stranger; for, during the three weeks' engagement, North was beaten but twice. Price took his discomfiture to heart and rushed into print in a challenge which he promulgated through the columns of *Bell's Life*.[50] Blackburn responded in behalf of North, accepting Price's cartel as printed. Price quibbled and then backed down, much to the disgust of "Gentleman Joe," who acquired an antipathy for Europe's greatest vaulter and to his dying day he spoke of him only in terms of contempt and as "the only man he hated on earth." On the contrary, amicable relations existed between the rivals and they in time became partners in business, as will appear hereafter.

The first appearance of North and Blackburn at Astley's is described in the following letter, which Joe Blackburn wrote to Thomas Atkinson of Louisville, Kentucky, from London, July 14, 1838. (The original is in the possession of Mr. North.)

> I will now give you an account of our success in business. We made our first appearance at the great place—Astley's Amphitheatre—two weeks ago, in vaulting; North as the champion of America, against Price, champion of all Europe, and my honorable self playing clown to the American party, having two springboards in the ring and two parties, American and English. You may well suppose I was much excited the first night. Such a brilliant audience I had never seen before, and was fearful North could be beat. The trial came. Price went on first and did twenty somersaults. The house rang with applause, they thinking North could not beat this; but the little Yankee went on and did thirty-three, the most that had ever been done in this country. Then the shouts came, and handkerchiefs waved all over the house. If I ever felt well, it was just about that time. We have played twelve nights since, and have only been beat once. So, you see, we have astonished the natives.

A postscript was attached in which another score was given, and opposite "41" is written "nine cheers."

North and Blackburn next appeared with Ryan's company in the provinces. During this engagement, Mr. North was presented with a medal by the members of the company.... Good Friday was the day selected, there being no performance at the circus. The presentation took place at a public dinner tendered him and the formal gift-maker was Richard Rivers, Sr. (father of the Richard Rivers who still is before the public) in the presence of about fifty guests, to which Blackburn responded in the recipient's behalf.

Up to this time, North had thrown fifty-five somersaults and it was to commemorate this event that he received the valuable testimonial.

The next engagement was at the Amphitheatre, Liverpool. Shortly after opening there, Blackburn returned to America. North returned to America in the fall of 1840 and opened with Welch's company, which was playing at the Bowery Theatre under the management of Tom Hamblin.[51] He filled an engagement of sixteen weeks, during which his trophies, a gold medal and a snuff box, were on exhibition at the Branch Coffeehouse, a favorite resort for equestrians, actors, and their admirers. This snuff box, a beautiful affair of solid silver, ornate with gold, and bearing in relief a representation of Mr. North in the act of vaulting, has the following inscription (unfortunately, it was robbed of its beauty and narrowly escaped destruction in the Chicago fire):

THIS BOX was given as a mark of esteem and merit to MR. NORTH BY MR. BATTY'S EQUESTRIAN COMPANY (presented by Mr. Hughs, acting manager), for the unparalleled feat of throwing 55 somersaults at one trial, at a morning performance at the Royal Leamington Spa, July 22, 1839, before Lord Dillion, Lord Manners, Countess Belgrave, Lady Paget, Marchioness of Devonshire, and other ladies and gentlemen of rank and fashion.

A local critic, commenting on North's performance at the Bowery, wrote:

What Fanny Ellsler or Taglioni is to the Ballet, North is to equestrian performances. It is not a mere execution of a number of difficult steps that can make a premiere danseuse, nor is it a number of extraordinary feats on horseback that can make the most finished rider. North, like the dancers we mentioned, has "caught a grace beyond the reach of art." There is a mind in almost all he does. In stature he is under the middle size, but well proportioned. His face is handsome and intellectual. He will be admired by everybody, but especially by the ladies. He is what Ducrow was in his prime—without exception, the most graceful and accomplished rider of the day. There are none who we have seen that can approach him.

Another scribe was quite as enthusiastic in the expression of his opinion:

There have been men of all ages of particular greatness, among all professions. Garrick, Betterton, Cook, Quinn, Kemble and Kean stood first in the drama. Thousands of females have equally excelled in the "fantastic toe"—but comparatively few have ever been what may be termed the "most brilliant performer in horsemanship." Mr. North stands out in bold relief of the Ring as did Kemble of the Stage, and far excels Fanny Ellsler in his graceful motions. We doubt exceedingly

whether there is a single individual can compete with Mr. North either in the beauty
or in the variety of his performance.

Mr. North's opening at the Bowery resulted in litigation. An action was brought by J. J. June and others for breach of contract and excitement ran high in regard to the young equestrian and his merits.

*   *   *   *   *   *   *   *   *   *

In the spring of 1841, North engaged to Welch for a season in the West Indies but on his arrival at Mantanzas [he] found that the manager had disposed of his interest but three days before. There was a marked increase in the receipts upon North's appearance, for he immediately arranged with the new proprietors. There was a gain of one hundred twenty-five dollars or more in the attendance in the Negro pit alone. The managers negotiated with North for the production in Havana of a Spanish version of "Timour the Tartar," for which he was to receive three hundred fifty dollars a week. The Cuban attaches of the theatre did not take kindly to young North, whom, by reason of his size, they derisively called "The Boy." But the refectory were brought to understand his position when they were told:
"Take the roof off if he tells you to."
At the very last moment, the leading actor revolted. He refused to risk his precious neck in the performance of any daring act of horsemanship.
"You will be **there**," remarked North, designating at a rehearsal the actor's position.
"I will be **here** if the price of my existence is twenty thousand dollars," the actor responded, "otherwise, I will be in my dressing room."
Mr. North was thus obliged to ride the "runs." The play opened to a $2,400 house but it did not prove a success. North rode for three weeks at three hundred fifty dollars a week.
Returning to New York in midsummer, he joined Jonas Bartlett at Baltimore. Bartlett was inexperienced in management and was shortly bought out by Welch. This Bartlett was interested with Welch at the time North was with the latter in Philadelphia. He was sometimes called "Pony" Bartlett and for a time was proprietor of the once famous Branch Hotel, New York City. This he disposed of to Tom Hyer and he then became landlord of the Washington Hotel at the Battery.

In the fall of 1841, North went to New Orleans and played with S. P. Stickney at the St. Charles Theatre, Caldwell being the lessee.[52] North went to New Orleans overland and, against the advice of Welch, sent his wardrobe by sea. As fate would have it, it was sunk to the bottom of the ocean.

Sol Smith was at the time playing the company of John Robinson, now a retired Cincinnatian and a heavy dealer in real estate. Ben DeBar, a slender fellow then, but afterward very corpulent, was a member of Smith's dramatic company. Smith organizing an expedition to Cuba, North joined it, John Robinson furnishing the ring stock and attractions. En route, Sol Smith suffered terribly from seasickness and, much to North's amusement, exclaimed:

"My native land! Oh, my native land! Oh, put me ashore anywhere!"

They survived the perils of the deep and arrived in Havana in the midst of the Lenten season. Fanny Ellsler was fulfilling an engagement there. Sol Smith was "out" on the speculation but John Robinson made a good thing of it by disposing of horses at a high figure.

North returned home on a fruit vessel and opened with Welch in Baltimore. In the company were Risley and his two boys. Risley excelled in everything he undertook. His "Risley Act" with his boys is known all over the world. Risley was equally successful as an athlete, a dancer and a shooter.

North visited England in the spring of 1842, taking with him an American trotting horse and a road buggy, both of which created a sensation and were objects of curiosity, the horse on account of its speed and the vehicle for its apparently frail construction.

Monday, September 19, 1842, we find Mr. North's American gray horse, Captain Tyler, entered in the East Surrey races, Rosemary Branch Grounds, Peckham, England, "under saddle" in the first race and "in harness" in the third race.

To visit his bride-to-be, Miss Sophia West, daughter of James West, North drove with his horse and buggy from Liverpool to Exeter, Devonshire, where his marriage took place. The fruits of his union were three children: Henry North, a non-professional, now living; Levi F., a promising boy who died in 1865 at the age of thirteen; and Sophia Victoria, prominent in the profession as a seriocomic vocalist. Mr. North recalls the fact that VanAmburgh, the American lion tamer, was at the time of his marriage performing in Exeter. The bridal tour was a buggy ride to London behind the American trotter.

What was known as the American Company, managed by Titus, June and Dick Sands, opened in Liverpool. North joined them there and also appeared under the management at the Opera House, London. In London an animal piece was produced called "Mungo Park," in which Carter, the lion performer, appeared, drawn in a chariot by a team of lions. A tiger fight was also introduced. Here North became acquainted with Mr. Dent, mine host of an inn in Brooklyn at the present time and their friendship extending nearly forty years is a solace to the veteran equestrian.

In the spring of 1843, North joined his old rival, Price, and put on the road Price & North's Circus. Leaving the circus in charge of

Price, he returned to the United States in 1843 and opened with Rockwell & Stone at Niblo's Garden.[53] But, the place being too far out of town, they removed to the Chatham Theatre.

Returning to England in the spring of 1844, he rejoined his partner, Price; and that autumn disposed of his interest in the show. After which, he appeared with the American Company at the Theatre Royal, Liverpool.

June 21, 1845, while a member of Franconi's company at the *Circus, Champs Elysees*, an institution subsidized by the government, he appeared by royal command before Louis Philippe, King of France, and the royal household, performing in the private riding school of that monarch. At the end of five months, he returned to the United States and engaged to Welch in Philadelphia.

In the summer season of 1846, he traveled with Rockwell & Stone. And in the winter [he was] with John Tryon, who was running the Bowery Theatre. William Kemp, who was the principal, is now a gold beater in New York.

Mr. North then played with the following managements: Welch, 1847; Jones, Stickney & North, 1848; Stokes, 1849; and from the winter of 1849 to 1851 with Dan Rice. He leased the Bowery Amphitheatre of the late Avery Smith in the summer of 1851;[54] and in the winter of 1852, conducted a circus in a riding school in Williamsburg, of which Harry Whitby was the manager. In 1853, North & Turner (Harry J. Turner, deceased) ran a canal boat show and in the winter season of 1853 and 1854, [he] leased the National Amphitheatre, Philadelphia. During the season of 1855, North & Turner traveled by wagon; and, in the winter, appeared in a circus which they had built in Chicago, then a city of 115,000 inhabitants. In 1856, North erected an amphitheatre on the site of the circus and, during the tenting season, turned it into a theatre and played there on "certainties" with the leading stars of the profession, such as Burton, Collins, the Keller Troupe, James Wallack, Jr., Mrs. Shaw and others.

Turner died during this winter, willing his all to his partner and cherished friend, Levi North. A fitting monument in Greenwood, erected by his surviving partner, marks Turner's last resting place.

In 1857, Mr. North was elected Alderman of Chicago and served his term of office. In 1858-1859, North's National Circus was on the road. During the summer of 1860, he ran a canal boat show and in the winter he played a star engagement with Spalding & Rogers at the Bowery Theatre, New York.[55]

The war excitement running high in 1861, North traveled in Canada with Alexander Robinson. In 1863, he associated himself with the late William Lake and Hod Norton, eventually disposing of his interests with his partners and in 1864 traveled with Haight & DeHaven. At the age of fifty-two, he made his appearance in Lent's New York Circus, in the iron building formerly situated opposite the Academy of Music, in his great specialty of the Sprite in the fascinating fairy equestrian legendary spectacle of the "Sprites of the Silver Shower," in which he appeared for eight weeks with marvelous success, astonishing his many admirers by the evident retention of his powers of his younger days.[56] Since that time, Mr. North has been principally in retirement, as there ended his career as an equestrian.

* * * * * * * * * *

CIRCUS MANAGERS
Some of the Old Time Sawdust Magnates, Showmen Who Have Visited New England, Reminiscences of Veterans. [Providence *Sunday Telegram*, May 17, 1885]

In writing of the circus magnates who have toured New England in the past and given pleasure to the lovers of the sawdust circle, I cannot begin with a nobler Roman than Lewis B. Lent, now living in retirement in New York. For many a year, Lent was a synonym of a first-class arenic entertainment. Mr. Lent was a first-class manager of a first-class show. The bills read "The New York Circus, L. B. Lent, director" and they told the exact truth. He directed.

In the minutest detail, manager Lent controlled. He dictated the space to be occupied in newspapers, ordered every sheet of printing, and fixed even the weight of paper for his programs. Every woodcut was drawn to a nicety and cut to a hair. Agents acted under written orders; they had just so much to do, no more, no less. They moved through the country in time-table order. His representatives were machines. He gave the orders. All he required was their execution to the letter and woe be tide the individual who did anything on his "own hook" not set down in the instructions. L. B. Lent may be called the

Hengler of America. His entertainments "on the road" and in New York were clean and models of excellence.

Circuses under the management of the "Flatfoots" have been given in Providence. Avery Smith, a leading spirit in active management, always remained in the background as far as the use of his name was concerned; and it is said that at the time of his death at Newark, N.J., many of his long-time neighbors learned for the first time that he was a "circus man." John J. Nathans, a "Flatfoot," has not been engaged in management since his retirement from the Barnum show some years since. Mr. Nathans was in the early days an equestrian and his many successful ventures have made him very wealthy. George F. Bailey was the manager of the Barnum show during the "Flatfoot" regime and has all the worldly goods he cares about. Mr. Bailey, it may be said, married into the circus business. His wife was a Miss Turner and the Turners were the "Pilgrim fathers" who "struck out" in the circus business at Danbury, Conn., when this century was young. Lewis June bettered his fortune by association and investment with Smith, Nathans, and Bailey and takes it easy at Ridgefield, Conn., with nothing else to do but cut the coupons off his bonds and he has to have the shears sharpened pretty often, too, at that.

Stone, Rosston & Murray were very popular in the Down East country. They were all professionals and got their start by a bold incursion into Vermont in the face of a law forbidding the exhibition of circuses in that state. Den Stone was a native of the Green Mountain domain, his father being the late Judge Stone and Den was named after Judge Dennison, a legal luminary of much prominence where snow and maple sugar grow. Den was designed for the bar but he ran away from home and became a circus clown. Stone had sufficient influence to "fix things" and the S., R. & M. show glided through Vermont and gathered in a "barrel of money."

Den Stone is "alive and well," at present the equestrian director of VanAmburgh, Charles Reich & Brother Co. Frank Rosston, one of the finest equestrian directors that ever handled a whip, died some years since, leaving his family well provided for. John H. Murray succeeded to the business of the firm and for a while prospered but the days of big shows came and he was forced to succumb. Ruined! Broke! That is a word, slangy though it be, that tells it best. Murray, proud and plucky, persevered and just as he was getting a foothold he was called away. His son, George H., a manly, handsome fellow, a living photograph of his father, is a successful and capable theatrical advance agent.

S. O. Wheeler is an eccentric character, who for a time existed and will be principally remembered for the large diamonds and very dirty shirts he wore.

James Kelley, a son-in-law of Daniel Drew, was long a factor in the tent show business. He made plenty of money in the show business but an ambition to be recognized as a banker proved his ruin. Kelley, Daniel Drew, and the Bull's Head Bank of New York all went down together. Mr. Kelley does not by any means seem to be suffering from any of the necessities of luxuries of life but the circus world in America lost one of its most capable managers when he withdrew of the control of tights and spangles. James Kelley was another manager who preferred to keep his own name in the background. Two of his best known ventures were the Central Park show and the London. He was in the possession of the London when he met with his reverses.

The elder of your readers will recollect Spalding & Rogers. They became interested in theatrical management in New Orleans, St. Louis, Memphis, and Mobile and acquired large fortunes. Spalding, familiarly called Doctor because he was once a druggist, has "gone over to the majority." Charles J. Rogers is enjoying the fruits of his labors in elegant ease. I think he is the best informed man living as to the early circus history of this country, although L. B. Lent remembers a good deal that other people have forgotten.

Levi J. North, the first man who ever turned a somersault on the back of a [running] horse, is also poor, very poor indeed, and living in Brooklyn, N.Y.

Rivers and Derious are both living; both, I am happy to state, well to do. Mr. Derious is very aged and resembles, with his flowing white beard, one of the ancient patriarchs.

George K. Goodwin combined pawn broking on a large scale and exhibitions of panoramas and circus management. At the time of his demise he was the manager of the Walnut Street Theatre, a dapper, natty gentleman, the Beau Brummel of the profession.

Some Middletown capitalists embarked in the show business a few years ago, resulting in the existence of the North American for two years. Mr. Stow, the manager, has since cut his way to fortune in wood engraving.

The Oriental, backed by a Boston horseman and managed by James Cameron of Providence lasted but part of a season and fell apart at Halifax, N.S.

Old John Robinson once made a "trial trip" into New England with an unusually fine company but the financial result was bad and he went West faster than any pioneer ever did looking for the promised land.

For years Adam Forepaugh fought shy of New England. He tried it once in the long back and oh! how he suffered. He was running a wagon show magnificently equipped but he flew by rail to Albany and landed, in spite of early reverses, over $100,000 to good business during the balance of the season. My friend of Philadelphia kept away from "Down East" many seasons, except an occasional drop into Vermont at the end of a Canadian tour. His movements and that of the Barnum show have been for several seasons by mutual arrangement.

Dan Rice's last tour of New England was made under the management of Adam Forepaugh, Adam paying the big-nosed jester $26,000 for twenty-six weeks' services. Daniel amused himself day after day by abusing his employer in the ring when he chose to put in an appearance, which was not often as he had a peculiarly drawn contract of which he took advantage. Rice made Forepaugh very tired of him before the termination of their relationship and Adam, who is a muscular Christian, wound up the engagement by threshing Dan's groom (a big, bulky brute), after which he drubbed Mr. Rice in a way that would have done honor to John L. Sullivan.

Adam Forepaugh was a butcher, a drover, and a horse trader and grew up in the Quaker City when a young man of spirit was frequently called upon to put up his hands. Only a few years ago, while the writer was in A. F.'s employ, he was grossly insulted by the pilot of a coal cart, who said very bad words at the showman. Adam got out of his carriage and whipped the fellow right then and there to the delight of those who had listened to the provocation.

"Well done, Adam. If you hadn't done it, I should have got out and helped you myself," said a white-whiskered gentleman in a carriage, an officer of one of the great trust companies who used to chum with "our Ad.," train with him, and run with the same machine.

"I'd take off my overcoat if I was going to try it again," remarked Forepaugh as he nodded to the crowd and drove off.

William C. Coup had a meteoric success as a manager. He found Barnum out of the swim, coaxed him from his retirement, and made a great deal of money until the Hippodrome venture, which proved very disastrous, Barnum's son-in-law, Hurd, George Bunnell, the museum manage, and Coup getting badly pinched in the squeeze. Dan Castello went out broke and never recovered. Coup's next venture was with Henry Reiche in the New York aquarium. Mr. Reiche put up money like a Prince and invested $85,000 in fish and water. Coup was bought out and Reiche continued. Coup again got a foothold in the circus business, prospered for a while, and was at last driven to the wall. One of the most likable men in the world, he was very popular with the press and I am glad to record that once more he is basking in fortune's smiles, controlling an exhibition of educated horses.

The Great Eastern for a few seasons was prodigiously prosperous under the guidance of Andrew Haight and George W. DeHaven, who were the originators of the two-ring business.

Howes & Cushing were very successful under the management of Seth B. Howes and Col. Joe Cushing. Howes is a many-millionaire. Cushing died a few years ago on his farm near Dover, N.H. The circus which last exhibited at Providence under the name of Howes & Cushing and wound up unfortunately was under the direction of Col. Cushing, Andrew Cullen, and Frank Howes (not Seth B.). Col. Cushing, I have been told, was originally a boss canvasman and secured his interest in the Howes & Cushing show by resenting an insult directed against his employer. The sound threshing he administered the infractor made him a partner in the show, which won great favor in England where they had the honor of appearing before the Queen and royal family.

The London, after its loss by Kelley, made several very prosperous seasons under Parks, Davis & Dockrill. The last two have been particularly unfortunate, and the former has been able to save no great amount from the wreck.

Now to come down to the billboards and the pictures displayed by the courtesy of Cornell & Haskins. I won't ask you to look way back to '20, the time of the organization and foundation of the VanAmburgh show. It might sprain your neck. To all the old folks, VanAmburgh is "as familiar as household words," if I may be allowed to use that very chestnut quotation. For many years the power behind the throne with this ancient and honorable institution has been Hyatt Frost, who has been connected with it for thirty-nine years. Frost says that the circus business is not his *forte* this year but it will be his *forty* next year.

The woods are full of showmen where Frost came from and today all the old inhabitants of Putnam and Dutchess counties, N.Y., traveled with the VanAmburgh show; and their progenitors were in the business with the Turners, Howes, Mabies, and Raymonds, whose names are a tradition in the history of the circus. Manager Frost has been associated at times in ventures with P. T. Barnum and James Kelley and was one of the proprietors of the last Barnum museum destroyed by fire. He has been rather backward in the way of personal advertising and for years he refused to sit for his picture, fearing that the camera might go off and spread his likeness broadcast.

Frost's old partner is also a modest man. I mean P. T. Barnum, whose face is quite as familiar as that of G. Washington. Phineas is a very nice-looking old gent. I don't know which I admire most, his face or his cheek. Mr. Barnum has combined religion, politics, cold water and clocks to advantage. He don't care anything for money. His partners have risen from the ranks. Hutchinson peddled the peanuts and he don't care shucks who knows it. Bailey was a billposter and "made haste with paste." Frost drove hogs out of Indiana when it was a new country and received his reward---thirty-seven and a half cents a day and found the hogs if he could. Said hogs were built to run and they could do as much space in a given amount of time as a quarter horse well gingered.

92

NOTES, PART ONE

1. Steele MacKaye's "Hazel Kirke" opened at the Madison Square Theatre on February 4, 1880, and ran for 486 performances. At that time, Daniel Frohman was business manager for the theatre. The play was so popular that during the 1882-83 season there were fourteen companies touring it.

2. Thomas Taplin Cooke brought his circus to America in 1836 and erected an amphitheatre in the Bowery, N.Y.C. He also performed in Philadelphia, Boston, and Baltimore. But Day must be referring to William Cooke, whose imported troupe settled at Niblo's Garden for a successful stay in 1860 under the proprietorship of James M. Nixon.

3. See Circus Personnel Reference Roster.

4. In September of 1841, Barnum was engaged as "puff writer" for the Bowery Amphitheatre but by December of that year he had secured Scudder's Museum. *The Life of P. T. Barnum, Written by Himself,* was published by Redfield in 1855. *Struggles and Triumphs, or Forty Years' Recollections of P. T. Barnum* was first published in 1869, with various editions appearing until 1888, three years before his death.

5. The Original Campbell's Minstrels was organized in June of 1847 by John Campbell. The group consisted of W. B. Donaldson, Jerry Bryant, John Rae, James Carter, H. Mestayer, and David Raymond.

6. Charles Graham Halpine (1829-1868), an Irishman, was a journalist and poet who came to America in 1851. He couldn't have been Barnum's private secretary for long because by 1852 he was co-editor of a Boston humor weekly, *The Carpet-Bag.* Jenny Lind's famous American tour occurred during 1850-52.

7. Arlington Minstrels was a new band that opened in Chicago, April 23, 1867, at a hall on Washington Street between Clark and LaSalle. Arlington and Pettingill were the end men. The group performed in and around the Chicago area for the next few years under various managements.

8. Born in London in 1826, Laura Keene made her American debut at Wallack's Theatre in 1852. She left Wallack's to start her own theatrical company in Baltimore and to become the first actress-manager in this country. This was followed by a tour of California and Australia, supporting a young Edwin Booth. In 1856 a theatre was built for her on Broadway, near Houston Street, Laura Keene's Varieties, which she operated for eight years. Later, her company had the dubious distinction of performing "Our American Cousin" at Ford's Theatre in Washington on the night of April 14, 1865. In 1869, the year Day joined her company, she had just assumed the management of the Chestnut Street Theatre, Philadelphia. The house opened September 20.

9. Sharpley's Minstrels and Sheridan & Mack left New York City in August of 1873 for a tour that closed October 3, 1874. Sharpley died two months later, after a painful illness from stomach cancer and ulceration of the bowels.

10. Charles Gayler was noted for his speed in dramatization. His *Bull Run, or the Sacking of Fairfax Courthouse* and *Hatteras Inlet, or Our Naval Victories* were both performed in 1861. His melodrama, *Out of the Streets*, appeared in 1868. There followed some thirty others during his career. Along with Bronson Howard, he was responsible for initiating the American Dramatists Club. The Mr. Pollock referred to must be Channing Pollock (1880-1947), whose dramatic pieces include *The Sign on the Door, The Fool*, and *Mr. Moneypenny*.

11. Newcomb & Arlington opened at the lower Apollo Hall, located on the north side of 28th Street, N.Y.C., a few doors west of Broadway, which they had fitted up for a minstrel hall, on April 17, 1871. Newcomb performed as Tambo, Arlington as Bones.

12. The *Sporting Times* was a Boston publication from 1867 to 1872. It was revived with a shortened format from 1884 to 1886. Stetson was a millionaire publisher, who at one time had been a champion ten-mile runner and had given pedestrian exhibitions in the circus ring.

13. The *New York Clipper* was first published on April 30, 1853, by Harrison Fulton Trent to serve as a theatrical and sporting weekly. Sporting subjects included boat racing, prize fighting, baseball, pedestrianism and even checkers. The paper's theatrical focus increased during the 1860's until, practically speaking, it was the only periodical in America dealing with show business news throughout the decade from 1865 to 1875; and it continued in the forefront as such until competition from the *Billboard* and *Variety* forced its demise in 1924. The paper was sold to Frank Queen in 1855. Under his guidance, the *Clipper* befriended the popular amusements of the day---minstrelsy, circuses, variety halls and concert saloons---neglected by other publications and became known in the trade as "The Old Reliable" and "The Showman's Bible."

14. Day's article, "Room No. 1, or A Night With The Circus Folks," appeared in the April 18, 1874, issue of the *New York Clipper*.

15. Mike Coyle was treasurer for John Hayes Murray in 1871, contracting agent in 1872, and general agent in 1873. Day's first season with the show was in 1872 as press agent. From 1866 to 1871, Murray was in partnership with Den Stone under the title of Stone & Murray's Circus. Murray then became the sole proprietor through 1878.

16. The Haight & Chambers Palace Show and Menagerie was organized in 1866. The company was to travel on the steamer *Coosa* out of New Orleans. However, floods made it impossible to meet most of their river bookings. At Henderson, KY, the boat's boilers burned out. At St. Louis, the troupe was quarantined due to cholera. At Pittsburgh, the vessel was run into by a tow boat and sunk. Having lost seventy-five thousand dollars from this venture, Haight sold his interests in the show and went into the hotel business in Memphis. His connection as agent for Stone & Murray occurred during the seasons of 1869-70, for which he was paid $50 a week.

17. G. G. Grady had his Old Fashioned American Circus on the road from 1869 to 1874. In 1871, Haight organized the Empire City Circus (also referred to as Wooten and Haight's New York Circus and Menagerie) with P. Bowles Wooten. Reference to this appears in the *New York Clipper* of March 11, 1871.

18. Tom Barry was with the Murray show from 1871 through 1877. See Reference Roster.

19. The "rebus" was a pictorial representation of the performance through a composite illustration of several of the acts.

20. Billy Burke was with James Robinson for the winter season of 1870-71 and the summer of 1871. See Reference Roster.

21. Ben Maginley was with Joel E. Warner's Great Pacific Menagerie and Circus during 1871-72. See Reference Roster.

22. Day is referring to the Leland brothers, proprietors of the Metropolitan Hotel at Broadway and Spring Street. They were the first to set up a hotel chain in the United States. The Metropolitan was one of nineteen luxury hotels built within a five-year period from 1850 to 1854. Unlike the St. Charles, the Metropolitan had accommodations for 600 guests, including 100 suites of "family apartments." Rates ranged from $15 to $100 a week. The hotel was demolished in 1895.

23. The famous marble and brown stone St. Nicholas Hotel was between Broome and Spring Streets. It had opened in 1852, built at a cost of over a million dollars. At that time it boasted of a novel central heating plant which piped hot air to every room. A block further up, at 550 Broadway, was Tiffany's; and on the corner of Prince Street, another jewelry establishment, Ball, Black & Co. Diagonally opposite was the Metropolitan Hotel, in the rear of which was Niblo's Garden. Passing on, one could observe the Olympic Theatre, 442 Broadway; between Howard and Grand Streets; the Southern Hotel, the New York Hotel, and Goupil's famous art gallery. Stewart's retail outlet was located on the corner of Tenth, above which was the beautiful Grace Church. Wallack's Theatre dominated the corner of Thirteenth Street. In 1865, the San Francisco Minstrels were located at 585 Broadway; opposite the St. Nicholas Hotel. By 1872, they had moved uptown to Broadway and Twenty-eighth Street. During that same year, the old location was occupied by Charles White's minstrel company and the place was called White's Athenaeum.

24. Progressing up Broadway from the lower tip of Manhattan, one encountered Herald Square, Longacre Square, Union Square, and Madison Square, each of which in time centers of New York's theatrical world as the busy houses of commerce worked their way uptown. At Fourteenth Street was Union Square, originally called Union Place and formerly an area of fashionable residences but now encircled with hotels and places of business.

25. The management team of John J. June, Lewis B. Titus, Sutton Angevine and Jerry Crane was given the name of "Flatfoots" when it openly threatened its opposition with the statement: "We put our foot down flat and shall play New York. So watch out!" The title was to stay with them for years. See Reference Roster for individual identification.

26. By 1860, the concert saloons were sharing a sizeable part of Broadway night life. Variety entertainments were performed in converted theatres and basements amid a barroom atmosphere, where the patrons were attended by "pretty waiter girls" who dispensed drinks

and engaged them in conversation and, in the less desirable places, made private arrangements with those who had money to squander on illicit meetings. The entertainment offered was of a varied and somewhat pleasing character, with each act on the program lasting about ten minutes; so that one could drop in, while away an hour or so, and leave. Prices ranged from six to fifteen cents for seats. Harry Hill's place was one of the most notorious of the lot. Located in a run-down two-story frame building on Houston Street, just off Broadway, it was a popular hangout for both the low and the high elements of society. Hill had been a bare-knuckle prize fighter in his earlier days. He was short and stockily built, yet well dressed and handsome, with immaculately parted black hair and a carefully barbered mustache. His quiet, gentlemanly manner was in sharp contrast to the raucous atmosphere of his establishment.

27. Thomas Byrnes was born in Ireland in 1842. After coming to America as a boy, he served in the Union Army. In 1863 he joined the New York City Police Department. By 1870 he was a captain. In 1879 he solved a multi-million dollar bank burglary, for which feat he was made commanding officer of the detective bureau. In 1888 he was elevated to the number two post in the department and a short time later to superintendent.

28. The St. Charles Hotel carried the following advertisement at this time in the *Clipper:* ST. CHARLES HOTEL, ON THE EUROPEAN PLAN, CORNER OF BROADWAY AND BLEECKER STREET. HEADQUARTERS OF SHOWMEN AND MEMBERS OF ALL PROFESSIONS. ONE HUNDRED GOOD ROOMS AT $1 PER DAY. HOTEL THOROUGHLY RENOVATED AND MEALS SERVED AT ALL HOURS. GEORGE S. LELAND, PROPRIETOR.

29. Harry Stanwood was an end man for Sam Sharpley's minstrel company in 1868-69. He was also with Newcomb & Arlington in 1871 when Charles Day was serving as press agent for that organization.

30. Jim (or Jem Mace, 1831-1910), a native of Norfolk, England, was the first world heavyweight champion, 1866-82. His scientific approach to the sport made him one of the "cleverest men who ever climbed inside the ropes." Because he was thought to have a Romany bloodline, he was often referred to as the Gypsy. Joe Coburn, an Irishman, was said to be "a man of the highest form of physical development." He had come to the United States as a child and grew up on New York's ough East Side. After claiming the American

championship, Coburn went to England in 1864 to fight Mace but the bout was called off when he insisted on using one of his friends as referee. The two finally met on May 11, 1871, at Port Dover, Canada, but seemed in no mood for fighting. They stalked each other for an hour and seventeen minutes before the sheriff and militia intervened. A rematch was held at Bay St. Louis, MS, November 30, 1871. Again, the two showed no inclination to mix it up. They stalled for twelve rounds to the jeers of the crowd until the referee stepped in and called the fight a draw. The unsavory event led to charges of fraud.

31. Andrew Haight was advance manager for the Great Eastern Menagerie, Museum, Aviary, Circus and Balloon Show, 1872-74, said to be the consolidation of Haight & Co.'s, Agnes Lake's, and George W. DeHaven's circuses and Col. C. T. Ames' menagerie. The show was one of the most extensively advertised on the road at that time. Meeting with enormous competition from other circuses, Haight and his agent, W. W. Durand, erected large stands of lithos and bought broadsides of newspaper space. With three bands featured in the parade and performances in two rings simultaneously, the show ran a continuous season of over two years. It was said to have cleared $100,000 the first year.

32. This is, of course, a reference to Shakespeare's gargantuan character of Falstaff and his henchman.

33. Charles T. White (1821-1891) opened the Melodeon at 53 Bowery, 1846. He was burned out twice, but each time he rebuilt. After a third fire, he moved to 585 Broadway. Pastor's New York management career began in 1865 when he opened the Opera House at 201 Bowery. He remained there for ten years.

34. William Donaldson was editor of the *Billboard* at this time.

35. Frank Rivers was a former circus performer whose injury led to opening the Melodeon Concert Hall, 539 Broadway, in the summer of 1859. This influenced a decided turn toward respectability for such places, for Rivers' offered a changing program of high-class singers, dancers and variety acts, competitive with other entertainment palaces along Broadway and appealing to the frequenters of the dramatic houses and the popular minstrel halls.

36. The New York Crystal Palace Exhibition opened in the summer of 1853.

37. Odell quotes from the *New York Herald* of January 31, 1844, which describes Franklin as "the beautiful, fearless rider and unsurpassed vaulter." It goes on to say that "his double somersault and his wild gallop on his bare-back steed are feats of the most extraordinary interest which can be conceived." By this time, the double-somersault must have been a regular part of Franklin's performance. Franklin was at the Bowery Amphitheatre, 37 Bowery, with June, Titus, Angevine & Co. for the season of 1840-41. Gardner was at the Bowery Theatre at this time as well. This may be the period of Donaldson's reference.

38. Forepaugh is said to have been the first circus manager to exhibit the menagerie under a separate tent. There are conflicting stories about the event. Joel E. Warner claimed to have contributed the idea to Forepaugh with the two tent exhibition being introduced in St. Louis in 1868. Forepaugh has it occurring in Louisville a year later.

39. The Barnum and Coup circus was organized as a wagon show for the 1870 season. The following year, P. T. Barnum's Museum, Menagerie, Caravan, and Hippodrome went out by rail. Coup left the arrangement in 1875.

40. Barnum's World's Fair on Wheels was an expanded version of the Coup/Barnum organization, taken on the road in 1873.

41. Lent's circus accident occurred September 28, 1870, on the Erie Railroad. The train left Middletown, N.Y., at 5:00 a.m., en route to Patterson, N.J., with seven freight cars and two passenger cars in the rear; but stopped at Turner's Station to check a heating "journal." While there, it was rear-ended by the Atlantic and Great Western express, coming at top speed. Harry M. Whitbeck, manager of Lent's New York Circus, had formerly been a successful businessman. He was about fifty when he died in the accident.

42. Day must be referring to William E. "Billie" Burke.

43. Forepaugh's season opened in the Exposition Building in Louisville for a stand of April 2-5. The circus followed with a tour of the mid-western and New England states.

44. Forepaugh's one-page *Clipper* spread appeared in the April 5, 1879, edition. The elephant puffery read in part: "Ponderous Asiatic Monarchs! One round dozen -- at a cost of $135,000. More of these Monster Forest Mastodons than are owned by any one man on the face of the earth. Dispute it if you dare!"

45. Swaine Buckley (1831-?) was an original member of Buckley's Minstrels, which opened in Boston, 1843. He performed on the banjo and the jawbone and was the principal tenor singer and comedian.

46. Spencer Q. Stokes, who gained fame as a horse breaker and trainer of riders, is credited with the invention of a device to enhance the safety of his novice pupils, called a "mechanic," comprised of harness and rope that disallowed injurious falls from moving mounts.

47. The writer spells the name as pronounced, without vouching for the accuracy of the orthography.

48. See *An Annotated Narrative of A CLOWN'S LOG*, edited by William L. Slout, distributed by The Borgo Press, P.O. Box 2845, San Bernardino, CA 92406.

49. Barkham Cony, called the "dog star," was born in England in 1802. He made his debut in America in 1835. His specialty was performing with his trained dogs, notably Hector and Bruin. Cony died in Chicago, 1858, at age fifty-six. William Blanchard, not to be confused with his English contemporary of like name, was an athletic performer, who for several years was connected with Cony. Their pieces included "The Cherokee Chief, or The Shipwrecked Sailor and His Dogs," in which Blanchard appeared as an Ourang Outang; "Jack Robinson and His Monkey," Blanchard playing the Monkey; "The Planter and His Dogs, or The Slave's Revenge," and "The Forest of Bondy, or The Dog of Montargis."

50. This appeared in *Bell's Life in London*, September 2, 1838.

51. The Bowery Theatre opened as a circus under the management of Welch, Bartlett & Co., January 11, 1841, with North as one of the feature attractions.

52. North was at the St. Charles, New Orleans, for six performances, beginning December 14, 1841, after which he removed to the American Theatre in that city, opening January 12, 1842, and performing nightly until his departure for Havana on the 24th.

53. The circus opened at Niblo's Garden, N.Y.C., on November 27, 1843 and closed January 13, 1844, the company advertising it was moving to Boston. Nevertheless, the troupe was back in N.Y.C., open at the Chatham Theatre, January 30, 1844, and remained until March.

54. North opened at the Bowery Amphitheatre on August 25, 1851. He was gone by the middle of November. He returned a year later, this time with R. Sands & Co. and J. J. Nathans & Co., beginning

November 23, 1852. In May of that year, he was in Brooklyn, Hoyt and State Streets, with Welch's National Arena for a few performances.

55. North was at the Bowery, along with his "stud of horses," beginning December 10, 1860. Prior to this he was in Brooklyn, on a lot opposite the city hall, where Levi J. North's Great Show opened on October 9, 1860.

56. The Hippotheatron was constructed of corrugated iron. The architect was Lawrence B. Volk; the contractor, W. G. Lord. James Cooke opened the building with his circus company on February 8, 1864. "The Sprite of the Silver Shower" was a feature during the week of February 12, 1866 at the Hippotheatron.

Part Two: Sawdust

From the Townsend Walsh
Scrapbook

1884

Signor Faranta, of New Orleans, is one of the old time performers who has prospered. He used to do, in his day, the best "bending act" in the business. I have not seen him in many a long day. Then we were "steady boarders" at the old St. Charles Hotel under the proprietorship of the late George S. Leland, as white a landlord as ever lived. Faranta, I am told, has grown white-headed; at the same time, he has become level headed. His new Iron Building in the Crescent City is spoken of as seating about 5,000 people. When Faranta struck New Orleans he had just eight Mexican dollars in his pockets. And they were valued at just eighty-five cents each.

In those merry days at the St. Charles, Billy Morgan used to carry his roll of greenbacks in the outside pocket of his magnificent seal skin overcoat. Seal skins were not so plentiful in those days and every biddy, chambermaid, and shop girl didn't wear one. You all read about poor Morgan's untimely taking off in the last issue of this paper.[1]

I see Dan Colvin called in to see you while in Chicago. Well, he's been prancing around in the sawdust for some time "in behalf of himself and others," sometimes a manager or a privilege owner and then again as a hired man. Although Colvin has had some reverses and been "bent" at times financially, he generally manages to save the pieces. It was a sad day for W. C. Coup when he lost Colvin's counsel and services.[2] Had he retained both, it is my opinion that he would not today be numbered with the great army of "has beens." E. D. made some money last season with Frank Robbins, and he is now watching the cat to see which way it jumps.

Ben Lusbie was another of the old St. Charles circus crowd. He has gone to join the great majority and, if Gus Hatch is to be believed, is just as busy over there selling pasteboards as he was on this side of the mysterious stream.[3] What a pity that poor Ben's last days were spent in harrowing poverty. Many was the dollar that he gave in charity. Through life he valued money as chaff.

I was reading a paragraph the other day, stating that F. M. Kelsh was the oldest circus agent in the business; and that set me to thinking of his side-partner, old "rough-and-ready," Uncle Charles H. Castle. We used to call them "Damon and Pythias" but what pleased them both best was the "Two Orphans." A warm friendship existed between these two men. Kelsh, the better educated of the two and of more polished and plausible address, was much admired for these gifts and graces by the blunt "Rucker" of Piety Ridge. The last time I saw Mr. Castle he was waiting anxiously to be called hence, that his earthly sufferings might be at an end. The mind was still bright and the language quaint and picturesque but the map of his coming route was the Holy Book ever at his side.

"Boy," he said pathetically, "I have made my last stand." Then a bit of the old time humor flashed up as he smiled and said, "There's a raft of them over there waiting for me---Avery Smith, Rosston, Murray, Mabie, Spalding." And he named others, whom he described as "billed ahead."[4]

"Where will they stop?" has been an oft-repeated question of late years in regard to the ever-increasing proportions of the big shows; but I guess that there is no doubt but that the halt has been called for the present, not only in the dimensions of the greater "tricks" but the wasteful over-advertising that has been indulged in of late years.

The report is again current that the Barnum party will send a show to Europe. P. T. is quite as well known in England as in America and his physog is no stranger to the pages of "Punch" and other humorous publications of London.[5] Then there is no doubt a good thing is to be made out of showing Jumbo.

Funny, isn't it, how things go in this world and in the show world in particular? Joel E. Warner bought Jumbo for the Barnum show and another man got all the credit for it.[6] Warner is well-to-do and has no need to travel. He has a fine farm and is something of a politician. He was once mayor of Lansing, Michigan, and, like Barnum, can write "Hon." before his name by right of office.

Mr. W. W. Durand is another fortunate circus agent who had laid up a dollar for a rainy day and I don't think friend William will be offended if I say that to his wife belongs the credit of lining the old stocking with greenbacks. W. W. has a farm at Bloomington, Ind., and

Jumbo at the London Zoo before the Great Exploitation

is a great admirer of Mr. Hendricks.[7] He is a sledge-hammer writer and, in opposition, goes in for knock-down blows and has more force and ability to a square inch than half a dozen inflated, self-conceited windbags, who call themselves circus writers.

William Henry Gardner was in luck when he struck up a dicker with Adam Forepaugh in 1880. James A. Bailey never let himself rest until he had collared and corralled W. H. and he has held tight to him ever since.[8] W. H. G. is a fine advertiser and a fair writer and, what is quite as good, a judge of good writing. The billposters in the country ought to get him up a gold medal for getting them good salaries. He has done more to raise their wages than any other man in the business.

George J. Guilford is writing for Pat Harris, the museum manager at Cincinnati. George is a particularly gifted man but he lacks industry; so less deserving men have come more prominently to the front. I have to tell a story about George (if he does get angry). Coup sent George down to Texas in his fatal tour of that state.[9] It was hotter than Ingersollville. And a journey to the interior of Africa in search of money would have been as successful. So you see I clear Mr. Guilford's skirts of all responsibility for the failure. It was the sun and the almanac. The tour was as unseasonable as strawberries in December. When Guilford arrived at the front, he met W. C. Coup's brother, George. George sized up the other George, and then he telegraphed: "W. C. Coup, Chicago. Another shade tree in Texas; send down another fat man."

The last time I was in New York I met Charles Gayler. He must have caught on pretty well with his spectacle which he wrote for the Boston theatre. He appeared somewhat thinner than of yore, except about the pocket; and was enjoying the goodly company of "Sam and Fred" at the "dice box" around the corner. Gayler made a dollar for the "Flatfoots" with his pen and had the good sense to know how to charge for it.

Charles W. Kidder is indulging in his old penchant for winter theatrical management. He went on to Omaha the other day to join the Fannie Mountcastle Dramatic Co., in which he has an interest. Kidder says that the two greatest men who have ever lived were Hyatt [Frost] and George Washington.

A good many of the boys consult their "Uncle" during the winter but Mike Lipman, once upon a time a clown and manager, is now keeping a "hock shop" in Cincinnati, the jester of the arena holding fort at the "sign of three balls." Well, it's quite a convenience in time of temporary embarrassment and I guess most everybody has been there, especially if he has been in the sawdust. The pawnbrokers have such strong safes that it is an inducement to deposit with them for safety.

Forepaugh's "Light of Asia" is dead. Well, I guess it would have been just about as well if it had died before it was exhibited. Not that I'm glad at my friend's loss of money but the people didn't swallow the "white elephant" business. It is laughable to think how the so-called scientists came forward to certify to the genuineness of Barnum and Forepaugh's sacred (?) beasts. No, no, that's wrong. It is mortifying to think that men of pretended scientific attainments volunteered in the deception; for, as the cat is long since out of the bag, neither of the animals exhibited by the great showmen were ever nearer Siam than New Jersey. It's enough to make one guffaw to think of Prof. Leidy, Dr. Boyd, Prof. Doremus and a lot of lesser lights lending their names to a gigantic sell. There was one little guy, Col. Sickels, who used to run around after the Barnum party, declaring that P. T.'s sacred beast was "just like those he had seen in the king's possession when he was Minister at Siam." He ought to have had a stuffed club. Now that the white elephant fever has spent itself, the price of sandpaper and whitewash will fall.[10]

Dave Thomas, who looks out for the newspaper people with the Barnum show, is running his printing office at New Haven, Ct. B. B. & H. have given him a single order for 500,000 circulars.

I was asking Jack Parks the other day what had become of his old partner, Homer Davis; and he told me that the last he knew he was soliciting for a sideshow down in New Orleans. Then Parks recalled some of Davis' original sayings. Homer was a Hoosier and had a quaint way of putting things. He had never seen a professional game of baseball and invited Parks to attend one. J. J. declined, so Davis went it alone. On his return, Parks asked his partner, "Homer, how did you like the game? What do you think of professional baseball?"

"Well," was the answer, "you take nine Frank Melvilles and give them a club and a ball, that's baseball." Davis hadn't a high opinion of Frank Melville's intellectual qualities and that's the point.

The *Clipper* says that Wooda Cook and his wife, née Mrs. James Cook (wife of the clown, not Big Jim of the English family), are going to Hengler's, London, England. I had never heard of a divorce from Millie Turnour, but, of course, there must have been one.[11] Millie was very pretty when she first came to work with Wooda for the Murray show. He was an apprentice with Charlie Noyes; and that was how he met Millie before he made her his wife.

Once with the Murray show, I recollected we showed at New Brunswick, N.J., and at the evening performance [we] were beset with roughs. Murray called on the authorities to protect him and an aged citizen arose in the audience and said, "Never mind the performance, Mr. Murray, protect your property."

"Hey, rube!" was called and made short work of the roughs. In the melee, Wooda Cook sought a place of safety just as he was, in his tights. After the disturbance, one of the boys found the brave Wooda seated at a restaurant table, quietly devastating a plate of cakes. He preferred to "snuff the battle afar off."

A New York paper says that James A. Bailey has bought a $15,000 pair of trotters. Well, he can afford it; and if he'll take an occasional spin on the road, it will do him good. I suppose I have tried to give Mr. B. about as many hard knocks as anyone in the business, in a professional way, but I have always been an admirer of the man's unmistakable abilities. He had it "collar-and-elbow" for a time but financially he's all right now.

Adam Forepaugh is a good storyteller when you get him "wound up" and his life written up ought to sell well. He had many a hard knock in his early days and is not afraid to work now that he has amassed an enormous fortune. He is one of the busiest men in Philadelphia. And if you want to fly around the city in a hurry, just join him in his carriage. He is one of the most reckless of drivers and as you ride he'll give you a chapter of his early experience, while he dodges here and there over the railroad tracks and gives you a lively shaking up.

Last summer the boys with the Forepaugh show played a prank on Billy Burke. William took part in the procession, made up as a clown, and drove a small pony to a little cart. The bad actors would tell the bad boys, "Throw things at the old clown and make him say funny things."

As the procession moved, the boys did throw sticks and dirt and stones and decayed vegetables at Burke. And the old clown did remark. You should have heard him revile at those boys. He would just grit his teeth and pour out a torrent of suppressed indignation and profanity as the boys rained sticks and stones upon him and made him miserable. Not satisfied with that, in the mule race they tied a pack of firecrackers to Burke's mule's tail and thereby hung a tale as well as the crackers. How that mule did cavort. He tried to stand on his head and his tail at the same time, while Burke cried, "Stop him!"

The mule wouldn't stop and that made the people and the actors laugh. A. Forepaugh, Sr., offered [a] "ten dollar reward for the man who put the firecrackers on the tail of Burke's mule," but no one wanted the money.

I spent a pleasant evening lately taking in the Kernell Brothers' new show and, as the gallery boy would say, "It is a corker." Then I ran against John at the hotel and we had a hearty laugh over the time he was with the Forepaugh concert in 1879. John had doubled up with William T. Bryant and was taking a summer excursion. The season opened in Kentucky and it was rainy, cold, and muddy. At Louisville the show had provided itself with a large quantity of bills to distribute in the audience, advertising the concert. It was one of my duties to see that the concert performers put out the bills. And I recollect that the rising, young Irish comedian was never to be found until after a thorough search and then performed the distasteful duty with great reluctance. As we got into the "dark and bloody ground," shotguns and revolvers of gigantic proportions became plentiful. At Richmond, John went on the seats and began the distribution of the bills of the Pinafore Concert Co., the first bill I ever wrote for the Forepaugh show. A Kentuckian of an inquiring mind asked John what use he should make of the papers. He received an answer. The next second the stranger whipped out a gun. Kernell fell through the seats, scattering his bills in every direction and, picking himself up, he crawled from under the canvas and did not stop running until he found shelter in the cook tent.

John was full of mischief and up to all kinds of pranks. So, not wishing to discharge him, the Forepaughs "put up a job on him." He was sent out in the parade to ride on a cage, wearing a Mardi Gras head and a fancy costume. Such costumes were generally "alive." John, greatly to the relief of the management, gave his notice and left us in Indianapolis one Sunday, shedding imaginary tears at the painful parting.

Fred Pride was in Baltimore the other day with the "dog-faced boy" and it recalled a caper of his some years since in Boston. Pride, Claude DeHaven, and Ferguson, of a Friendly Tip fame, met up on an occasion in a lagery opposite the Boston Hotel and quaffed the foaming beer. Pride "set them up" and put down a dollar note for the first round. DeHaven called for another and, as Pride's money still remained on the table, paid therefrom and so continued to do until the "case" was exhausted. Now Pride pretended to be oblivious as to what was going on but he was not. He watched his opportunity and when DeHaven was off his guard, sneaked out with his coat and pawned it for one dollar in the nearest pawnshop. When Pride rejoined the throng, DeHaven was still sipping beer and spinning yarns in his shirt-sleeves, for the weather, let me say, was hotter than blazes. Ferguson, though, was "on" and had seen Pride's exit with DeHaven's coat. When the party broke up, DeHaven made a search for his coat. Explanation was made and the party accompanied DeHaven to the pawnshop, where he recovered the garment upon the payment of $1.20 in the "coin of the realm." Of course, further libations thereupon ensued.

Often the circus folks get a "rough deal" at the hotels where they are quartered. Last summer Forepaugh's company put up at an inn at Streator, Ill. Prior to the appearance of the company on Sunday, the landlord gave this verbatim notice to the guests, "During the stay of the circus there will be no napkins." And to the waiters, "Never mind what they ask for, just sling it to them."

Billy Burke says that he once knew a giant who, although the tallest man in the show, was always the shortest before the end of the week. He'd borrow money the very next day after salaries were paid.

Adam Forepaugh has a habit at times of speaking his mind in a general way so that the party for whom the conversation is intended can put on the coat if the garment fits him. On such an occasion, "the Governor" was addressing himself to Matt Leland but Matthew did not seem to take in the drift of the talk. The confab took place at the Chestnut Street office, Philadelphia, but it was wasted eloquence as far as Leland was concerned. Oblivious of the fact that he was the subject of the lecture, he came over to my desk and as innocent as a lamb asked, "I wonder who the Old Man means?" You must know Matt and have listened to one of the great showman's rakings to appreciate the point.

Few circus performers have got along in the world better than Fred Levantine (Though I believe he now writes it F. Levantine Proctor.). Becoming interested in a variety theatre in Albany, he secured sole control and has ever since had an uninterrupted season of prosperity. Joining in the dime museum rage, he has, in conjunction with Mr. Jacobs, been particularly fortunate and is now in the full tide of prosperity. Fred always was an artist as well as a gentleman and is justly held in high esteem in Albany. He has had quite a romantic matrimonial experience and must rejoice that in his prosperity he is reunited with "the one" of the early days.

William G. Crowley, the circus writer, who died but a short time since, had none too much love for the former owners of the London before it came to be merged with the Barnum show and he showed his spite in a funny way while working at the dime museum in Baltimore. Chee Mah, the Chinese dwarf, who travels with his fellow countryman, Chang, the giant, both of whom are with Jim Davis, formerly Barnum & Co.'s foreign agent (There's a sentence for you worthy of Evarts, William M., or Harry, take your choice.), wanted a biography written up and secured our friend Crowley to produce the nickel volume. Crowley began with a general reference to dwarfs and then went on to say, "Amongst the most famous little folks may be mentioned James A. Bailey, James L. Hutchinson, and Merritt Young. The smallest man in the world is James E. Cooper."

Curious, isn't it, how performers and agents take to particular hotels and saloons and no inducement can get them to give their patronage elsewhere. You can recollect, Mr. Corbett, how "Doc"

Metchear drew all hands about him in Providence, R.I. Pray and Boston were synonymous at one time. Mr. Pray probably knew every agent and circus performer in the business. The same can be said of Col. Pleckner at the old Allegheny in Philadelphia. Mr. Palling of the Commercial, Chicago, was a great friend of us show folks. Matt Mitbeck of the old Franklin in Buffalo, everybody liked. Then way down in Calais, Maine, was a one-legged landlord named Young, who always bonded the shows to enter New Brunswick at St. Stephens across the bridge. The old St. Charles of New York I have written of by the column. It was a choice lot of spirits met there in the halcyon day. An Englishman named Earnshaw used to get the boys' budge-money at the Delmonico in Philadelphia and Charlie Burrows took up the name at a late date and planted himself at Ninth and Arch Streets.[12]

Burrows always was a conniver, as long ago as he was committee on hay and oats with Forepaugh. He managed to save some money and after the Den Stone show ceased traveling at Chicago, while George Bronson went home to Kansas to see the hogs and other members of his family, Burrows concluded to get out of the sawdust and make dust.[13] Since then he has, as they say in the Quaker City, been "keeping tavern." Right well has the tavern kept Burrows. Hagar, Campbell & Co. came along and opened a dime museum right under his nose on the other corner and, having a monopoly on Bradenburgh's twenty-five cigar trade, he has prospered. Here gather all the circus and museum folks to chin and hold sessions of the "turn-over club." There is one peculiarity at Burrows---he has no slate. Trust died before C. S. opened shop. The only person he has any confidence in is the scrub woman, Krao's mother,[14] "the homeliest wench ever permitted to breath." But when it comes to a bit of sensible charity, "Cucumber," as the boys call him, will put his hand in his pocket and produce his full share. In your own city of Chicago is Billy Gilliam, who has loaned money enough to dead-broke showmen to buy the entire lake front. At the same time, he has built up a comfortable fortune. As William is a real estate owner, he is often called on to give bonds for managers and come to the front as a solid man in legal disputes. The Antonio Brothers, formerly managers and artists, are located in St. Louis, adjoining the Everett House, and always enjoy a good patronage. Tom Barry, the clown, has several times embarked in business with the hopes of getting out of the sawdust, quit traveling, and settle down for life. To that end he on divers occasions started restaurants and saloons to see his investments turn out the wrong way; for Tom has much of the English professionals desire to run "a public" and surround himself with friends to whom he can recall the past as he serves a glass. Once on a time Frank Whittaker opened a place on Fourth Avenue, New York, but closed because the slate was not large enough. Lafe Nixon long conducted a restaurant. William Ducrow was quite successful for a time in dispensing fluids. Billy Porter, the ex-clown, is a permanent and successful tavern keeper in Philadelphia. Mazoni, for a time, kept a little place in Cincinnati, called "Side-Pocket," just room enough for one man to turn around in and crook his elbow. Gus Hatch has been a saloonist and hotel keeper ever since he retired from management.

I note with regret that George H. Adams has been unlucky, and for a time will give pantomime a rest, going out with Gardener's "Zozo." He was ambitious and persevering as a boy and deserving and meritorious as a man. As a boy with the old Murray circus, he could do almost anything in the ring and do it well---leap, tumble, ride and play clown, a good all-around performer, as the Cooke blood in his veins entitles him to be.[15] With Murray I took a great liking to the boy and delighted him with a three-sheet clown bill got up in the senior Sam Booth's best style. After a while George got to playing stage clown; and I have often heard him tell with a laugh how William E. Sinn came over to New York to witness his efforts at the Theatre Comique and gave as his verdict that young Adams wouldn't do. Well, George has done for the whole nation and William E. Sinn included, since the days of the Brooklyn manager's adverse opinion. Nothing would please me better than to see Tony Denier and George once more in double harness. I really think it would be a good thing for both parties. What does the Chicago real estate holder think of the suggestion?

So Fred Lawrence don't go with Forepaugh next season and the engagement of Warner, Cooke, and Durand crowds Fred out. But he'll catch on with some one no doubt. Fred lives up in a queer little place in New Hampshire, London Village, a short stagecoach distance out of Concord. There he whiles away the winter, gunning and fishing through the ice for pickerel. They have about as much snow and ice up there as Greeley encountered in the Arctic regions; and it is enough to make one shiver to hear Fred's description of the snow banks, when he merges into civilization in the spring. He tells a pretty good story about himself that I will take the liberty of repeating. There was a revival going on at London Village and Fred took it in, along with his better half. In the course of the evening the good pastor made the usual appeal for those who loved Jesus to stand up. Either from flinty hearts or bashfulness the entire assembly remained seated. Again, the pastor addressed the sinners, this time varying his request, "Let those who love their Maker stand up."

Up stood Fred, to the astonishment of the good man and all his flock.

"I am glad to see," spoke the minister, "that you are one, Mr. Lawrence, who loves his Maker."

"A man would be a son of a __ that didn't," responded Fred. A solemn hush came over that meeting in short meter.

Fred has got a mania for big trunks. Before the 250 pound baggage limit order came into effect, Fred's cut trunks looked like small boxcars minus the wheels. When it came to loading them onto trains, it generally took the confined efforts of the local baggage agent, station agent, loungers, and the train brakemen to get them aboard. Crowley was his assistant one season and used to relate with great gusto how one day they carried away a whole railroad platform and the conductor swore that by all that was holy they could lay there in the ditch. Crowley went around the station to laugh, while Lawrence coolly remarked, as he expectorated a half-pint of Gravely tobacco juice, "It is immaterial to me. You can let the trunks lay there if you want to. The railroad is good for their contents, I guess."

"What's in 'em?" inquired a curious bystander.

"Three hundred thousand dollars worth of jewelry, that's all." The iron-bound trunks were put aboard on the double-quick.

Adam Forepaugh is a great joker and as a "leg puller" is a success. We were going from Philadelphia to Fort Wayne as witnesses in a lawsuit and had picnic all the way. The Governor was full of fun and he made it warm for Fred all the way down there and back. At every dining station Mr. Forepaugh would inform the man in charge that Fred was a dangerous lunatic and to put an extra waiter at his elbow to see that he did no damage, also to guard against his escape by the door. The extra attention or annoyances were sure to set Fred off and when he turned one of the guardian angels over they were more than ever convinced that he was a crazy man. At Fort Wayne the parties of the suit were non-sated, having failed to appear; but the great showman kept up the fun by telling Fred that a new suit would be brought and that warrants were now being prepared for the arrest of the whole party and there was safety only in flight. So all fled to an inn at the depot, where the hours were whiled away until the hour of escape and the one o'clock train came along. On the sleeper the porter was "fixed" and Fred got a deal all night and the more he kicked the more he got it, the patience-tried porter remarking in bitterness of spirit, "Deese crazy men traveling is a heep of trible, sah."

The *Clipper* stated in its obituary of the late Charles H. Castle that he was the originator of the trademark "4-Paw" as applied to the

Forepaugh show. I don't know where they got their information but Mr. Castle himself often told me that it originated with the late Richard P. Jones, the famous bill writer, and I have heard Mr. Forepaugh say the same.

John H. Murray had many successful seasons in New England and, after the Barnum rage, his business dropped and for two or three years he struggled on poor business. Meeting Harry Bloodgood one day, he remarked, "I saw the Murray show last night."

"How was business," I asked.

He replied, "Well, if the performers had been a mind to they could have hissed the audience out."

How nicknames stick. There's S. S. Smith, the lecturer and ringmaster, known to all his professional friends as "Sunday School Smith" on account of his double-S initials. James L. Hutchinson will always be known as "Hutch," in spite of his acquiring a fortune in co-partnership with Barnum. Adam Forepaugh, to his old horse-dealing cronies and butcher friends, will always remain "Our Ad." John B. Doris, the rising young manager, is "Hunky Doris" to all who know him best, just as in the days he peddled barber-pole candy on the seats or cried "Peaches!" in the streets of Albany. James E. Cooper might be worth a million and still would answer to "Jimmy" Cooper. Dr. Spalding used to be known as "Old Pills." And his surviving partner, the man with three theatres in New Orleans, is "Dave" Bidwell. E. Darwin Colvin is "Dar" Colvin"; and Benjamin Maginley's familiar "Ben" of the old clown days is still his prefix in the holy Madison Square company.[16] John F. Robinson is "Jack" and his father, the veteran, is proud to be called "Old." D. W. Stone, who mortgaged the show to Susan, is "Den" for Dennison. Coup, the circus manager, in his sideshow days was plain "Bill Coup" and when he came to be a rich circus manager, W. C. Coup, as the bills read, some of his Indiana friends mixed his title and dubbed him "W. C. Bill Coup."

When I was with Mr. Coup, who was running the memorable season of that neat little show, the "Equescurriculum" in Philadelphia, he one day got mixed up on my name. Harry McCartney was the treasurer and a great stickler for red tape. I had used him for some money, and he turned and asked:

"Shall I give some money to Day?"

"Who do you want to give it to?" asked Coup.

"To Day," reiterated McCartney.

"Well," demanded Coup, irritated, "Who do you want to give it to today?"

"Why, Charlie Day," explained McCartney.

"Today to Day," mused Coup. "Confound it, yes!"

1885

Clowns have ever been familiarly dealt with. Sam Long, Joe Pentland, Sam Lathrop, Sam Stickney, Ben Maginley, Dan Rice, Billy Burke, etc. The big shows have rather shorn the "Joeys" of their old privilege, the songbooks. Well do I recollect the fat thing Gus Lee had of it in the big bonanza days of the Barnum-Coup show. His songbooks cost him nothing, being furnished by the Vinegar Bitters Company. Then Gus Lee was bathing in wine and rolling to and from the show in carriages. The last time I met him in Chicago he was imbibing five-cent beer and, in blackened face, guying the swinging fairies of the first-part of a female minstrel show. If we only knew when we were well off we would adhere to our dust and become rich and prosperous.

Ike Reed, a New York Bohemian, contributes several columns of slush to the *Mercury* every week under the signature of "Harry Hill" and he manages to revamp about as many "back numbers" and "chestnuts" as anyone I know of. In Book Second, Part Third, Chapter XXVI, he goes on to tell a cock-and-bull story about "Old Man Adams," the father of George H. Adams, of circus and "Humpty Dumpty" fame, running a concert saloon in company with Paul Berger called "Adams' Eden Saloon."[17] All this is said to have occurred in the days of the Hone House, long enough before Adams, Sr., ever came to America. Mr. Adams was first connected with French's circus after his arrival in America, afterward with Donnelly of Brooklyn variety fame, and later still with John H. Murray's circus, but never did he keep a saloon, "Adams' Eden" as related by Reed.

Rummaging among a lot of odd papers in the bottom of my trunk, I came across a memorandum in the handwriting of L. M. W. Steere, written upon a bill-head of the City Billposting Co., Cornell, Haskins & Co., 21 ½ Washington Street, Providence, R. I. It is not dated but must refer to 1875. A footnote runs: "Above are a few of the circus agents, press agents, lithographers, etc., in advance of circuses that have been visiting 'Pop Steere,' who has charge of the City Billposting Co. in the absence of C. F. Haskins." The agents mentioned are L. B. Lent, F. A. Keeler, C. W. Fuller, Ed Tinkham, George M. Tiffany, Mike Coyle, Richard Fitzgerald, William S. Irving, Charles H. Day, Claude DeHaven, C. F. Haskins, C. M. Perry, Reed Howes, and Uncle John Tryon.

Editor Corbett of the *Journal* was at the time publishing a Sunday paper in Providence and he will bear witness that it was a merry party gathered there. L. B. Lent is still hale and hearty and was out ahead of Frank Robbins' last season. F. A. Keeler is billposter at Albany, N.Y., likes Lew June and hates Charles Gayler. Ed Tinkham was with Barnum last year. Tiffany is retired. Charles W. Fuller was with Forepaugh last year. Mike Coyle, ditto. Dick Fitzgerald is a dramatic agent and bulldog raiser. William S. Irving is at Booth's Printing Office. I am _____. Claude DeHaven is editing the *Indicator*. Charley Haskins is still at the head of a billposting firm in the same place. Perry I have lost track of. Reed Howes and Uncle John Tryon are both no more. The names of eighteen lithographers, etc., appear in the list. Among them is J. M. Fuller, now superintendent of Fuller's Detective Bureau, N.Y.

Quaint, genial Pop Steere passed away years ago. He was an old attaché of the New York Circus in its palmy days. Steere's initials were L. M. W. and he received the title of "Little More Whiskey" Steere from the late Ned Kendall in one of his funny effusions, "The Pockmarked Brotherhood."[18]

Kendall was an old time circus agent himself and a man of most extraordinary ability. There was another Steere in New England, a drummer for a manufacturer of fireworks, whom all the people and circus folks knew. To designate him, he was dubbed by Kendall, "the other Steere."

Col. T. Allston Brown could tell many a funny story about Kendall and Steere if he saw fit, for the Colonel can write and was one of the early founders of the *Clipper's* prosperity when it hid in an Ann Street garret, long before Frank Queen made a fortune and put up his newspaper palace opposite his old newsstand location in the days of his poverty-hood. Brown was with Jim Nixon and Noah just after the flood.

Jim Nixon could furnish reminiscences enough of his own career to fill a volume and a right interesting one it would be, too. Nixon did a very shrewd thing once when he set New York wild with Ella Zoyara (Omar Kingsley), who was riding a female principal act.[19] Business was tremendous at Niblo's and Nixon was coining money, when out comes the New York *Tribune* and gave the whole snap away--- told the truth that Ella Zoyara was not a beautiful girl at all but a real man. Did the sly James go to fighting the *Tribune* and contradict it and all that? No such thing. He just covered the dead-walls and billboards with posters quoting the *Tribune* exposure entirely, word for word. Result: no one believed the *Tribune* article and Nixon made more money than before.

It is amazing how professionals in every walk of show life will stick to the business, many coming to the front again after a respite from their labors. Even at this writing we have the spectacle of a Ristori again treading the boards in an endeavor to renew the triumphs of the past. But to drop from high tragedy to sawdust, Hyatt Frost is again to take the road and once more unfurl the banner of VanAmburgh to the breezes, having formed an alliance to that end with the immensely wealthy Reiches, the German animal importers of New York. Francis M. Kelsh, "the Captain," as poor Castle, dead and gone, loved to call him, has left the "swift and sure" of Doris and will make the railroad contracts. Charles W. Kidder will make the other contracts, and H. B. Knapp will be the advertiser. E. D. Colvin will be the manager and run all the privileges and Herman Reiche, treasurer. There's a team for you and plenty of bullion at the back of it.

John W. Hamilton has got the red wagon fever and wants to go on the road again. Jack served with Barnum and the London and was particularly successful in New York City. When he left the business to manage the Mt. Morris Theatre, his brother, Tody, took up the place left vacant by his brother's retiring. Jack is fiery and pugnacious and never so happy as when engaged in a newspaper broil. Tody is perhaps a little more *pliable*, as they say Down East.

David B. Sickels, who made a donkey of himself last summer by endorsing Barnum's white elephant, is writing a series of articles on Siam for the *Current*. If his accounts are as truthful as his yarns about

Charles Reiche

that sandpapered beast, Mr. Wakeman ought to present to every purchaser of the *Current* a pound of salt.

Shed LeClair died abroad a short time ago in a lunatic asylum. He was brought to America in 1873 by John H. Murray with John LeClair and three of the Leopold Brothers, who are now achieving a great success in "Frivolity." He married one of the Stuart Sisters, who were with Sheridan, Mack & Day in 1875.[20] In 1874, Murray opened the season in Newark, N.J., and for the first performance Shed LeClair volunteered to go in and do George H. Adams' act of the previous season---the tall stilts. Shed got along very well until he came to the finish where he drops the dress, dons the bonnet, and appears as a very grotesque giantess. Just at that moment he stumbled into a stake hole with one stilt and down he came kerslap! It took four property men with Tom Barry, the clown steering the stilts, to get the discomfited performer out of the ring and into the dressing room. Manager Murray, who was dignity personified, had to join in the explosion that followed and performers and audience laughed until they were sore.

John H. Murray first brought over Whimsical Walker in 1875. In 1880 he came over again for Forepaugh. James A. Bailey would like to see him again but I don't think the climate agrees with Whimsical. When Whimsical was with Forepaugh, he had a quarrel with Wooda Cook over a game of billiards. So the same afternoon he came to Mr. Forepaugh, who was reading a newspaper at the circus entrance, and said, "Beg pardon, Mr. Forepaugh, but I'm going to lick Wooda Cook."
The main guy hardly looked up from his paper but he chuckled a low, quiet laugh and said, "Oh, that's all right. I have no objection."
Away went Walker, full of fight, as fierce as the British lion on the rampage. To every performer and acquaintance he met about the show en route to the dressing room, he remarked, "I'm going to lick Wooda Cook. The Governor is willing."
Everybody smiled and advised him to do it. Five minutes later Walker returned to the front door and he was a sight to behold. His mug looked as if he had been hit by a cyclone. His nose was bloody and out of shape and both eyes were in mourning. He stood a speechless figure of misery before his manager, who removed his gold-rimmed eyeglasses for a moment for a better view and made the consoling remark, "Well, I see you did it."

"Happy" Jack Lawton, I see, is down South auctioneering. I have a little bit of a story about Jack. Years ago Billy Burke and Ted Croueste were clowning with Mike Lipman, your uncle in Cincinnati at the sign of the three gilded balls. The countrymen used to call Ted, Croset; and the Joey was about as much out of humor with his name as W. C. Coup is with his. Lawton was outside orator, stentorian solicitor, in front of the sideshow but had an ambition to be a clown. Hearing that S. O. Wheeler was in want of a clown, he on the quiet put on some of Burke and Croueste's togs and, wearing them under his street dress, turned up in Wheeler's dressing room with the big conundrum, "Do you want to hire a clown?" They did.

"Well then, here I am, " said Lawton, and off went the outer garments and he stood before them, a clown all ready for the ring. That was the first appearance of "Happy" Jack Lawton in any arena.

Years and years ago, Van Orden, a very talented gentleman, was press agent for Spalding & Rogers. (That must have been about the time Charles Gayler was studying law. I believe he was related to Dr. Spalding but that is neither here nor there.) He was traveling down the river, bearing with him a large sum of money and, participating in a game of "draw," he dropped every cent of his own money and Spalding & Rogers' to boot. How to face the Doctor he did not know but, after due deliberation, he went about it in this way. On meeting Dr. Spalding in New Orleans, he "passed the time of day" and then went on to say, "Doctor, suppose I was coming down the Mississippi on the steamboat and should dabble a little in cards, using your money, for instance, and win a good deal, would you be in with it?"

The Doctor cleared his throat and exclaimed, "Why, to be sure, Van. It was my money and it would be no more than right that I should be in with it."

"Then you have no objections to my having risked your money?"

"Not in the slightest," returned the Doctor, quite sure that Van had won a pile.

"Well then, you are in with it?" questioned Van Orden.

"Yes," answered Spalding.

The answer, to Sullivanize, knocked the Doctor out, "You are in with it. I lost every dollar."

There will be a most decided frost for those who follow Hyatt Frost next season. He is going right back to our grandfathers' days, when all the elephants and accompaniments were to be seen for a quarter of a miser's soul. The VanAmburgh show will be put on exhibition at twenty-five cents.

Mr. Frost has directed the destinies of this time honored institution for many a year. In its rejuvenation it will indulge in all the modern improvements. No longer will its performers eat the one o'clock breakfast and hasten along the railway over mountain and dale to make the next stand. In its own special cars, it will be steamed from place to place. Hyatt Frost will hunt up country as of yore. Captain Francis Kelsh will buzz the railroad magnets and [their] counsels. The advertisers will have no time to nap under Knapp and no kidder will kid Kidder, who is anything but a contracted contractor. E. Darwin Colvin, the Doctor, will manage the fabric and dispense lemonade (the clear juice), peanuts (meaty ones, not hollow mockeries), candies and ginger cakes to rural belles and beaux. Mr. Colvin will also control the freak tent and the grand after-show, "which will take place, etc. Price ten cents."

When grandma and grandpa read the name VanAmburgh on billboard, they'll become coltish and kittenish and take their grand-children to see the show that pleased them so much in their courting days.

Frost is backed by a lifetime's experience and the ducats of the Reiche's, who are enormously wealthy and live in good shape at Hoboken, N.J. They are the extensive bird and animal importers and have grown rich selling stuff to all the shows in existence since I can recollect, including Burr Robbins. The Reiches have had almost a monopoly on the canary bird trade and if any reader has a pet canary in his cage, it is pretty safe to wager that the Reiches made their percentage on it. One of the Reiches was associated with William C. Coup in the establishment of the New York Aquarium. Den Stone also went to Germany under their management with a party of American Indians. Frost's outlook is good. Yankee snap and German thrift will tell.

Ben Maginley is a "May Blossom" with the Madison Square traveling company, playing Belasco's latest and best. When I see Ben on the stage I can see double, without going out "to see a man" between the acts. The double is Ben's other self---the clown of the circus ring as I used to know him; and when the well dressed villain of the play walks the stage, I look in vain for the ringmaster's whip. Wonder if Parson Mallory of the Holy Madison Square ever saw Benjamin in the fool's motley.[21] I don't believe he did. Well then, he missed a sight. Ben used to crack a pretty wheeze expressly for the little folks; and then he'd sing a song that would make Col. Mapleson of Her Majesty's Marines sick with envy. In Ben's circus days he was manager and often is the time he has been stuck in the mud in the early spring and addressed words of consolation to the tired mules. As a circus manager, he was often liable to be blown down. As an actor, he might be blown up by the critics but the scribes will take kindly to the rotund comedian. Ben is a jolly soul and it is "worth the price of admission" to hear him laugh.

Last winter Benjamin was out West "acting out," as the natives called it, in one of those truly good milk-and-water plays of brother Mallory. Attached to the theatre was an old cully who had traveled with Ben in the days of the Maginley & Carroll show.[22] His nibs was acting as the gallery officer and was proud to greet his old employer. It is probably a fact that the gallery guardian worked up half the business of the night by sounding the praises of Ben Maginley.

The eventful night came and Ben's most enthusiastic admirer was the best listener in the house. But as the fates would have it, an intoxicated individual created a disturbance. The officer tried to pacify the infractor. Then the intoxicated individual argued the point, interrupting one of Ben's best scenes. The play went on. So did the drunken guy. Then Ben rung into his lines the circus war cry, "Hey rube!"

The only cully in the gallery prickled up his ears. Ben again interlarded, "Fake!"

The veteran complied with the request, to state it mildly. He knocked the noisy chap down and there was peace.

Tom Barry, who first made a hit in this country by playing Irish clowns with L. B. Lent in the old Iron Building, returns to the foolscap next season with the VanAmburgh party, having been lured thereto by Hyatt Frost. Tom used to be a great favorite in New England and the lower British provinces in the days of the Stone & Murray and the John H. Murray shows. Mr. Barry has always been both a jester and gentleman and one of the emigrants from abroad who has never boasted of his intimacy with the Queen and the royal family at 'ome or made himself odious in the dressing room by relating how much better everything is done "over there."

Last summer Tom was factotum for one of Dr. Heeley's many medicine shows, Dr. Barry being located in Brooklyn. At the beginning of the season, the patrons of the great Sagwa combination were inclined to be turbulent but they soon came to understand that Mr. Thomas Barry, M.D., by brevet, meant business and that he could not only heal the flesh but bruise it, too, as their noses and eyes gave good evidence. Tom was his own bouncer and it was the best act on the program of events.

It is recorded that Johnny Patterson is to clown with Lloyd's circus in Belfast, Ireland. Everybody knows Patterson, who made his appearance and hit in this country with the London show under Parks, Davis & Dockrill. Afterward he was for a long time with Doris.

Lloyd must be the James Lloyd who was engaged by Sam Watson and brought to this country for Forepaugh. Lloyd long enjoyed the reputation of being the best hurdle rider in England. His sons also rode and did the tight-rope. Lloyd had plenty of money and Watson one day in London, finding himself unexpectedly called upon for a large amount, was proffered the loan of the sum by the saving circus rider who had the money and to spare.

Lloyd's economical ways were a constant source of amusement to the people with Forepaugh. He would call for one oyster stew for the two boys, then get an extra plate and spoon and divide the refreshments, swelling the supply by adding a glass of milk. Sunday he would retire to some shady nook and the boys would divest themselves of their shirts and underclothes while their parent washed them in the adjacent brook or stream. After the raiment had dried hanging on the bushes, the boys would redress and follow their pa back to town.

Charles Forbes advertises himself in the *Clipper* as a circus bill writer and twice in his own announcement commits a couple of most ridiculous grammatical errors. No one doubts that Mr. Forbes is "a close, calculating businessman, just the one to make billboard contracts, hire lots and the like ahead of a show"; but, when it comes to writing anything except his name to a check and filling out a statement of local expenses, he is as much at a loss as William W. Durand would be in writing biblical poetry. Charles Forbes is just as much of a circus bill writer as Harry Cordova and neither one could produce an original bill in six months to save their lives.

There are writers in the circus business. They are men who can make their living by their literary abilities. Charles Stow writes costic verse and is an editor. William W. Durand is an ex-city editor of the Louisville *Courier Journal*. Both the Hamiltons were journalists. Poor Crowley was a reporter and a good one, too. Dave Thomas has been a journalist. Charles Gayler is a journalist, dramatist, and novelist. The late William Adams was Dana's right hand man on the *Sun*. Fred Hunt enjoyed a long connection with the Cincinnati press. Even William C. Crum could write more or less, especially less. Perley, Louis E. Cooke, Joel E. Warner, and Peter Sells, Jr., are writers who write---although none of them, I believe, set themselves up as literary men. Warner has written some clever letters from abroad to the papers of Jackson, Michigan, where he resides.[23] Joel E., like Stow, is a born orator and most entertaining talker.

It always makes me hot to see a man set himself up for a writer who does not know "B" from bull's foot. Fred Lawrence is one of the "ancient and honorable" who can write right and I shall be disappointed if he does not "catch on." Matt Leland can write a bill and pretty poetry to his girl. William H. Gardner can drive a quill if necessary. George K. Steele is perfectly honest about his bill writing. He says, "Murray and I set down in the barn and write our bills with scissors and paste-pot. We just pick out all that's good in all of them."

Hutchinson and Colvin could give Holland, Sanger, and Hengler points on peanuts. Doris knows more about gingercakes or "the juice" than all three together. What chance do you suppose Holland would stand swapping horses with Adam Forepaugh? Sanger will never know so much about billposting as James A. Bailey, and Hengler wouldn't be a patch as an advertiser to P. T. Barnum. The Sangers may have jaunted around some in their days but they will never live to equal Hyatt Frost as a circus traveler.

I have spoken of P. T. Barnum as an advertiser and he is an originator and a producer and a constant suggester to his retained writers and continually supplies them with hints written down on bits of paper, old envelopes, and, for that matter, the first thing that comes handy wherever he may be---at home in his library, in the cars or the strange hotel. Every line of the stock letter press that is prepared in the winter, he sees and criticizes and he is not loath to drop a word of judicious praise. It is related that once late-in-the-winter-time the manuscript for the couriers and quarter-sheets was sent up to Bridgeport for his perusal and, as the scribes did not enthuse over the "Greatest Show on Earth" with any degree of uniformity of statement, the whole mass was packed up in a soap box and shipped to Madison Square Garden with the request, "Please lie with some uniformity."

Barnum, Bailey, and Hutchinson are very appreciative employers, from the fact that they are competent judges of good work. Barnum himself is a writer. Bailey has a nose for advertising, the same as a good reporter has for news or an old maid for scandal. Hutchinson was once a compositor. He knows good writing and is a critic when it is in cold type or in proof. A great majority of the cards that appear in print during a circus war, or in the advance advertising of the Barnum show, are written by P. T. himself and he has a knack of doing them.

How some circus folks do wander. For instance, there is George Loyal and his wife Ella Zuila. They are never so content as when in the diamond regions of Africa, the old-eating land of Greasers, or some out-of-the-way end-of-the-earth place. I have been led to these remarks by looking over the route book of the Watson Family, returned to America to join the VanAmburgh & Reiche Bros.' Shows. They opened with Chiarini's Royal Italian Circus at San Francisco, August 7, 1879. September 29 of the same year they sailed for Aukland, New Zealand, beginning a tour of the world; returning to America after an absence of four years, five months, and seven days, having traveled 82,118 miles.

I doubt if any of the famous travelers ever made so extended a tour, visited as many strange lands, or covered as many miles in the same time or at all. Chiarini is one of the most venturesome and, at the same time, one of the greatest circus managers of the day. The sea journeys were long; San Francisco to Aukland, 3,907 miles. The next voyage made was 1,169 miles. Skimming over the record, I find figures of ocean trips: 500 miles, 800 miles, 544 miles, 420 miles, 750 miles, 1,346 miles, 550 miles, 1,411 miles, 600 miles, 800 miles, 1,182 miles, 945 miles, 1,480 miles, 1,280 miles, 3,940 miles, 1,292 miles, 963 miles, and 3,020 miles. These figures I have jotted down at random as I have turned the pages of the record.

Jumbo Leaving England for the Land of Barnum

Talk about "jumps," that beats anything I ever heard of in the circus business. Of course, their wanderings took them hither and yon, right and left, and here and there; but Mr. Frederick Watson informs me that when he made a jump home of 3,020 miles and reached New York, he had been one and one-half times around the globe. The Watson Family visited professionally the Sandwich Islands, New Zealand, Australia, Java, India, China, Siam, Manila, Spain, England, and other parts and places too numerous to mention.

Some other of our circus people have swung about the circle quite extensively. James Robinson has rode in almost every land and before the crowned heads and block heads of every nation. Charles W. Fish has done the best of Europe. Charles Reed is now considered one of the best horseman abroad. John Worland has seen circusing pretty much the world over.

Down in James Reilly's printing office is a picture of Frank Farwell, the founder of the house that was in the days before Bacon or Clary and Reilly. A son of Bacon's is a job compositor at the old stand and the venerable Thad Anderson, the foreman, is an heirloom handed down to the Doctor with the good will and the plant.

Castle was also a great favorite about the printing houses but up to all sorts of tricks to gain information and, if he was not watched, would be all over the sap bush, poking his nose into every nook and cranny. Coming on to New York one time to order some printing of Farwell, he found that the boss had gone on to the Rice show to see if he could collect some money. If the truth has been told, Daniel was never any too prompt in paying at any stage of his career. Be that as it may, Farwell's patience had become exhausted and he had gone on to the show to make a raise. Mr. Farwell made a failure. Rice did not pony up, so he telegraphed home not to ship any more printing to Rice. The dispatch was delivered at Farwell's place of business bright and early in the morning. Castle was there and captured the dispatch. Its tenor was: "Ship no more printing to Dan Rice."

Castle pocketed the dispatch, ordered a goodly supply of printing in great haste, saw it boxed and shipped, and then went up town to his hotel. When he was quite sure that the printing was well on the road, he sent the delayed dispatch down to Farwell's office. Of course there was an explosion when the printer got home; and Dan Rice, politician, philanthropist, and jester, had to ante before he got any more pictorial paper.

In 1872, George F. Bailey threw a bombshell into the managerial camp by exhibiting for twenty-five cents. John H. Murray, Howes' London show (James E. Kelley, manager), and L. B. Lent's show were all going East. Kelley had in his employ one Capt. Hughes, a so-called writer about the literary caliber of Harry Cordova or Charlie Whitney. He was in a great state of anxiety about the Bailey show and got his desired information by slipping into Booth's printing office at the dinner hour. He found an electrotype plate all ready for the press, read the fat line, "Admission Twenty-Five Cents," and sneaked out to report to his master.

When Billy Burke strikes Ohio, he draws largely. William E. fought and bled in one of the regiments of that state and it is wonderful how many boys in blue fought shoulder to shoulder with the old clown. The veterans waited on him in such numbers this winter at the United States Hotel, Columbus, that he had to conceal himself in the solitudes of Sellsville to save himself from their good natured importunities. Bill has relations in Ohio and during one of his visits they came down on him in whole families. There was a blooming cousin of the fair sex, with red hair just like Bill's only more of it. Bill is badly bald. The clown invited the whole tribe to supper. They joined. The contracting agent had made a mistake and the show was stopping at a good hotel. That agent, let it be remarked, rarely makes a mistake. I hate to see injustice done to any man. This was a slip. "Slips don't count."

Bill's cousin sat at his right hand and she chewed through the bill of fare until the waiter asked, "Miss, will you have some of the fruit, canned peaches?"

Bill's carrot-ty cousin simpered, "Yes, I'll take a can, if you please."

A late number of the Indianapolis *Journal* contains an alleged interview with John B. Doris and compresses about as many mis-statements as I ever saw condensed in the same amount of space. I've heard that Mr. Doris has been unwell of late. He must have been very sick at the time the reporter came in contact with him and almost gone. He begins by relating that Adam Forepaugh and the Sells Brothers began life by selling concert tickets and lemonade on the seats of the circus. Well, to answer temperately, they did not. Doris is made to say that circus people call each other "rubens." The reporter will please call one of Doris' canvasmen a "ruben" when his show opens in Indianapolis, first selecting a soft place of ground to lie down on. A "ruben" is a "jay," a "gawk," a "gill"; not an attaché of the circus, but a patron who has come to town to see the show without first combing the hayseed out of his hair.

Doris, in the interview, credits W. C. Coup with being the inventor of the railroad show. "Oh, me! Oh, my! Oh, me!" L. B. Lent, Spalding & Rogers, and others ran railroad shows when Coup was a sideshow talker and Doris was selling peaches in a huckster's cart in Albany. Doris is a good fellow, if he does have the gout like thunder. Perhaps he had an extra twinge that day and talked a little reckless to the pencil pusher.

That quaint character, Bill Devere,[24] sometimes called "Big Foot," is singing his songs in New York and reciting his ordinary poems in his own inimitable way. William is a poet that could tackle Joaquine Miller in a six-day go-as-you-please at rhyming and come up smiling at the end of the last lap of the last day without turning a hair gray. Bill is chock full of talent but hasn't the exact faculty of applying it. A rough diamond of the first water. He has written some good things, as your readers know. Perhaps if Bill had let his hair grow and oiled his soap locks and called himself Ywilliam Deverequin, he would have been more of a success. Devere could be the poet laureate of the sawdust, as Miller is the poet laureate of the plain. Burns liked the allurements of the tavern and Bill is at home surrounded by the fumes of the burning weed, the merriment of the roysterers and the oysterers, who exclaim, "The world is mine oyster," and go out after dark hunting the shell fish. Devere rhymes with wit, sense, and pathos, but for reasons best known to himself he mounts his fancy at times to ride in pursuit of dreams. Bill is not much of a saint or much of a sinner but when his last trump is called I guess he'll pass.

Frank Ashton does a very clever hand balance act and he found his accomplishment quite handy one day last summer while laying off at the St. Charles Hotel in New York. Ashton, it appears, had suffered an injury to one of his ankles and on that account could not walk upon his feet; but when he wished to visit the hotel office, he simply reversed the order of things and walked on his hands. One day during his stay at the St. Charles, a regiment of militia came gaily marching down Broadway with colors flying and band playing. Ashton heard the music and, throwing up his feet, he marched down stairs ahead of all the rest.

A chronic borrower struck Francis, the leaper, at the St. Charles just after supper for a loan.

"Haven't got a cent," answered Francis.

The loan solicitor appeared incredulous but Francis convinced him by standing on his head and remarking, "You can have all that drops out of my pockets."

Most of the circus agents and managers know Vanderbilt of the firm of Crane & Co., the wood engravers. Van has in his day dabbled considerably in the show business. One of his latest ventures was a panorama of "Uncle Tom's Cabin." The manager found that the public did not take kindly to his moral show. They expected to see a play and not a painting; and, in their anger, they made rude remarks and threw the chairs and benches at the work of art. Vanderbilt sold the panorama to Doc Healy, the patent medicine showman, [who] painted out the Negroes and changed them into Indians.

P. T. Barnum's hobby is still his autobiography. At the opening of the show at the Madison Square Garden, William D. Hagar of the privileges showed me a letter from Barnum covering two closely written pages of note paper, giving him pointers how to work the book.

A friend of mine, on arriving in Gotham last fall, called on the bankers and made a deposit of his summer earnings. It was one of those peculiar monied institutions where the more you put down the less you take up. This winter, the man who had monkeyed with the tiger, met a professional friend, who remarked, "I think next season will be a tough one."

"It couldn't be any worse for me than the last one," was the reply. "I worked all summer for a suit of clothes."

A veteran manager was telling me the other day that he looked forward to the time when the circus managers would all meet in the winter and equitably divide up the territory. I inquired when he expected that time to come.

He answered, "At the millennium."

Before Tom Barry came to America, as the biographers have it, "he had a large and varied experience abroad," having roughed it with the small shows in his early days and started later on with Hengler, and the other circus lights.[25] About '55 or '56, Thomas was with a small trick called Hayes & Brothers', following the fairs and taking in the smaller towns. They pulled down at Redditch at night after the show, so as to reach Banbury on time for the fair next day. One of the Brothers Hayes, had a peculiar twist to his neck, caused by falling from a balloon during an exhibition ascension and was a peculiar character at the best.

As they set out on their all night journey, Tom ventured to make the inquiry, "Who knows the way? How are we going to get to Banbury?"

Hayes, with a neck awry answered, "I'll steer you proper, Tom, or I'll travel by the moon."

So they set out and traveled near to morning. At last the guide called a halt. He dismounted and took a survey. Tom Barry remarked, "If I'm any judge, we are ten miles from no place on the direct road to nowhere."

The managerial pilot took an observation and peered in the darkness all around, then looked long and anxiously at the moon.

"Well?" spoke Thomas.

Then the manager made answer, "Tom, blow my heyes hif we ain't on the wrong bloody side of the moon."

Tom Barry is going to try on the Irish clown again with VanAmburgh next summer. He made a success of it in England and a hit with L. B. Lent at his first appearance in America at the old Iron Building on 14th Street. When Tom was playing Hibernian clown with Hengler in 1864, he took a benefit and announced it in verse:

> The greatest of our modern wits
> When pressed to longer tary.
> Exclaimed, "Oh no! a legacy
> I leave you in TOM BARRY "
>
> A maiden, spotless as the snow
> And just about to marry,

> Was led to take so wise a step
> By list'ning to TOM BARRY.
>
> If you but listen to his jokes,
> You quickly grief may parry;
> "By thunder, smoke, and jibbareens,
> Here's luck to bold TOM BARRY."
>
> So haste, dear Phil, and Mike, and Pat,
> And you, young dancing Larry;
> Be quick, wake up and patronize
> Your countryman, TOM BARRY.

March is a very long month when there is no money to be borrowed of the manager and the landlord begins to look anxious. Managers are not advancing money to performers as they once were, all on account of a few individuals who forget to pay, especially a Joey who went to England and forgot to come back at all.

Den Stone tells a yarn of the early days, along among the back numbers. Rockwell's Native American Circus and Menagerie went South from New York and in the course of its trip made Charleston. In the "city-by-the-sea" lived a livery stable keeper who had in his day and generation been a lecturer on the wild beasts in the menagerie. Many time and oft' had he related his oratorical triumphs of the past to his newer neighbors. Upon the coming of the show, they all, with one accord, implored him to favor them with a sample of his eloquence. The Rockwell agents-in-advance favored the airing of the resident's volunteer eloquence and zoological information and the proprietor was nothing loath. Of course the showman made known all the particulars in the local press and the Charlestonians turned out in goodly numbers to greet the show and give ear to their townsman.

The livery stable keeper and ex-animal lecturer acquitted himself with honors and got away with the peculiarities of the beasts in good order until he arrived in front of a large specimen of the tapir, an animal which he had never before seen. He got as far as, "This animal, ladies and gentlemen," then he stopped and said, "Hem-m-m!" He cleared his throat and remarked, "Haw!" After an awkward pause, he commenced again, pitching his voice in a very high key, "This animal, ladies and gentlemen, is a hog and it is probably the Gdddst hog you ever saw!"

When Hyatt Frost, who was with the VanAmburgh & Co. Floating Palace Menagerie on the Mississippi River so long ago that it would make you tired to think of it, there was in the collection of animals a number of young panthers that were very playful and very pretty. Capt. Schote had learned them a very clever hat trick. It was a good thing for those who had hats to sell and a demand for head covering was created whenever the show exhibited. The Captain would show the gawks how the panther could be made to jump and play by moving a hat in front of the bars. The lookers-on tried it with an unvarying result. The panther never failed getting the hat and demolishing it to the immense delight of the wicked Captain and the showman. The waggish Captain kept up this practice until the show ran aground and remained there stuck fast on a sand bar in the Ohio River three months.

Hyatt Frost, still at the head of the VanAmburgh show, has a superstition about sevens. He made arrangements to run away from home in '37 and was well warmed for his first endeavor to embark in the show business. In '67 he went broke by destruction of the show in winter quarters. He thinks twenty-five is a pretty lucky number, so he is going to show for a quarter of a dollar.

Old Sport Clifford was too fluent for the Barnum show.[26] You might as well try to stop Clifford's blab as the flow of the Niagara. Bailey invited Sport to accept two weeks' notice and told him in a brief note that the two weeks' salary was waiting him if he would only accept it and quit at once. The proposition delighted the leaper from Binghamton and he reported to the St. Charles Hotel to relate his good fortune.

"Why don't you go out with Maybe?" asked Col. Charles Seeley.

"Who's Maybe?" inquired Sport.

"Maybe!" exclaimed Seeley, "Haven't you heard of him? Lots of the boys will go out with him this season."

Sport has been looking for Maybe ever since. Maybe he will find him. Maybe not.

One summer Sport was out of a sit, when the Forepaugh show struck Cincinnati. To obtain a penny, he opened a beer joint in proximity to the canvas and dispensed lager to the thirsty. Trade was not rushing and one of his comrades of his other days remarked [as much] to the proprietor of the "beererey."

"I've got one advantage," responded Sport. "If I don't sell much beer, I get what I drink myself at wholesale."

It was a great saving.

I will wind up with a short sermon to the circus billposter. My friend, you have hired out to perform a very important duty and will receive very fair salary for the same. You will often be sent to bill country routes. Presumably, you know the importance of billing the country. With a circus, that is what **tells**. Let the town be filled on show day with the country people and it can well be left to take care of itself. The manager and the agents will see all that is done in the towns. You are trusted with the country, work that is the manager's main hold. You are expected to put up all the paper you can on your route and make a truthful report of the same. I have known men to ride out to the edge of the town, burn their paper, and sleep away the day in the shade instead of faithfully putting up their bills. Don't do that. Then be honest about your tickets. Put them where they belong. Don't barter "comps" for "budge." Don't cover a rival's paper. There is nothing in it. It only creates retaliation and both managers suffer in the end. Don't be afraid to wear a clean shirt. I have seen billposters who were. Blacking will improve the appearance of your shoes. Don't go in a hotel dining room without a collar. If you must chew tobacco, don't do it about the tavern. The less rum you drink, the more money you will have next winter. I know this to be a fact. Don't see any of the company's property go to waste, not even a program. Avoid slang and profanity everywhere. Don't talk loud. Don't be fresh. If you are "strictly business," you will be "all right in the fall."

You will never know, reader, what comfort is until you travel ahead of a circus. Now when a circus agent has worked hard all day, he likes to get a good night's rest.... I ran into a town the other night so close to New York that you could smell the great city. I was tired enough to lie down. The landlord's name was Doll and a healthy **doll** was he, a clever Dutchman about five-feet-eight standing up.

The hose company was going to give a ball. Some of the boys in the barroom were brawling for beer already. At nine o'clock the festivities began. The fiddlers agitated the cat gut. The firemen and the girls began their grand promenade. And I went off to bed. So did Jimmerson. The fiddlers sawed and the boys and girls danced. At first the music rather pleased me; then I got tired of it and wished they were all in Harlem---both revelers and dancers. I dropped off to sleep, to dream. I dreamt that the *Journal* circulated one million copies a week and was printed on satin; turned over, and woke up as the dancers made the building shake. During the intermission for beer, I again departed to the land of Nod; dreamt I saw P. T. Barnum and Adam Forepaugh locked in each others' arms and exchanging the kiss of brotherly love. That made me so tired that I slept for some time. When I was awakened next, it was by a butcher-fire-boy striking the floor and turning around in the dizzy waltz with a good girl weighing two hundred pounds. Too tired to keep awake, I was again carried to the realms of slumber. Then I awoke. Then I slept. Again I awoke. And then swore, mildly. The boys and the girls were having a good time and I was having a Bob Ingersoll time. Along toward morning the program was varied. A fire was started in an adjacent building. That was done to put out the firemen who were balling. The firemen who put out, went out and put out the fire. Then they returned to Doll's hotel, balled at the bar, resumed the ball and shook the light fantastic until it was time to read the morning papers. I felt as if I had had the gloves on with Sullivan when I arose. That's how one Day, a circus agent, put in one night.

Jimmerson jumped ahead of the red car the other night to tell a landlord that we were coming, and to prepare breakfast for thirteen men with appetites; also to tell the livery man that some of our numbers wanted to take a sunrise ride into the country. When Jimmerson spoke about the hour for breakfast, Boniface said he couldn't get it ready so early, adding, "I don't keep a hotel for working men."

The "main guy of the pecking castle" looked as if he had worked on the railroad not so long ago. Come to size up this hotel and guests during the next day, we found that he had just two guests beside ourselves. One hadn't planted his potatoes yet on account of the late spring and the other juggles freight on a Hudson River dock when the steamers are running. How some folks put on airs.

The circus billposters are a fly lot. We stopped at the Nelson House, Poughkeepsie, over Sunday and Bain knows how to keep a hotel. I wished Yank Adams was there. From soup to ice cream, it pleased the boys. The colored gentlemen were particularly attentive to them. One of the waiters in taking Skip's order suggested, "Roast duck."

"Naw," answered Skip, "I been eatin' duck all winter."

Skip would have eaten cold beef, rather than to have had that waiter think for a moment that he had not lived off the fat of the land all winter.

Jimmerson says that the way to recollect anything is by association. At Peekskill, he sent Skip up to the livery stable on an errand.

"What's the name?" asked Skip.

"DeKay & Anderson, " replied Jimmer.

"I'll forget that before I am half-way there," replied Skip.

"No you won't," replied Jim. "Associate decay with DeKay and you'll not forget it."

Away went Skip. As he went up the hill he began to associate things, carrying out J.'s theory.

"DeKay, decay."

Then he thought of "rot," and by the time he got to the stable he was all mixed up. Walking into the livery office he asked, "Mr. Decay, is Mr. Rot in?"

Hyatt Frost relates that in '53 the Raymond & VanAmburgh show leased two giraffes of P. T. Barnum, paying him twenty percent of the gross receipts of the attraction. I recollect the show myself without straining my memory. They traveled Down East and I guess the giraffes were about the first of that kind of animal in that section, outside of picture books and circus posters. The giraffe-Raymond-VanAmburgh show with Hyatt Frost ran against Spalding & Rogers' railroad circus (Mr. John B. Doris' attention is called to this paragraph.) and Van Orden, who was a writer from Writersville, made it unpleasant for the giraffe show. S. & R. knocked the spots out of the giraffes.

The receipts fell off and Mr. Phineas Taylor Barnum's agent, who collected the twenty percent, thought the ticket boxes did not turn up enough, so he had printed a muslin sign which read: POSITIVELY NO MONEY TAKEN AT THE DOOR! This rag was displayed conspicuously at the main entrance, directly over the head of the ticket-taker, who happened to be Woods, of Vermont, who is now a trusted employee of the Estey Morgan Co. Woods thought it did not tell the whole story, so he added: AND D——D LITTLE AT THE WAGON.

That is one of Hyatt Frost's stories and he is fuller of them than a sailor's boarding house is of bed bugs [or] a wharf-dock of rats. The New England route awakens many pleasant memories, as well as some sad ones.

L. B. Lent is enjoying retirement but has not lost interest in circus affairs. He resides in New York. George F. Bailey has all the money anyone but Jimmy Cooper needs. G. F. B. and George Francis Train both tie up with the Ashland House.[27] John Nathans has got everything, except health. Lew June is at his ease at Ridgefield, Ct. Ben Maginley is "acting out." John H. Murray and Avery Smith are dead. Chester Clarence Moore, who used to write for Lent and Murray, crossed the ferry a long time ago. Mike Coyle, one of the whitest Irishmen that ever lived, is with Forepaugh. Claude DeHaven is editing a newspaper in Providence. Charles Gayler is writing plays, which he does not read to Shook, and telling funny stories to "Shed" and Sam Booth. Uncle John Tryon is over there. S. O. Wheeler still lives, with less diamonds. Hitchcock "went out" some time ago.[28] Gus Hatch is keeping tavern in Kansas. Joe Cushing made his last stand and closed. Kelley, once the millionaire manager (and first-class manager, too), is in retirement. Fred Couldock has no need to work. Fred Keeler is posting bills and minding other peoples' business at Albany, N.Y. Charlie Haskins is billposting at Providence. Bill Metchear left us to "pave the way."

How the paste brigade would kick if Kidder put them up in a beanery such as one that the Forepaugh show stopped at in Stamford, Ct., in 1879. They fed in a bakery on bean sandwiches. Fact!

A newspaper friend remarked to me at Peekskill, "Have you got a William O'Dell, circus rider, with your company?"

I answered, "Yes."

"Well," he answered, "he's Tom Hadley, that's his name. He used to polish stoves here. I thought he never would amount to much."

"So," I returned, "because he became a circus rider, William O'Dell, at one hundred dollars a week, has not amounted to much; but if he had remained at Peekskill polishing stoves at one dollar a day as Tom Hadley, he would have been all right. Can't see it."

I don't care about polishing stoves any more than Tom Hadley did and he made "a move in the right direction" when he became a circus rider. Sometimes we miss our callings. Some lawyers ought to be sawing wood, some preachers breaking stone, and some politicians doing time. John O'Brien was truly fulfilling his mission when he was peddling porgies. The circus business would have been the better if he had never been in it.

Now there's my friend Corbett, our worthy editor, if he had remained at Providence, R.I., he might have been taken with the cholera or the collywobbles and carried off with too much clam chowder. Now he is doing good and making money polishing the *Journal*. FOR SALE AT ALL NEWSSTANDS. TEN CENTS.

Fortune has also favored Yank Adams; he has never lost his appetite. Does me good to see my partner eat. The bull in the china shop cannot compare with Yank in the dining room. Now just imagine Mr. Adams, with that appetite, polishing stoves up at Peekskill at a dollar a day. It would be dreadful. He'd have to eat pig-iron to fill up.

I had occasion today to fire a man for selling complimentary tickets. It would be well if managers had photographs of all billposters and lithographers and when a man was detected in the destruction of paper or the sale of complimentary tickets, his mug could be furnished to [other managers]. As Mr. Dana of the *Sun* would say, "Turn the rascals out!" The man who will buy a complimentary ticket is worse than the seller. I would not care to leave a horse tied at his hitching post. He is a "fence." A fence is a receiver of stolen property and "the receiver is as bad as the thief," only more so.

There is a good deal of fun with the circus. Circus folks enjoy hunting for the "sleeper" when it is a mile up the railroad track, hid behind numerous freight cars and your life is in danger every minute you are playing "needle in the haystack." It's fun going to the lot after dinner on a hot day, with the dust as deep as last winter's snow. When the managers arrange to bring the lots down to the hotels, it will be different. It is funny when it rains and you don't know whether "the bottom has fallen out" from the mud or you will have to swim for the water. Then it's funny to hear the kickers kick. Some of them can kick over the top of the center pole and not half try. How pleasant the kicker makes it for the manager and the "layer out." Poor devil, I pity the L. O. Ben Lusbie was a daisy; he could "lay out" a kicker in a sulfurous manner. "Top doors!" "Close up!"

Sandy Spencer is dead. Some of the newspapers spoke pretty harshly of Sandy but he was a good-hearted, charitable man, yet as rough as a bear. I could spin yarns enough about Sandy to fill an entire issue of the *Journal* set in agate. Sandy had a pretty rocky experience during his final managerial career at the Globe Theatre. One of the last attractions that he put in the old church was a circus, in which Jim Nixon was interested. George J. Guilford wrote the bills. Judge Hilton and A. T. Stewart, the rent collectors, were in a great state of excitement because Sandy put in the sawdust and the horses; but Sandy was stubborn and in they went in spite of all threats, protestings and arguments. The circus did not pan out well and an inquisitive reporter of the New York *Sun* asked the lessee, "What was your share, Mr. Spencer?"

"Two barrels of horse manure," was the frank response of Sandy.

At Hartford on my return trip, I met Charlie Stow at Calhoun's printing office and, as we did not put on the gloves, we spun a few yarns for Higgs. Charlie told one on Gaylord, our deaf friend who is in Frisco with a trained animal show. I believe it occurred while Gaylord was with Cole and took place in a go-as-you-please mining town in Colorado. Gaylord, Hayden (now with Keene, the tragedian), and a number of the advance agents fell to playing pool and, as they were all well healed, for the edification of the gawks they pretended to play for money. It was all make-believe but it was carried out as if in dead earnest, the greenbacks passing to and fro in bundles and the sums bet made the jays' eyes hang out on their cheeks. After a while, having tired of the sport, Gaylord stepped up to the captain's office to settle.

"Five games," said Gaylord.

"Five games and the house's percentage on winnings. One hundred and thirty-five dollars." Gaylord looked. "Rules of the house," said the room keeper.

Gaylord planted the money like a man, one hundred and thirty-five dollars, and has not played any make-believe billiards for money since.

Ben Snow, one of the old time Snow Brothers, of the Stone & Murray show and for a long time with Coup during the run of the Equescurriculum and William C.'s later ventures, has trained ten enormous St. Bernard dogs to give a delightful performance. Ben favored Stow and myself with a private seance. It is a **dog gone good** show and Mr. Snow must have in**curred** a good deal of labor in their education. Ben says that they are not like most actors; they never kick but they **growl** once in a while.

The names of Fred Lawrence and George Fox Bailey came up the other day in conversation and, of course, out came a new story about Fred and Fox which must be repeated. Fred was press agent with the Barnum show and his earliest morning duty at every stand was to pay the newspaper bills, bestow the deadhead paper, and gather up the cuts. For this purpose, Frederick of London chartered a jehu and a chariot. To this expense, George of Danbury objected. Frederick argued the point and dwelt on the weight of the coin, the weight of the cuts and the bulk of the comps to be toted. Then Fred went and chartered an express wagon, a rickety, worn-out old vehicle drawn by a plug that would have made Bergh shed tears. The harness was a combination of leather and rope, principally rope, and the driver was in as poor a plight as his steed. Bailey saw the turn out. After that, Fred rode in a carriage in his morning rounds and Bailey said not nay.

Funny thing occurred when the VanAmburgh-Reich-Frost-show was at New Brighton. Colvin had a racket of running out the big Zulu and letting him cavort on the lot in front of the sideshow painting. Whenever the barbarian appears in this way (in native costume and bearing his javelin), all hands cry aloud, "The Zulu's escaped!" And yell at the top of their voices.

At New Brighton, the giant's sudden appearance created an immense sensation and the crowd ran helter-skelter, while the showmen yelled, "Run for your lives."

A policeman in full uniform started first. The Zulu selected the policeman for his victim and brandished the javelin and gave vent to his native war cry. The policeman made excellent time, with the Zulu in hot pursuit. The show folks roared with laughter and then the townspeople, seeing the point, screamed with delight. If the Zulu had been mounted on Maude S., he might have caught that copper.

Talking about sideshows, let us turn back to the early reign of Hyatt Frost and see how they used to do it "in our grandfathers' days." In 1849, Hyatt Frost and Charles Townsend, the famous elephant keeper, ran a six-and-a-quarter-cent side with Raymond & VanAmburgh. They traveled with a one-horse wagon and the show consisted of a seven-banded armadillo, one big snake, and four rattle snakes. As the California fever was at its height, the armadillo was known as "the big bug of California."

In '51 and '52, Frost ran a concert in an outside tent, a sixty-five foot round-top. In the company were C. L. Wheeler (now president of the oil exchange, Titusville), Ned Davis, John Brown, Morris Edmonds, and E. M. Dickinson and wife. Ned Davis was long a popular minstrel. Afterward he became agent for Tom Thumb under Sylvester Bleecker's management and toured the world. Bleecker long managed Wood's Minstrels and was the author of many minstrel sketches. Frost paid him half the profits for the night to run this trick. The tariff was twelve and a half cents.

Frost at one time ran the bar and candy stands on the Floating Palace on the Mississippi, for which he "turned up" one hundred dollars weekly to the management. Frost says that one of the luckiest hits he ever made in the privilege business was in the purchase of two boatloads of conch shells at New Orleans at three cents each. He took them up into Tennessee and sold them for dinner horns at half a dollar apiece. I asked Frost the other day to give me a "back number" in the privilege business. He thought for a moment and answered, "In '47, Hank Holloway paid $600 for the candy stands with one of the VanAmburgh shows."

Some years ago a *Clipperite* wanted some items. George J. Guilford favored him with some. This one created a sensation: "John O'Brien has not yet disposed of the clothesline privileges." The bit of news escaped the argus eye of Frank Queen and created a good deal of fun among the habitués of Room No. 1 at the old St. Charles.

With the decline of the "all tent" show, we can look for the return of the circus with a clown. And, by the way, do you recollect

Hyatt Frost

David Seal? Wasn't he a slick one. Just the *beau ideal* of the "King's Jester." Charlie McCarthy says he saw him in England and he is as fine as silk.

The elephant market is overstocked. The Barnum party has no less than fourteen on the shelf at Bridgeport.

George Loyal and his wife Zuila have gone to Europe and will probably appear at the Hippodrome in Paris. Loyal is both a producer and a hustler and his wife is one of the smartest and bravest little women who ever put on tights or attempted feats of skill and daring. Their engagements with Forepaugh were very successful and they filled several winters to advantage in Cuba and Mexico. The Loyals have traveled almost all over the world and speak numerous languages. They have seen life in all kinds of climates and braved epidemics and revolutions in the outlandish parts of the earth. They have acted at the theatre in times of yellow fever, cholera, and plagues; undertook long and perilous voyages; experimented in the performance of difficult and dangerous feats; and succeed where others have failed. George Loyal was one of the few to make any money out of the cannon act. As the "human cannonball," he was a success. Farini tried to monopolize the act but his bluffs did not go and Loyal did the act "in spite of his teeth."

Got some printing of John Stetson's "Boston Job Print" and that reminded me it is not so many years ago that Stetson was a professional runner and a champion "ped" with a first-class record. In those days he used to run foot races in circus rings as an extra attraction. John Stetson is a man who can keep a good many irons hot at the same time. He piled up a fortune out of the *Police News*. He was long the successful manager of the Howard Athenaeum and put upon its stage some of the greatest combinations of talent ever massed. As for salaries, he was a perfect angel. Stetson is now best known as the proprietor of the Globe Theatre, Boston, and the Fifth Avenue, New York. He has also managed Modjeska and Salvini and runs a "Monte Cristo" company on the road.

Charles H. Duprez, who for many years was a prominent minstrel manager, is keeping a hotel at Lowell. Duprez left the road or, perhaps more correctly, the road left him. In many things Duprez reminds me of circus manager John H. Murray. Both were very attentive to business, dignified and straightforward, and both in their respective lines got to running very queer shows. I don't believe that Duprez ever thought that he at any time in his career gave a tart show. I know that Murray never for a moment suspected that he had a quisby circus. I once asked Oscar Rahn, Duprez' agent, a graduate from the circus advance, "Does Mr. Duprez really think that he has a good show?"

Rahn answered sadly, "He does."

It was painfully bad and Duprez, with all his experience and successes, did not know it. He was blind to the imperfections of his own entertainment. I was talking not long ago with a life-long friend and admirer of Duprez. He said, "Duprez wrote me enthusiastically of his show and described it as the best he had ever had and pictured it in glowing colors. Why, it was the worst I ever saw and I don't think the man ever suspected it."

Now how would managers so shrewd, so smart, and experienced as John H. Murray and Charles H. Duprez come to think their own bad shows good? Nine hundred and thirty-nine out of a thousand friends asked in regard to the merits of an enterprise will praise it to your face, mislead you, and warp your judgment. Murray played "Dick Turpin" three seasons on the New England circuit. In '75 he had proposed to do "Mezeppa" but at the last moment threw it up and adhered to the worn-out program. When I mildly suggested that "Dick Turpin" was worn threadbare, he said, "Why, my friends tell me that it is worth a half dollar to see Black Bess die."

Black Bess died all the next season to poor business. It's pretty tough to tell a man his show is rotten but if he asks my opinion he's going to get it. It's a good thing for a manager to get about and see other peoples' shows. I don't suppose Duprez ever took in Thatcher's, Primrose & West's, or Barlow & Wilson's. He ran in his own groove until it ran out. Duprez keeps a good hotel. Murray is in the good place.

In route West, I stopped overnight in Boston at the old Boston Hotel, kept for so many years by landlord Pray, so well known to all circus folks who traveled the New England circuit. Pray was very popular with the arenic patrons but that is not saying that he kept a good hotel. He ran a good, clean, orderly house, and managed it with the strictest discipline but the bill of fare was none too rich and was methodically cast iron.

In the springtime, you could see in the office about meal hours, or in the evening, L. B. Lent, occupying a double space; George F. Bailey and his cane; Avery Smith, puffing a bad cigar; Col. Joe Cushing, smoking a good one and indulging in an occasional nip in the narrow, contracted, hide-away barroom; Charles W. Fuller, big with whiskers and any amount of self-esteem; Uncle John Tryon, full of good humor and the rheumatism; Mike Coyle, lathy, long and good natured; Claude DeHaven, a Dundreary in dress and poetical; S. O. Wheeler, from way down in Maine; big, handsome John H. Murray and his brother, Jim; John J. Nathans, calculating and business-like; Lew June, looking like a farmer; Chester Clarence Moore, the writer, almost a double for bluff Ben Maginley; Fred Keeler, asking questions; Matt Leland, busy quizzing, dressy and frisky and quite inclined to guy; William C. Coup, with his Indiana dialect; Richard Fitzgerald, the Irish terrier, making more noise than any man in the room; Andy Cullen, weeding Spanish and telling of marvelous adventures in Cuba and Mexico; Fred Couldock, hard-working and "h" dropping; Charlie Haskins, a walking fashion plate, just as he is today and not looking a day younger; and not by any means to be forgotten, Sgt. Curtis Trask, of the Boston police, the circus man's best friend in Beantown.

Fred Keeler of Albany is well posted in the ancient history of the American arena. Fred says he wants someone to find him a later back number than this one: He says that in 1851 Stone & Madigan traveled in the West and Northwest by rail. Den Stone has often confirmed this statement. W. T. B. Van Orden was the writer of the concern. Fred is a great admirer of the late Dr. Spalding and cherishes his memory. Fred joined Spalding & Rogers as treasurer at $25 a month. The first week he was insulted by a rube, licked him, and was fined $22. In 1850, Spalding & Rogers opened in Boston. Fred says it was a great show with a great outfit, a 110 foot round-top, the largest used at that time, with a 17 foot extension, laced all around, 27 tiers of built seats, admission 25 cents. About '56, Spalding & Rogers made an experiment. They constructed crate cars with low, small wheels, such as one sees at the ferries between New York and New Jersey and Philadelphia and Camden, in which baggage is transferred. The show was advertised as the "Crystal Palace Circus, All Iron and Glass." The truck cars were to be unloaded from flat cars drawn to the lot and loaded after the show. They proved a failure. The wheels were so small and the crates set so low that once stuck in the mud they remained there. Fred says that S. & R. used the first quarter poles he ever saw. Each had a bale ring. At first, four were used; afterward, eight. Keeler traveled before the days of the dirt-bank ring, when they carried their sectional curb with the baggage. Sometimes it persisted in wobbling or bobbling up and bothered the riders. That was indeed a curb to proud ambition.

I never miss a number of a bright, gossipy paper called *The Journalist*. I began to read it under the regime of Byrne & Richardson, who are always readable. In a late article about "press agents," it refers casually to the circus scribe and mentions the two Hamilton's as if they were the only successful ones and then winds up by referring to the "mere circus agent, who has to work eighteen hours of the day and live very much like a dog and who, on top of it all, receives usually a poor salary." Now, as it goes in most of the newspaper offices, the New York press believe that all the literary work of the Barnum & London shows was from the pens of Tody and Jack Hamilton. All the country editors thought that Dave Thomas wrote all the bills and advertisements. The truth is, for years they were written by Charles Stow and W. W. Durand and, as each received $6,000 a year, I doubt that either "lived like a dog."

The success of Jack Hamilton in New York with the Barnum and the London was great. Tody proved equally popular. I don't want to detract one iota from the reputation of good fellows, deservedly belonging to both the Hamiltons; but the highest salaried men in the circus-writing profession are not the men who make it pleasant for visitors to the show but the men who write up the show and its attractions. All tolled, they are but a handful. They not only can write, but they are **showmen**. They understand how to write to bring out the people. They scheme, they originate, they boom, they write to draw money. P. T. Barnum himself understands the art. He is a practical writing advertiser. I know an A-one, first-class journalist who tried it last season. Honestly, he did not in all the summer write a line that drew ten cents. Press agents, **Mr. Journalist**, for the circus or the theatre, are not made, they are born.

It is no secret that last winter James A. Bailey (of Barnum, Bailey & Huchinson) and Stow were out. Fred Lawrence was solicited to write up the season's bills. He declined. A virtue was made of necessity and they were written by Charles Stow. Why? Because there was no one disengaged considered competent for the task. If the editor of *The Journal* would go out of New York and see the vast amount of circus literature put in circulation, and its infinite variety, he will come to the conclusion that circus bill writing, together with the illumination thereof, is a specialty that no tyro need try his hand at.

George M. Clark, the Vermont clown, is dead. He was a minstrel manager and ran a grist mill with equal success. He was also a song writer and composer. As a clown he was not possessed of any humor but he sang with sentiment that caught on in the ring and he was a favorite in New England. For many years he traveled with "the Flatfoots." Being thrifty, he got along in the world. Whitmore & Clark's Minstrels were for many seasons a Down East success. Mr. Clark successfully conducted a grist mill and by a business transaction one winter appeared in a court of justice as a witness. It is an old story long current in the Green Mountain state but it will bear repeating. The lawyer, as most lawyer's will, began to belabor Clark on his being a minstrel and circus clown and wanted to know in thundering tones that made the justice's wig dance on his bald pate, "Are you not ashamed of your disreputable calling?"

"My father was engaged in a worse one," quietly responded the clown, minstrel and miller.

"What was your father?" screamed the attorney.

"A lawyer," replied Clark.

The browbeater sat down, the justice laughed his spectacles off, and his wig turned halfway 'round and back again. The audience yelled and the justice entirely forgot to preserve the dignity of the court. Clark won his case. The lawyer has not heard the last of it to this day. Hiram Atkins published it in the Montpelier *Patriot* and the story is a Vermont classic and is related at every session of the legislature.

I ran across a small show the other day struggling with fate. There was no management. The show was in eminent danger any day of passing the agent. An attaché told me that they actually ran into one town where no arrangements whatever had been made. The last I heard, the boss agent was three days ahead of the show with a five dollar note. If the show comes to grief, it will probably be claimed that they were on the wrong route or had bad luck. Bad luck is called to account for the asinine stupidity of some people. I always feel sorry for people with such a handled trick. They are bound to be brought up standing when they are stranded and the fabric goes to pieces. The performers are out for the season, lose their salaries, and are liable to find their trunks in hock with the landlord. It is a remarkable fact that several would-be managers take the road every year. Balloon! Oh, everybody. Stick the printer; leave performers, working people, all in a lurch; let the agents and billposters walk home; and the very next season they again take the road and rope in more victims. With gall as their only capital, they assume to manage and drag out a brief and miserable existence. Result: "Same as last season." Chief mourner: the printer. First assistant mourner: the agents, the performers, the musicians, the working people. Undertaker: the sheriff. Let her R.I.P.

I'm sorry to hear that both Sells Bros. and Forepaugh paid an extravagant license at Minneapolis. It would do no good to state the amount here. It would be a good day's receipts for a small show. It would have been better to have let Minneapolis go without a circus. Cedar Rapids has an attack of the high license fever. They wanted the earth and two or three comets. Forepaugh arranged to show in a nearby town and they fell to a sum of six times too much. I only hope that he sticks and refuses to show in Cedar Rapids at all. The town is not worth the powder. Forepaugh showed there last year to no great business (a moderate day's work), paying a $100 fine for parading the burgh and exhibiting without the city limits. Since then they have extended the limits. Merchants and the local authorities of towns and cities will often appropriate large sums to subsidize horse trots, balloon ascensions, displays of fireworks, agricultural exhibitions, and the like, to make business. But when a showman comes along and assumes all risks, some of these same parties will put an obstacle in the way, in the way of a robbing license. Skip the high license towns, Mr. Managers, and let the councils of those burghs encourage the cultivation and growth of grass on the highways.

One season when I was with Forepaugh, a committee of citizens from Three Rivers, Michigan, came on to see the showman to induce him to come to their town. They guaranteed him free license, free lot, free billboards. They were live businessmen, full of snap, life, energy, business. They were "up to snuff." Forepaugh went. Business was immense, both for the showman and the trades people. Both were more than well paid.

Waterloo, Iowa, is a fine town. Its merchants are "red hot and still a heating." They have a piece of ground in the heart of the city for public use. They have purchased it and set it aside for that purpose. They seek the showman, they want him, and they must and will have him. And it is a fact that last season they wanted to entertain Forepaugh's company at a hotel at their own expense. They couldn't do too much for the show and the showman. Forepaugh took pains to pay off at Waterloo and everybody connected with the show felt like buying of the wide-awake, public spirited, go-ahead merchants of Waterloo. Keep away from your Minneapolis, Cedar Rapids, and skin towns until they feel better. The railroads, the newspapers, the billposters, the lot owners, hotel keepers, and merchants will remedy the matter in due time if you only give them the go-by.

Levi J. North is in the "cold, cold ground." In paying his last respects to the memory of Frank Pastor, he hastened his own demise. Mr. North will ever be remembered as the first to ever accomplish a somersault on horseback and one of the most finished equestrians the world ever knew. The old gentleman's latter days were saddened by bitter poverty. Some years since, I wrote for the *New York Clipper* an extended account of his most brilliant career at home and abroad. It was with much difficulty and only after the most persistent persuasion that I succeeded in securing from his lips the necessary data. He was morbidly sensitive about his reverses and cited the instance of a representative of the Chicago *Daily News*, who wheedled him out of an interview on the ground that "Chicago readers would be interested in an old residenter." The Chicago scribler enlarged in detail on Mr. North's poverty and he was wroth thereafter. Howard or Fontaine of the *Herald* afterward tried to get from the veteran's lips the events of his professional career and, although his warm friend, William J. Florence, interceded, the ex-equestrian's consent could not be obtained.

Mr. North's recollections of his apprentice days were vivid and complete and he rattled off anecdotes and facts as fast as I could note them down. Of his extraordinary successes in Europe and on his return to New York, he related in glowing and enthusiastic language; but when it came to his more recent days, his memory faltered and he said, "There is not much worth recollecting." The dates of some of his most recent ventures and his last appearance in New York I had to obtain from others. I read him the manuscript as I completed it and he seemed well pleased with my treatment of the triumphs of his better days.

Frank Queen had long desired a biography of North and I left the manuscript in the charge of Evans (who was then the manager of the *Clipper*) in the morning on my way down town to attend a meeting of the "Turn Over Club" at the counting room of Dr. James Reilly. On my return to the hotel about three o'clock, I found a note from Evans, saying that Mr. Queen had accepted the biography and the price was waiting for me at the office. It is needless to say that I immediately chartered a Bleecker Street car and rode to Centre and Leonard Streets, returning by the same route with the cash in my pocket. There's many a pen driver misses Frank Queen. He was a great friend to writers, paid promptly and liberally, and was both friend and patron. Many a time he has paid me money when I was indebted to him. Alas! Queen, the editor, and North, the rider, are numbered with the dead.

I have just received a letter from George Loyal in London. His wife, Ella Zuila, is appearing at the Crystal Palace there. She performs but once a day and then in the "centre transept" at five-thirty p.m. I think Loyal's idea was to do a trapeze act when he went abroad. He writes: "I found that the trapeze was played out here, as there are millions here, good and bad, and some very bad." Zuila's opening on the 8th of July was well received and complimented by the management. The daring lady exhibits on a wire 300 feet long, stretched 90 feet above her audience, which is out-Blondining Blondin in his own field. The Loyals will take in some of the other European capitols ere their return.

One of the press associations reports the new deal of the Barnum show, hinted at by us in a late issue of the *Journal*. As stated and probably with official sanction, James A. Bailey retires and henceforth the title of the show will be Barnum, Cole & Hutchinson.[29] The telegram referred to credits Bailey with the possession of two million dollars. There can be no doubt that Bailey is "well fixed," as the saying goes, but one million dollars, except in a circus bill, is a good deal of money. Of course, the report says that the Cole show will be merged with the present Barnum show and it is quite certain that it will be in the bills.

The Barnum party have long been courting Cole and the present wedding will not surprise some folks so very much. W. W. Cole possesses many of the qualities that made James A. Bailey a success. Mr. Cole is both a router and an advertiser.

What will become of the high-hired men of both shows is now a question that will interest the present incumbents. Some may be chosen and some may be left. Or will the Cole show continue in the field, sailing under another name?

If the Barnum show extends its next season to California, Cole has been there before, knows all about it, and his experience will be invaluable. There is no doubt the Barnum name would draw largely in Australia and Cole knows a l about the Antipodes.

Should the printer "carry" lame duck shows? Successful managers who pay the printer promptly argue that the printer should not keep alive the struggler.... Jones has capital and cash, Smith has gall and no cash. His show is mortgaged and he is in debt up to his eyes. But for the printer, Smith would not be on the road to eat up country, stick agents and performers, and finally "climb the golden stairs." Smith invariably runs a faking show, leaves the country burned up, the people raw, and is a positive injury to the good name of all reputable showmen.

One Western manager has retrenched in his billing expenditures, having hauled off his second car and put a couple of program men ahead in lieu thereof. Perhaps if he'd keep his only advertising car nearer to the show than when he ran two, he may get along quite well, provided he is running in territory free from opposition. It is a fact that in many instances the country patronage does not pay for the double and often treble livery hire in addition to wages of the billposters and the paper they put up. Country billing pays less every year. The return grows smaller and smaller. Take, for instance, the billing out of Kokomo today: five livery teams, 1st brigade, $20; five billposters, wages and board, $10; 1,200 sheets of paper, programs and couriers, $80; liveries, 2nd brigade. $20; billposters, wages and board, $10; paper, pictorial and small bills, $50; paste for both brigades, $10. In summation, billing country out of Kokomo, $200. The privileges save many a manager from bankruptcy and there is not one of them but would be glad to rid himself of the peddler of the peanut, the server of the lemonade, and the dispenser of the barber-pole candy and the cornucopia. The "annex" and the "grand after concert" are indispensable adjuncts in this country and earn many a penny that helps pay the printer and the lithographer.

Billy Burke broke "Sid," the clown elephant without the use of a hook, a club, or any manner of cruelty or punishment whatever.

As I sit in the office of the red advertising car and look out of the window at the reddening woods, I am made aware that "the autumn days am here."[30] The streamer date reads "October." The time is not far distant when we will turn in the last expense account and begin to pay our own board bill. When the show closes it breaks up many a pleasant association. With the advertising car sidetracked, we are scattered from Kalamazoo to Kalamazac and another season we may meet under other banners. Skip, when he leaves for Michigan, will not ride home in a side-door pullman or a flat car, but first-class all the way without missing a meal. Townsend, the paste-maker and chambermaid, the man-who-shaves-himself, is of an economical turn of mind and with his accumulated capital and talents could put out the three balls of the pawnbroker and the barber's pole and conduct a brisk trade in Putnam county, this state. Cohen will have a smaller postage stamp bill after the season is over and the postmaster at Albion will have much less to do.

The death of Jumbo is an irreparable loss to the Barnum show.[31] P. T. has received no greater setback since the burning of his two museums. I was amused to hear a gentleman remark at Towanda, N.Y., "Barnum had him killed purposely for an advertisement." And the New York *World* remarks in an editorial paragraph, "Sweet are the uses of adversity in advertising."

It appears that the railroad officials at St. Thomas were at fault in informing Byron Rose, the careful and able manager of transportation, that there was "nothing in the way"; neither did the train make any signal by whistle or bell of its approach and came within an ace of wiping out the entire herd of elephants.

The Barnum show has a racket on the lithograph comps that works to a charm. The certificates when the lithographs are first displayed in the windows do not grant an admission to the show but are exchanged for a ticket that does if the lithographs are kept up until the day of the circus. Manager Hutchinson has the list in hand at the main entrance and the "elected" enter while the "foolish virgins" are referred to the ticket wagon, which is painted red.

Henry Barnum, of the Barnum show, takes the world philosophically. When he was one of the proprietors of the London show, he thought himself worth at least $80,000. Alas! Kelley, his partner, failed and carried his partner down with him. Mr. Barnum has always had both the sympathy and respect of the entire profession.

The Barnum advance for 1886 will be engaged by W. W. Cole, who will manage the route and advertising matters in advance of the big show. Mr. Cole is also particularly happy in combining an entertainment, as his present exhibition gives good evidence. Cole's own policy always has been an aggressive one and he has made many a magnificent fight in opposition. He is a peculiarly closed-mouth man, not at all given to wind, brag, or bunkum. Heretofore he has declined to permit the publication of his portrait but with the Barnum, under the new regime, we shall, of course, see his phiz as the middleman of the new firm.

I met a manager the other day who complained that he was doing no business. He had a neat little trick but how could he do any business? He promised fifty cages of animals in the menagerie and a "half-mile track" under his canvas. He did not have a dozen cages of animals and as soon as his parade appeared on the street everyone knew that his big promise in the way of animals was false and the sight of his canvas proved that the "half-mile track" must have been left in the last town.

Over-advertising was not the only thing he suffered from. He harbored an army of fakirs who commenced their pilfering early and continued late, ruining the business of the show and driving the country people out of town. This would-be manager says there is no harm in "doing up a countryman." Indeed, then, it is just as honorable to rob a hen roost or clothesline. A thief is a thief and such a manager should be tied to a whipping post and be given a couple of dozen lashes on the bare back, the medicine to be repeated until a perfect cure is affected. It is strange that such outlaws should be permitted to roam while there is such a quantity of tar and feathers handy in the land and stone piles that need recruits.

exchanged for a ticket that does if the lithographs are kept up until the day of the circus. Manager Hutchinson has the list in hand at the main entrance and the "elected" enter while the "foolish virgins" are referred to the ticket wagon, which is painted red.

Henry Barnum, of the Barnum show, takes the world philosophically. When he was one of the proprietors of the London show, he thought himself worth at least $80,000. Alas! Kelley, his partner, failed and carried his partner down with him. Mr. Barnum has always had both the sympathy and respect of the entire profession.

The Barnum advance for 1886 will be engaged by W. W. Cole, who will manage the route and advertising matters in advance of the big show. Mr. Cole is also particularly happy in combining an entertainment, as his present exhibition gives good evidence. Cole's own policy always has been an aggressive one and he has made many a magnificent fight in opposition. He is a peculiarly closed-mouth man, not at all given to wind, brag, or bunkum. Heretofore he has declined to permit the publication of his portrait but with the Barnum, under the new regime, we shall, of course, see his phiz as the middleman of the new firm.

I met a manager the other day who complained that he was doing no business. He had a neat little trick but how could he do any business? He promised fifty cages of animals in the menagerie and a "half-mile track" under his canvas. He did not have a dozen cages of animals and as soon as his parade appeared on the street everyone knew that his big promise in the way of animals was false and the sight of his canvas proved that the "half-mile track" must have been left in the last town.

Over-advertising was not the only thing he suffered from. He harbored an army of fakirs who commenced their pilfering early and continued late, ruining the business of the show and driving the country people out of town. This would-be manager says there is no harm in "doing up a countryman." Indeed, then, it is just as honorable to rob a hen roost or clothesline. A thief is a thief and such a manager should be tied to a whipping post and be given a couple of dozen lashes on the bare back, the medicine to be repeated until a perfect cure is affected. It is strange that such outlaws should be permitted to roam while there is such a quantity of tar and feathers handy in the land and stone piles that need recruits.

In Buffalo I met Mike Coyle, my old side-partner and employer with the Murray show. Mike "put me in the business" and for four years we meandered through New England, New Brunswick, Nova Scotia, and Canada. Mike had acted as treasurer of the show and '72 was his first year in advance. He made it a point to leave no complimentary tickets and was continually using mine, until I discovered a way of circumventing him. I had a lot printed, signed "M. Coyle," and when he asked for tickets he got his own and it was weeks before he discovered the dodge and when he did he laughed heartily thereat. Then, when Mike would make a particularly bad contract, he would say, "Charlie, please give the gentleman a contract and check." I did, but I signed each check, "M. Coyle, per day" and it was months before he got onto it.

In those days I wintered in New York and Mike and I used to take in all the sights and scenes of the great city by gaslight. We went to bed early (in the morning), usually taking breakfast with the milkmen in a Bleecker Street restaurant. John Murray used to call on us on his way downtown to Booth's Printing Office and several times he found us "just getting up." We said so and he believed us, until one morning he "dropped" and remarked dryly, "Go on and undress. I see you are just going to bed." We'd forgotten to muss the bed.

Did you ever know that Mike was a sailor? Yes, sir, a sailor and a captain at that. I have no doubt that he could have commanded the "Pinafore" and the whole navy. Mike was the captain of a canal boat and a terror of the tow path. If you don't believe it, sing out "Low bridge!" the first time you see him. You can bet Mike has had many a stormy passage on the "raging" before he dropped anchor in Buffalo or Syracuse. Uncle Charlie Castle was also a canalman before he "joined out" with old Dan Rice.

The paint brigade were readying the papers in the advertising car and one sitting in the office was forced to hear their converse and comments. At last Cochran's eye ran onto the heading of a patent medicine advertisement and he read and remarked, "Distress after eating, did any of you fellows ever have it?"

"I have had distress before eating," spoke up Skip, "because I didn't know where the grub was coming from."

Clever souls, the billposters. We were at Weedsport, New York. It was a cold, solemn morning and the boys gathered about the fire under the boiler, by the aid of which Townsend, old, slow-and-easy, one-quarter, James L. Hutchinson and James E. Cooper each one-eighth. Ever since Cooper was crowded out at the London-Barnum wedding, he has sighed for a piece of the Barnum show and now he has got it. Cooper's admission to the firm makes one change. James E. will himself attend to the "doing up" of the show in winter quarters and Frank Hyatt will have a lay-off at Connersville, Ind., until the robins come again. Cooper is a good deal of a horseman and a very close figurer. In fact, in a deal he can skin a flint; and his partners may rest assured that the "litter" on the lot will always find the highest market price.

Poor Charlie Noyes has gone over to the other shore.[32] He had been to the height of prosperity and in the depths of dispair. Mr. Noyes had many good qualities and was a well-meaning but unfortunate man. It is well enough for those who never met with reverses to carp but a dose of his experience will take the starch out of any man. Besides financial difficulties, Charlie Noyes had another sorrow that bore him down. It's all over now!

William E. Burke of Ohio is about to blossom forth as a stage clown under the management of Allen Sells (son of E. Sells) and Harry Amlar, himself an actor as well as for many seasons manager of the candy stands of the big Sells' show. Burke wanted R. B. Hayes to join as Pantaloon but Mrs. H. wouldn't let him. Besides, he couldn't leave his chickens. They would be lonesome.

A characteristic story is told of Jimmy Cooper of the Barnum show. He discovered that the roof of the winter quarters at Bridgeport leaked a bit. And off he rushed to Barnum.
"Mr. Barnum," said Cooper, "the roof of the building leaks in several places. I wish you would get it fixed at once."
Barnum looked at the new partner a moment and then answered, "Mr. Cooper, my managers attend to such small matters. I never bother about anything except where thousands of dollars are involved."

In 1876, the "Flatfoots" were running the Barnum show. My employer was sore on them for billing him everywhere and wanted a pill for their stuffed giraffe. I prepared the following and sent it on its travels around the press:

A good story is going the rounds among the show folk about P. T. Barnum and the stuffed giraffe he is said to have on exhibition with his "World's Fair." Ever since Phineas embarked in the clock business, he has had a mania for mechanics and is forever getting up something that runs by clockwork. A giraffe is set up by a skillful taxidermist and, as the eyes, tail, and ears were moved by the machinery within, the animal had every appearance of the living beast. Proud of his work, the great showman was gazing upon it with admiration with his partner, the venerable Avery Smith, when the spring which operated the movements [snapped] with a loud thud, ripping the skin of the giraffe clear up the back, deluging the showmen and spectators with a bushel of bran, and filling the eyes, mouth, and nose of P. T. and grandfather Smith. After this unfortunate *contretemps*, it was decided not to wind up the zebra in any other cage and the giraffe, it is said, was sewed up after the movements were taken out.

1886

Edward A. Tinkham fainted from the bursting of a blood vessel while listening to a minstrel performance at the Grand Opera House, Rochester, January 8, and died two hours afterward at his boarding house. A wicked, paragraphing journalist declares that poor Ed's demise was occasioned by the end man telling a new joke. Tinkham was the son of an elder of the church and his home was in Lima, N.Y. He held good positions with Cooper, Bailey & Co., Barnum & Coup, and W. C. Coup. Ed could talk faster than Maud S. ever trotted or the *Journal* ever sold and wrote left-fisted to keep time with his tongue tangle.

In 1877, when I was Pilgriming with Uncle Charles Castle, ahead of the sainted John O'Brien's, we drove with the bill wagons and contractor's carriage from Akron, N.Y., into a stand (some Falls or other). But the people of the Falls took a tumble and did not want the "Irish Brigade," as Castle called the show, within its limits. On the contrary, it did not object to the cholera, yellow fever, small pox, or itch. Jim Robinson,[33] Castle, and myself talked and talked but, as they say Down East, the authorities "sot and sot." Well, we camped there for two days and then came Tinkham, who was laying off that season and selling hymn books at camp meetings. The select men were glad to see

"Brother Tinkham" and in a few moments he succeeded in persuading them that "Brother O'Brien had met with a change of heart and come over on the Lord's side."

Sally Stickney is dead. For four months she was cared for by the Actors Fund, who also put her under Mother Earth. The fund includes circus folks in its good offices and every member of the circus profession should become a member and in a small way help along the good cause. Remit two dollars for one year's fee to Benjamin A. Baker, Assistant Secretary, Actors Fund, 12 Union Square, New York, and he will put you on the books. At the same time, inform him of your line of business, as non-professionals are not eligible.

Barnum & Co. have bought Alice, the companion to Jumbo, and she will be brought over in the spring and billed as the best girl of the late lamented. There ought to be considerable curiosity to see the beast and she will be worked up for all she is worth.

Death, the reaper, has been ever busy of late. Again I am called upon to chronicle the departure of well known professionals to the unknown spheres. Horace G. Nichols, the ringmaster, died at St. Mary's Hospital, Hoboken, January 19, aged 68. Mr. Nichols was fatally injured by a fall from the stoop of his house a fortnight previous. The veteran had seen long service and was an antique and honorable member of the hair-dye brigade under the banner of "the fleet foots."

Most of the cheap theatres and museums are managed by circus folks. John A. Forepaugh holds forth in Philadelphia; Kohl and Middleton have three establishments in Chicago; Drew & Co., one each in Providence and Indianapolis and two in Cleveland; Herzog & Co. at Richmond and Washington. Old Thad Barton, of Washington, is also an old circus cully from way back. Pat Harris, the "Monarch," holds forth at Baltimore, Pittsburgh, Cincinnati and Louisville. Keith and Batcheler of Boston; George B. Bunnell of New Haven and Buffalo; Garwood and Brady of Toledo and Fort Wayne; Signor Faranta of New Orleans; and many others are all from the circus fold, not forgetting Jacobs and Proctor.

A bold operation. Doctor Watts, of Boston, trimming the tail of a Reiche Brothers' tiger.

Dr. James Reilly, the popular show printer, died at his residence in Brooklyn, January 25. He was the successor of Clany & Reilly, and formerly the bookkeeper of Bacon, the printer, at the old Spruce Street stand. Clany was a practical typo and died many years ago. I believe that Mr. Reilly got the title of "Doctor" while clerking on a Mississippi boat from his kindly dosing of ailing passengers or crew. Years ago he was the treasurer of Bryant's Minstrels, when Dan, Jerry, and Neil were all three playing. He was a courtly, genial gentleman, an able businessman and a staunch friend and will be greatly missed by the managers and agents who were wont to meet at his office.

After the failure of Kelley of the London show, Dr. Reilly carried it on his shoulders until it finally fell into the hands of Cooper & Bailey. It was a heavy load but the Doctor managed with rare skill and came out all right. His departure for the land of hereafter was not unlooked-for. Mr. Reilly was a victim of Bright's disease and he had long since arranged his business, knowing that soon his call must come. Peace to the ashes of an honest man, a kind husband and father, and the staunchest and truest of friends.

How Thad Anderson, the old foreman, will miss the Doctor! Thad dates back to the Farwells and was with Bacon. He has lived to see all his employers pass off the scene of action. I know not what change in Thad's affairs the Doctor's may make but hope Thaddeus of Brooklyn will remain as he has for a lifetime, a fixture at the old Spruce Street stand.

Just previous to the death of the late C. W. McCune of the Courier Co., there was a plan on foot for the organization of a gigantic printing company which would have absorbed Dr. Reilly's concern. It would have been located in Jersey City and have been far larger than any establishment in the world. James Reilly would have been the managerial head of the monster affair.

I am informed that John A. Wood, circus agent, has been called to his last home. John was many years with the Robinson show, a couple of seasons with Forepaugh, with the London show, and last with Myers & Short. John was a man of ability and most positive convictions. In the "Beauty" season with Forepaugh, he was my "right bower." Peace to his ashes.

Perhaps you recollect when it was the fashion to part one's black hair and bring the soap locks over the ears in front? Bob Stickney has always glued his hirsute that way. This is what "the Giddy Gusher" has got to say about the peculiarity in the New York *Mirror*:

> I cannot account for Robert Stickney's being with this company. He may want practice or has a horse he desires to keep up to business. Certainly he seems mighty out of place among these artists, showing his fine form and graceful riding to a handful of ragged boys and a baker's dozen of women and children. Stickney is a splendid figure of a man, as Aunt Hannah would say. If someone would disturb the awful bandolined rigidity of his hair that is thrown up on one place and plastered down another, I would go on and say he was handsome. But no man can be good-looking and resemble a barber's block so closely.
>
> It's funny to note the sincere admiration the troupe have for this equestrian Apollo. Down to the man who holds the banners and the toughs who sell popcorn candy, every topknot is laid out, soaped down and parted like Bob's.
>
> I can always tell you the distinguishing features of the most celebrated man in a company or a band or a club before seeing the Admirable Crichton. Just hear Barrett's company bleat before he comes on. Note the lingering nasal tremor of Irving's gang. Catch onto the near-sightedness of the principal cornet players. Hear the catarrhal snorts the satellites of Clara Morris indulge in. John Sullivan came on a tear to New York with a hideous indigo-blue shirt on. The following week every pug was standing up in cerulean calico as near the tint as he could get.
>
> So when I saw the candy butcher at the Cosmopol, with his head ornamented with hair scroll-work, with scallops on his brow, I would have layed an **egg** it was my Robert's capillary vagaries that set the fashion. Take down your hair, Bob. Try a simple bang. You are a darling in the pastoral days of Mlle. Arisna Felicia and you are today the best formed man in the circus business.

I was at Cincinnati the other day and by the courtesy of Mr. Morgan went through the vast establishment of the Russell & Morgan Co. As the proprietors are the familiar "Bob, Pick, and Young John Robinson, circus folks may be glad to know something about their old friends in their new building. The printery is 75 by 230 feet and the floor space measures two and a half acres, six stories. Seven large vaults insure safety to cuts, etc. 450 names appear on the payroll. Heat is distributed through eighteen miles of steam pipes. All the inks are manufactured on the premises, six large mills running continually. Two systems of electric light are in use. Forty-seven presses are in constant use. Show printing and the label business no longer monopolize their attention. The Russell & Morgan Co. is now the largest manufacturer of playing cards in the world. But as my readers do not know anything about "keards," it is not necessary to remark further.

Hyatt Frost is much put out at the use of the VanAmburgh name in California by a snide show. He writes:

I have worked hard for forty years to become sole manager of the menagerie and circus and title of VanAmburgh & Frosts Shows and I have no interest whatever in the so-called show now in California and never did have. I would not, under any circumstances, permit the public to be deceived under the name of VanAmburgh & Frost by paying their money to see an imitation show, owned and run by men who have so grossly [pilfered] me of my good name and title. Many an old "forty-niner" now in California is personally acquainted with me and is well aware that I never had anything to do with any show but the best.

The worst feature of the larceny of the title of VanAmburgh is that it is connived at by Mr. Hyatt Frost's nephew, Frank.[34]

You don't know how glad I am to hear that Charlie Corbett, one of the founders of the *Journal*, is much improved in health and is once more in the newspaper field way Down East in old Providence, R.I. It was there I first scraped acquaintance with Charles, when he was on the *Sunday Dispatch*. Then he started the *Sunday Telegram*, afterward a daily and prospered marvelously. I opine that Mr. Corbett has not put his trust in Providence in vain in his new venture.

Corbett was always a favorite with the show folks, especially the circusites. And if Bill Durand don't give C. C. C. a good advertisement for Forepaugh's, he is not the W. W. D. that I used to know. When the flowers of May were on the way, the circus agents used to meet Corbett at the Adams House and the Washington Tavern, along with Sam N. Mitchell, the song writer; Hopkins, the variety manager; Archie Stalker, the only man in New York who knows how to make a clam chowder; and dead and gone Dr. Metchear; and the prince of billposters, Charlie Haskins; and ex-fireman, Sam Cornell. Oh! dear! Talk about clams and oysters and sich and the Rocky Point roasts!

There's Gus Hatch, prospering in Kansas City and standing in with the real estate ring that are coining cash. Before he was ever in the circus business he was a whaler. Now when he tires of Armour's beef and Baltimore oysters in the tin, he buys a New York *Herald* for a change and reads the "Marine List."

Kansas City is enjoying a great boom. Real estate is a ballooning. Mel Hudson says there is no telling how fast fortunes may be accumulated here: "A man made $15,000 the other day while he was changing cars at the Union Depot."

It is a wonder that circus folks get their mail at all. This very week I called at a post office for my mail and secured but a few letters. I walked away half satisfied that more were in the office, as letters of importance were not among those received. Arrived at the hotel, I called a messenger boy and dispatched him to the post office with a polite note and in short metre he returned with a fist full of communications. Next I unearthed a batch at a hotel. It is no uncommon occurrence to come in possession of one's mail by installments. Rival hotels divide it, the billposter may have some, and it is no uncommon thing to be told, "All the show mail goes to Mr. So-and-so's store." Why should it? What in the deuce is the showman's mail doing scattered all over town? Some years ago I dropped off the train at Bridgeport, Ct., and on calling at the general delivery of the post office I was informed that, "The clerk that takes care of the show mail has it locked up in his drawer. He has gone to supper. You will have to wait until he comes back."

I didn't wait though. I demanded my mail, the drawer was broken open, and the mail produced. Down at Calais, Maine, they once had a turnstile affair and everybody helped himself, which was about as good as locking it up. The clerks in city post offices have a racket of burying the mail and holding it until the arrival of the show and then turning it up in a mass in hopes of getting tickets.

Ere these lines are in print, the particulars of William W. Durand's sudden taking off will have been heralded. Perhaps his greatest success was with the "Great Eastern" or the "Large Eastern," as the coons Down South used to call it. His old comrade, Andy Haight, was laid away but about a year since. It is a satisfaction to know that he left his family well provided for.

It is detracting nothing from the laurels of the late William W. Durand to say that you have been misinformed, Mr. Editor, in regard to his salary. It was not $7,000 a year and there are no $7,000 a year salaries flying around in the circus business. Probably the highest he ever attained was $5,000 and a royal figure was that. I understand that at his decease he was receiving $125 per week from Mr. Pat Harris. But William did not feel at home in theatricals but sighed for the red wagons, as one always will when he has followed them for years.

The *Journal's* kind obituary also makes an omission by not referring to Durand's successful connection with the London show. When Parks, Davis, Dockrill, and the late James Reilly took hold of the London after Kelley's failure, it was pretty tight papers for the outfit but Charlie Fuller had the nerve to push the London show east in the face of the Barnum show under "Flatfoot" management, and W. W. D. whooped up the tricks to an immense success---much to P. T. B.'s disgust, the king of Bridgeport fairly frothing at the mouth with envy and chagrin. That was the smartest thing Col. Charles W. Fuller ever done in his life and he ought to have been promoted to Brigadier General then and there.

1887

So Grady is going to tackle the circus line again. He had quite a start at one time. Peter Sells relates that when Grady was traveling over the road he had a great deal of trouble to keep a certain bear in its cage and as the show moved over the country the "bar" would jolt out and then the word would be passed all along the line, "Bear fell out! Bear fell out!" Every cage being brought to a standstill until bruin was recaptured.

Tom Barry is now first engineer of one of Peck's Uncle Thomas companies, of which my side-partner, A. Bailey Knapp, is the man that goes ahead and tells the people that the donkeys and the rest of the jack asses are on the way. I suppose that Tom will have his hands full seeing that Eva gets to heaven every night in a blaze of red fire and that the donk don't kick to be starred. Peck has made as much as four quarts of gold dust with his shows this season and I'm glad to hear it; for he is a large patron of Sam Booth, who is a solid friend to a showman, as John B. Doris and Frank A. Robbins will testify from experiences. I pity the first gill that attempts to be fresh when he goes to see "Uncle Tom's Cabin," Eva, the dogs and the donk. Why, he'll go out on his head.

And if the hall is on the second story I should be sorry for him, as Tom Barry is just such a bouncer as John L. Sullivan would be if he was traveling with two Evas, two Marks, and two Topsies, besides the livestock.

Peck, Barry, and Knapp are doing missionary work in the dramatic field and who knows but that those who go to snort, to snivel and to whine at the illustration of Mrs. Stowe's masterpiece may be some day induced to go and see "a play." But that would be wicked!

I suppose that Peck could get a front seat now, way up on the "amen row," but don't you recollect that Thomas Thumb and not Uncle Thomas was the paying card. And you, Harry Knapp, I suppose are dodging about the country seeking even the basement of churches and school houses for your Uncle Thomas. And as for you, Mr. Barry, in the language of John Healy, Wally Ward and his son Joe, I say "Sagwa!" You may be making money on the road, Mr. Barry. That is pleasant. But now, really between you and I, in this frigid weather, where it's cold enough to freeze the ears off the donkey, wouldn't you rather be gathered in at "the dice box" at Howard and Crosby's at the lunch and wet hour with congenial Charles Gayler, Sam Booth, Snook, Sneden, Boyd and Hagar and have a bit of circus chat? But, when you get lonesome, I suppose you make the best of it with the donk and the country editors.

At this writing, William Sells is due in New York, having completed his engagement at the Covent Garden, London. During his absence abroad, he has perfected himself in a new act called "The Sculptor's Dream." Young Sells' ambition is to be commended. Having an idea he wished to carry out and knowing no one here particularly fitted to instruct and perfect him in it, he crossed the ocean and accomplished his purpose. Work makes the artist and many an American performer who warms a chair all winter might better himself in money-earning capacity by buckling on the harness and getting down to business. Then they would not have any cause for growling because American managers hire foreign talent.

New York is full of circus folks and down at the old St. Charles tavern, where so many memories cluster, things are lively. Col. Charles Seeley is keeping open house and "unveils the statue" for arriving guests with liberal frequency---so frequent he thinks of buying a jug. What's the matter with a barrel? For romantic, terrific, unparalleled, first-class liars, commend me to the mob that hovers about that old stove. Perhaps not so boisterous a one as assembled during the stay of King Richard (Fitzgerald) or Harry Stanwood (he of the banjo and good humor), but just as good, every day, go-as-you-please truth stretchers.

I have received a visit from J. J. Showles, whose full front name is Jacob. He is not the other Jacob of the same name who is an old circus rider.[35] This J. J. is an ex-circus agent. The "honest farmer" traveled his first season with Noah in the ark and then joined Raymond & Waring early in the present century. Jake has got an egg factory at Port Elgin, Ont., and breeds fancy poultry for profit. He must be the chap who lays those large eggs on the editor's table of which we read.

J. J. advanced in his time ahead of Jerry Mabie, VanAmburgh, Howes' London, Spalding & Bidwell, Hilliard & DeMott, Burr Robbins, Adam Forepaugh, and Cooper & Bailey. With Cooper & Bailey he made a tour of the world; with Burr Robbins he gazed on Janesville. [He] piloted J. H. Haverly, also the Forresters when they were making money by the bushel. And I forgot to remember the Commonwealth Circus, a cooperative institution that sent into the ring thirteen star performers, each one brilliant. Showles was with Bartholomew, the great horse trainer, when he first came over the Rockies and joined the equines to the forces of Dan Rice. J. J. is now in advance of the prosperous Celtic star, Joseph Murphy, one of the wealthiest actors on the American stage.

I put in a week in Detroit and it is a nice place to tie up to, especially if you stop at the Griswold House. Detroit is opposite Windsor, Canada, and is famous for its Jim Kelly and the *Free Press*. Kelly is a living city directory. He knows everybody in the city and everybody knows him. Just now Kelly is a literary freak in a dime museum and is editing the several newspapers in the city. Kelly is a conscientious advertiser; he will never tell a lie when a falsehood will answer just as well. There is a rumor going about that Kelly is Irish, but Frelich, of the *Free Press*, declares that it needs confirmation.

At Detroit I met John D. Walker, who I knew in the back number of 1868. At that time he was one of the few billposters in the country possessed of means and did business on business principles. John and I blabbed several hours about "old time rocks," Ned Kendall, the agent, and many others.

By the way, "Granville," your Washington correspondent, in relating to an anecdote of Ned Kendall, the bugler, mixes the musician with the agent. My Ned Kendall was one of the greatest advance agents that ever piloted a show in this or any other country. He was what used to be called "a working agent"; could put up a stand of bills and delighted to do it, knew the country to a dot, wrote with fluency, and had a legion of friends. Ned Kendall could inject about as much wormwood into a paragraph as any man that ever put a pen to paper.

In the days when Walker flourished, much depended on the billposter's friendship and the agent who stood well could often "bill out" a rival.... John D. Walker was a prime mover in the establishment of the National Printing Co. in Chicago, of which McConnell, then of the Detroit *Post*, became the head. Walker was foremost also in the formation of the organization of billposters, which still continues in existence.

And now let quip and jest and chat be hushed. L. B. Lent is dead! The dates all filled, the last stand made! Perhaps everyone did not understand Lewis B. Lent as well as I but as long as I live I shall cherish his memory. For many years he was my true, good friend. If the world had been harsh with him he did not repine. Quite the contrary, he bore up bravely under reverses. There was no whine in his composition and he lived the life of a philosopher. It is a great satisfaction to know that no penury or pressing want pursued him in his old age. He died in comfort with happy home surroundings and those he loved best at hand. L. B. Lent was deeply attached to his family and their sorry must be as great as was his affection for them.

Inclination would dictate that I should pen a fitting tribute to my departed friend but my time is not my own, business duties press, and I have only time to say this much and add, "God bless his memory!" If, as some like to believe, we may resume "beyond the river" the duties and the life of this world, what a gathering there must have been on the golden shore to greet the veteran. Welch, Quick, Angevine, Titus, Sands, Cushing, Murray!

What a blessed thing is memory! Now as I write, my mind reverts to the great days of Lent's New York Circus, its triumphs in New York, its successes on the road. Still, as the scythe-bearer rushes on, we are apt to be forgotten or exist only in the recollection of a cherished friend. Lewis B. Lent and John H. Murray both did much for arenic

170

amusements in America. Clean, respectable shows were their hobby and for many a year to come they will both be remembered as managers who had an exalted standard and maintained it.

CHARLES H. DAY
by C. M'Donald
[*Sporting and Theatrical Journal*, May 23, 1884]

In the days of "Adam," all were taught
That remotest corners of earth were sought
For curiosity strange, most monstrous creatures
To spring on the "natives" as novel features.
And when secured, who announced them, say
In blood curdling sentences?--CHARLES H. DAY.

Our alphabet has been twisted and turned;
Over-worked scribes have their money earned
In futile attempts to down this man
Who writes up headlines as none other can.
Any startling sensation in the show line may
Be safely attributed to CHARLES H. DAY.

Who when the sawdust circle had lost,
In a certain measure, its former caste,
Racked his brain, and with heart aglow,
Gave the $10,000 beauty to the Forepaugh show?
You anticipate my answer to the question, eh?
You're right! 'twas the only---CHARLES H. DAY.

Who was it when Forepaugh with chagrin bent
Because "Barnum" had got a "white elephant,"
The ocean crossed, search glade and dell,
Until the "old man" had another as well?
If my data's wrong, excuse me pray,
But a good many thought 'twas CHARLES H. DAY.

For many a "DAY" has he worked intent,
The very best years of his life been spent,
That others might garner the harvest of gold
Brought to their coffers by the tales he told.
If the laborer is worthy of his pay,
A fortune is due to CHARLES H. DAY.

May his years be many and without stint.
May his brain invent "fairy tales" for print.
When death o'rtakes him as it surely will,
His eulogy we'll post on a three-sheet bill
In colors, that all who pass that way
May raise their hat to the genius of CHARLES H. DAY.

NOTES, PART TWO

1. Morgan was murdered in Arkansas on October 30, 1884, by Douglas Post.

2. Colvin was manager with W. C. Coup's United Shows, 1877-80. He bought an interest in Burr Robbins' circus in January of 1881 and went out under the title of Robbins & Colvin's Great American and German Allied Shows. Another source indicates that Colvin and Coup split in 1882.

3. Lusbie died in Columbus, OH, on July 8, 1884, after a period of ill health.

4. Castle died at his home in Syracuse, NY, September 25, 1884.

5. The circus was taken to London's Olympic Coliseum in the winter of 1889-90.

6. James R. "Jumbo" Davis (1852-1886) was the agent who represented the Barnum show in purchasing Jumbo and was for some years the purchasing agent for Barnum abroad. Davis has been given credit by some for the fortuitous acquisition of the big elephant..

7. This is a reference to Thomas Andrews Hendricks (1819-1885) who was elected vice-president on the ticket headed by Grover Cleveland in 1884.

8. Gardner left Forepaugh for the Barnum & Bailey show in 1881 and served as general agent for that organization continuously until 1892.

9. Guilford was director of publications with W. C. Coup's New United Monster Show, 1879-80.

10. The "white elephant" is merely one with albinistic traits, with the dark pigment absent, giving the skin a pale color. Because such phenomena were rare these beasts were venerated in Siam and Burma and considered sacred. Barnum's "white elephant" humbug set up a war of publicity between Barnum & Bailey and the Adam

Forepaugh shows which, although ridiculous as one looks back, successfully created the desired public attention.

11. James Cooke married Miss Helen Cooke while with the Barnum show in 1874. Wooda Cook and Millie Turnour were married at Shreveport, LA, in March of 1872 while with C. W. Noyes Crescent City Circus.

12. This would be Charles S. Burrows, the gymnast. See Circus Personnel Reference Roster.

13. The reference is to D. W. Stone's Grand Circus and Musical Brigade, 1878, which had an unsuccessful season and an early retirement.

14. Krao, "The Missing Link," was an attraction developed by Signor G. A. Farini, who suggested she might be the link in Darwin's theory. She was purported to have been found in the jungles of Laos and advertised as having "prehensile feet," pouches, hair over most of her body and other simian characteristics.

15. George H. Adams was the nephew of James E. Cooke. He married Rosina Cooke, daughter of Henry Cooke and niece of W. W. Cole.

16. After retiring from the ring, following the 1877 season with Barnum's Greatest Show on Earth, Maginley spent several years performing on the stage as a character actor. He supported Lester Wallach in "Rosedale," McKee Rankin in "The Danites," etc.

17. The reference is to Charles H. Adams. See Circus Personnel Reference Roster.

18. This Kendall is not to be confused with Ned Kendall (1808-1861), "The Magic Bugler" and band leader for many circuses.

19. This occurred in 1860 while Kingsley was performing with Cooke's Circus at Niblo's Garden, NY. On the question of sex, the *Spirit of the Times* editorialized, "If the person is a man, the humbug is a very dishonest one; if a woman, for the sake of all parties, the point should be settled."

20. Day's memory has failed him. LeClair came to America with Howes & Cushing, 1870, as one of the LeClair Brothers. See Circus Personnel Reference Roster.

21. The Mallory Brothers, G. S. and Marshall, were financial backers of the Madison Square Theatre. G. S. Mallory was a clergyman and editor of *The Churchman*.

22. Maginley teamed with Barney Carroll in a circus venture. Maginley, Carroll & Co., in 1867-68. Maginley had married Carroll's daughter, Marie, in 1864.

23. Day may mean Lansing, MI.

24. William Devere was a banjoist and singer in variety halls.

25. Barry made his professional debut with Pablo Franque at Free Trade Hall, Manchester, in a pony race, 1847. He then apprenticed to Ned Briarly to learn clowning. Subsequently, he performed alternately with Bell's, Pablo's, Hengler's, and Newcomb's circuses. He also had his own show out for a short time in 1865 but inevitably went back with his former managers.

26. Day is referring to Thomas Clifford.

27. Train, a treasurer, was killed in the 1893 Walter L. Main Circus railroad accident at Tyrone, PA.

28. This would be Lyman A. Hitchcock. See Circus Personnel Reference Roster.

29. W. W. Cole closed and sold his circus at auction on the Canal Street lot in New Orleans to become part owner with the Barnum & Bailey show and to look out for James A. Bailey's interest. He sold his share of the Barnum & London show to Bailey in October of 1887 and retired. However, in 1898 he purchased a quarter interest in the Forepaugh-Sells Bros.' Circus and the Buffalo Bill's Wild West Show and acted as governing head of these organizations while the Barnum & Bailey Circus was touring Great Britain and the Continent. With Bailey's death, the governing board of B. & B. elected Cole managing director for one year. At its expiration, Cole permanently retired.

30. The car in which Day traveled had a stateroom on one end which also served as an office. Behind this was a section where advertising paper was stored and prepared for posting. Bunks were arranged in that part of the car at night. The space could accommodate as many as thirteen men.

31. Jumbo's death is well recorded. The tragedy occurred in 1885 at St. Thomas, Canada, where the Barnum & Bailey show had performed. Byron V. Rose, master of transportation, had been given assurance by the Grand Trunk Railway that the tracks would be clear for loading the circus. Relying on this, Jumbo and a dwarf elephant were walked down the tracks in the direction of their rail cars. However, suddenly out of the night's blackness the blinding lights of a locomotive signaled the sudden and unexpected approach of a freight train. A collision was unavoidable. The dwarf elephant was thrown down an embankment and sustained a broken leg. Jumbo took the full impact, derailing the locomotive and rail cars.

32. Noyes died October 20, 1885.

33. There were at least five James Robinsons in the circus business around this time. Day is most likely referring to James A. Robinson, the contracting agent. See Circus Personnel Reference Roster.

35. Jacob A. Showles is the performer referred to. See Circus Personnel Reference Roster.

LOTTIE WATSON, "THE WOMAN WITH THE IRON JAW," in Albany, NY, with the Van Amburgh, Charles Reiche & Brother show, June 30, 1885. The act of holding a cannon by her teeth while it was being fired went awry when one of the pulley ropes broke, causing Lottie to tumble to the ring. She was rendered unconscious, her mouth was cut, two teeth were knocked out, a hand was badly bruised, and she suffered internal injuries, but recovered to perform again.

CIRCUS PERSONNEL REFERENCE ROSTER

George F. Bailey, (1818-1903) showman, nephew of Hachaliah Bailey, began in show business with the "Flatfoots" before joining Aaron Turner's circus. He married Turner's daughter and, when Turner retired, Bailey took control of the show and changed the title to reflect his name. After several years of solo operation, he went into partnership with "Flatfoots" Avery Smith, John Nathans, and Lewis June. Bailey retired around 1880 after forty years of circus involvement and with the reputation of being one of the great showmen of his generation.

Richard Guy Ball, (1844-1905) contracting agent, began his career as a candy butcher on L. B. Lent's circus, 1859. The following year he joined the advance of Gardner & Hemmings under William H. Gardner, with whom he remained until 1863. Following a stint in war service, he was connected with such shows as James L. Thayer's, John O'Brien's, Cooper & Bailey (for their Australian and South American tour), Forepaugh's, and Barnum & Bailey. He started in the business for $10 a month and ended up as one of the highest salaried agents. He was considered superior at contracting bill posters, hotel proprietors, liverymen, and city and state officials.

Henry Barnum, (c.1826-1902) showman, was Hyatt Frost's manager with VanAmburgh & Co. for several years. In 1873 he purchased a tenth interest in James E. Kelley's Howes' Great London Circus. Debts caused the show to go under in 1876. Following this, he held managerial positions with Cooper & Bailey (1880), Forepaugh's (1893), Barnum & Bailey (1895), and was purchasing agent for the Buffalo Bill Wild West Show (1902).

Tom Barry, (1839-1909) was a rider and manager as well as a clown. Born in Manchester, England, he came to America in 1870 to join Lent's American Circus on Fourteenth Street, New York City. He was with the Murray show from 1871 through 1877.

George H. Batcheller, leaper, began his circus career with Isaac Burtis in 1843. This was followed by engagements with various organizations throughout the 1840's and 1850's. He developed into one of the best leapers in the circus world of his day. In 1863 he became associated with John B. Doris in the management of privileges. Later, the two men took of a circus under their names and operated it successfully for several years.

David Bidwell, (?-1889) theatre proprietor, went into partnership with Spalding & Rogers in 1856 when the men took a ten year lease on the Pelican Theatre, New Orleans---the Spalding & Rogers Amphitheatre, later renamed the Academy of Music. Bidwell continued his association with Spalding after Rogers' retirement until around 1875. In 1873 Bidwell bought the St. Charles, New Orleans; and in 1880 he became lessee of the Grand Opera House (formerly the Varieties Theatre). With these acquisitions, he controlled the amusement business in that city until his death.

William E. "Billy" Burke, clown, who sang comic songs and tumbled, was connected with the circus business as early as 1866, when he was with Mike Lipman's show. He was later engaged with such organizations as Forepaugh's, James Robinson's, Montgomery Queen's, Sells Brothers', and Barnum & Bailey's. He was active as late as 1896 with Rice's Circus Carnival.

Charles H. Castle, (1816-1884) agent, like many a circus man was first engaged by Dan Rice (1851-53). He entered into management in 1853 with Harry Whitbeck and Wash Kidwell to form Whitbeck & Co.'s One-Horse Show, an enterprise that lasted only a season. Subsequently, he was connected with Spalding & Rogers, Thayer & Noyes, Goodwin & Wilder, John O'Brien, John Robinson, Batcheller & Doris, Barnum's Traveling World's Fair, and Sells Bros. Lovingly called "Old Roughhead," companionable, a good story teller, a fair singer and jig dancer, he was one of the best known circus agents of his day.

Dr. C. S. T. Chambers, agent, was connected with Andrew Haight in the ill-fated Haight & Chambers' Palace Show and Menagerie which was launched in New Orleans and traveled up the river on the steamer, *Coosa,* 1866, until flood, cholera, a sinking disaster terminated the venture. The following year he was attached to the C. T. Ames' Menagerie, Museum and Tropical Bird Show. In 1869, he left the business to keep a jewelry store in Charleston, WV.

Birkit "Kit" Clarke was a circus press agent who, like Day, submitted articles to various weeklies. Born in N.Y.C., he was connected with Satterlee & Bell's Circus at age 13. Later, he was agent for such shows as Forepaugh's, VanAmburgh's, and O'Brien's.

William Washington "Chilly Billy" Cole, (1847-1915) show-man, was the son of British circus performers William H. Cole and Mary Ann Cooke. Four years after his father died in 1858 his mother married Miles Orton of the Orton Bros.' Circus. Cole grew to manhood learning the ins and outs of circusdom and in 1871 he launched his first show, the Cole & Orton Circus. He sold his holdings at auction in 1886 to become part owner of the Barnum & Bailey organization. Two years later he sold his share to Bailey and retired until 1898 when he purchased an interest in the Forepaugh-Sells Bros. Circus and the Buffalo Bill's Wild West Show. With Bailey's death, the governing board of Barnum & Bailey elected Cole to a one year term as managing director, after which he went into permanent retirement. He is said to have been the first person to have earned a million dollars from his operation; indeed, he died leaving assets of around five million dollars.

E. Darwin Colvin began his circus career as an assistant treasurer with Sands, Nathans & Co.'s Performing Elephant, G. C. Quick's Hippopotamus, Herr Driesbach's Menagerie & G. F. Bailey's Circus. In 1870 and 1871 he was the manager of Adam Forepaugh's aggregation. In 1872 he managed G. F. Bailey & Co.'s Circus.

James Cooke (Patrick Hoey), (1836-1880) clown and general performer, born in Dublin, Ireland, began performing with fair theatricals in feats of acrobatics and contortion before turning to clowning. He made his American debut in 1863 for J. M. Nixon. In 1865, he joined John Wilson's circus in California and for an Australia tour. He was back East in the 1870's, where he performed with many of the principal circuses. His last appearance in the ring as a clown was with Stickney's Imperial Parisian Circus at the Aquarium, N.Y.C., during the winter of 1879-80; and as ringmaster for the Barnum show at the American Institute the following spring. His engagement with John H. Murray for the summer season ended as a result of his death from pneumonia.

Louis E. Cooke, agent, entered the profession in the late 1870's and became one of the most prominent agents in the business. His career began with W. W. Cole, with whom he accompanied on the famous trip to Australia. Later, he served with James A. Bailey as confidential agent and manager for over twenty years, during which time he was responsible for bringing about some legendary circus deals. He made the arrangement for organizing Buffalo Bill's Wild West Show under Bailey's management. He was responsible for the consolidation of the Forepaugh and Sells Bros. shows. He brought about an amicable business arrangement between the Ringling and the Barnum & Bailey shows.

William Cooke, (?-1886) general performer and proprietor, was the son of Thomas Taplin Cooke who brought the Cooke circus company to America in 1836. William performed as clown, strong man, rope walker and vaulter. He gave up performing to direct equestrian spectacles---succeeding Batty in management of Astley's Amphitheatre for several years.

William Cameron Coup, (1837-1895) showman, formed a partnership with Dan Castello, 1869, and took a boat circus around the Great Lakes. The following year the two men induced P. T. Barnum to join them on a circus deal, P. T. Barnum's Museum, Menagerie, Caravan and Hippodrome. At the end of the summer season, 1872, the organization branched out: sending a unit into the South and opening a second at the Hippodrome, Fourteenth Street, N.Y.C. The southern tour proved a failure and was closed. The Hippodrome burned down on December 24 of that year. The outfit was expanded, 1873, into P. T. Barnum's Traveling World's Fair. Coup worked for the erection of a new Hippodrome, which was opened to the public on April 27, 1874. In 1876, with Charles Reiche, he erected the New York Aquarium, Broadway and Thirty-fifth Street, and a similar one at Coney Island. In 1878 he took out Coup's Equescurriculum and remained involved with the show until his death.

Mike Coyle, (c.1838-1918) agent, etc., was connected for many years as publicist for P. T. Barnum and was one of his close associates. He was a picturesque and unique personality with a wide circle of friends and admirers. Along with agenting, his many assignments included positions as treasurer, and business and transportation manager.

James Crockett, (1835-1865) wild beast tamer, began as a circus musician for Sanger's English company and inadvertently became a handler of wild animals. Through his fearlessness and physical ability, he was soon a leading performer in England and Europe and was brought to America by Seth B. Howes in 1864. In Cincinnati the following year, his young life was ended as he succumbed from heat prostration in his dressing room following the parade.

Col. Joseph Cushing, (1818-1884) showman, graduated from candy concessionaire to sideshow operator to taking control of the entire show, which he built from a single wagon to an aggregation of forty. He formed a partnership with Seth Howes in 1856 and took Howes & Cushing's Great American Circus to England. He sold out to Howes in 1860, but returned to form a circus for Germany. Howes & Cushing continued to tour Great Britain until 1862 when Cushing returned to America. Cushing retired to his farm in 1879.

George W. DeHaven, (1837-1902) showman, beginning in 1858 he equipped a circus with Oliver Bell. Four years later, he took out a boat show along the Mississippi and its tributaries. This was merely the beginning; for during his career, he organized and put on the road some thirty-three different circuses. He was one of the first to send up hot air balloons as an outside attraction. He claimed to be the first to introduce Roman hippodrome racing into the circus program and the first to inaugurate the railroad circus.

John B. Doris, (1848-1912) showman, joined the Dan Rice circus as a fourteen year old run-away. In 1863, with George Batcheller, he purchased the privileges for the Rice show. Two years later Doris and Batcheller took out their own circus, which operated successfully for the next twenty years. In 1881, Doris bought out his partner and continued on the road until 1889, after which he dabbled in theatrical management.

Herr Jacob Driesbach, (1807-1877) wild beast tamer, entered the circus business around 1840 with Raymond & Waring, and continued under Raymond & Weeks and later with VanAmburgh & Co. for some twenty years. It has been said that he was the first man to train a leopard. He would walk the streets with one attached by a rope. Shortly after his marriage, around 1856, he turned to farming in Ohio. He also kept a hotel nearby, which became a refuge for itinerant showmen.

William W. Durand, (1837-1886) agent, after working as a printer and journalist, entered the circus business, 1867, to become one of the best writers of his profession. He worked for many of the large shows throughout his career. His last engagement, before his sudden death, was managing a museum in Indianapolis, IN.

O. J. Ferguson, showman, was connected with VanAmburgh & Co. for many years in various capacities: advertiser, treasurer, manager, and co-proprietor. Following the close of the company in 1881, Ferguson was manager with Nathans & Co. (1882), Cooper, Jackson & Co. (1883), proprietor of Ferguson's New York and New

England Circus (1884), general agent with Frank Robbins' Circus (1885), assistant manager with the Adam Forepaugh Circus (1887), general superintendent with Sig. Sautelle's Circus (1898).

Richard Fitzgerald, (1842-1889) amusement agent and manager, was born in what is now Wheeling, WV. His professional career began in 1865 as proprietor of Parker's Opera House and Virginia Hall in Alexandria, VA., and later as manager of the Canterbury in Richmond. That same year he was with Spalding & Bidwell at their Academy of Music, New Orleans. In the summer of 1866, he was business manager for Metcalf's Circus. In the fall of that year, he became associated with James Conner in a dramatic agency. When Conner died he returned to work for Spalding & Bidwell at their Olympic Theatre, St. Louis. Next, he returned to the dramatic agency business at the corner of Houston and Broadway, N.Y.C. Shortly, he took actor T. G. Riggs as a partner and moved to 512 Broadway. In 1871, he managed the Charles M. Barras "Black Crook" Co. and later Kiralfy's "Humpty Dumpty" Co. For two seasons he was agent with Cameron & Co.'s Oriental Circus and Tubbs & Co.'s New York Circus; after which he returned to the dramatic agency business in N.Y.C. He was said to be a most companionable man with only two weaknesses--- "his large-heartedness and his love of Masonry, Lodge No. 273."

Adam Forepaugh, Sr., (1831-1890) showman, was one of the great circus magnates of the 19th century. After beginning his working life as a butcher, then a horses and cattle broker, he was forced to take a share of John O'Brien's circus in 1863 as payment of a debt that had been incurred for the purchase of horses. He went out under his own name for the first time in 1867. By 1880, the show was traveled on three trains of railroad cars, had sixty cages, 290 horses, 400 employees, and a daily expense of $4,000. Forepaugh was the first to incorporate the wild west spectacle with his ring performance, the first to exhibit the menagerie under a separate tent. He carried more animals in the menagerie than any other circus of his day. He paid the highest prices for European talent. He was said to be "the master of his business as no man before him was, and as no man will probably be in the future."

James M. French, showman, organized the Oriental Circus and Egyptian Caravan in 1867. The show featured a team of twelve camels, the first ever broken to work in harness without the assistance of horses. His great elephant, Empress, imported in 1869, was said at the time to be the largest ever brought to America. He is given credit for importing the first troupe of Arabs. French sold his circus property in 1870, but the show was reported back on the road the following year. In 1876 he organized a circus with L. B. Lent and served as general manager. He acquired an ample fortune and, after retiring from active trouping, he rented out cages of animals.

Hyatt Frost, (1827-1895) showman, began at age nineteen, working for the candy privilege man with Raymond & Waring. He later worked for VanAmburgh & Co. under Raymond's management as an advertiser. When Raymond died, Frost and James Kelley purchased the show and continued as partners until around 1873 when Frost bought out Kelley. VanAmburgh & Co. was put up for auction in 1881. After 35 years in the circus business, Frost thought he needed a rest. His last venture was with the Reiche brothers under the banner of VanAmburgh, Charles Reiche & Brother, 1885. Shortly after that he retired reasonably well off.

Frank A. Gardner, (1855-1905) leaper and rider, began as a pad rider with the James T. Johnson circus. He was connected with the VanAmburgh show in 1871, when he first turned a double somersault over ten and twelve horses. While with Dan Rice's Paris Pavilion Circus the following year, the *New York Clipper* announced that he was the second man ever to double-somersault over thirteen horses abreast. He toured South America and the West Indies for several years with his own company during the 1880's and 1890's. Small in stature but well-proportioned and strong, he is considered one of the greatest leapers of all time, on a par with Fred O'Brien and William H. Batcheller.

William Henry Gardner, (1842-1906) agent, was the eldest child of the famous Gardner family of circus performers. He began agenting for the Gardner & Hemmings circus, 1861, and remained with the show until he sold his interest to Harry Whitby, 1867. He was general agent for Gardner & Kenyon (1868-69), advertiser with James Robinson (1869), agent for John O'Brien (1870-71), general director for James E. Cooper (1872), Cooper & Bailey (1873-74). He had the privileges with the latter show when it went on its Australian and South American tour (1875-77). He was general agent with Anderson & Co. (1879), Forepaugh's (1880), and with Barnum & Bailey (1881-92). He acquired an interest in the Pawnee Bill show (1893-94), was contracting agent for Walter L. Main (1894), general agent for Buffalo Bill's Wild West Show (1895-97), general agent for the European tour of Barnum &

Bailey (1898-1901), and was with Forepaugh-Sells (1903). In 1904 he bought the Hagenbeck show and became its general agent.

Charles Gayler, (1820-1892) agent, was connected with various circuses from the 1860's to the 1880's, including Howes' London Circus, VanAmburgh & Co., and P. T. Barnum's Greatest Show on Earth. Although beginning his career as a lawyer and journalist, he moved into the areas of acting, theatrical management, reviewing and playwriting, along with his circus connections.

G. G. Grady, (c.1831-1895) showman, was proprietor of Grady's Old Fashioned Circus , 1869-74, until the show was attached by the sheriff in Shelbyville, IL. In 1879, he was out with Grady & Beatty's Circus. The following year, he was giving sideshow performances at political meetings in Indiana. He retired from the business about three years before his death.

George J. Guilford, (?-1900) press agent and bill writer, at various times connected with George F. Bailey, DeHaven & Haight, W. C. Coup, and Sells Brothers. In his later years, he did not travel but settled in Cincinnati and wrote for many shows from his home.

Andrew Haight, (1831-1886) agent and showman, left a successful mercantile, real estate and hotel keeping business in Wisconsin to join forces with Claude DeHaven in a circus enterprise, 1865. He had interest in various shows until he retired to operate the City Hotel in Chicago, 1879. But, shortly, he returned to arenic activity as advance agent for Forepaugh, Coup, and Barnum's London show.

Dr. Richard Patrick Jones, (1826-1869) agent, was born in Philadelphia and educated as a doctor of medicine. But he soon became an actor and minstrel performer, and finally a circus writer. He continued in the latter profession until his death. It was said that "no one in the business was better posted in all the little dodges of the profession."

Sampson H. Joseph, (c.1833-1910) agent, worked for forty years as general agent for the John Robinson Circus. He was also connected with Mike Lipman's (1866), George DeHaven's (1869), Lake's Hippo-Olympiad (1871), American Racing Association (1875), Cooper & Bailey's (1880), and with Sells Bros.' (1884).

James E. Kelley, (c.1826-1892) showman, bought out James Raymond's menagerie along with Hyatt Frost, which became known as VanAmburgh & Co. He operated it successfully into the 1870's. Kelley bought an interest in Howes' Great London Circus in 1873 and selected

Henry Barnum to manage the acquisition. Debt, caused by economic conditions, forced a sale of the show to John Parks and Richard Dockrill.

Gus Lee, clown, was with Barnum's Traveling World's Fair (1872), L. B. Lent's New York Circus (1874), W. H. Harris' Nickel-Plate Shows (1885).

Prof. J. M. Langworthy, (c.1811-1871) wild beast tamer, was with VanAmburgh & Co. for six years in England, performing the elephant Bolivar. He remained with that concern for over twenty years, until the time of his death. He was also connected with Raymond & Co. (1854), Mabie's Winter Garden Circus (1862), Dan Rice's (1866), and Forepaugh's (1867).

Lewis B. Lent, (1813-1887) agent and showman, was agent for June, Titus & Angevine's Menagerie by the time he was twenty-one. That same year, 1834, he bought an interest in I. R. and W. Howes' Menagerie. From this beginning he developed into an all-around circus man and one of the best general agents and routers of his day. He was connected with many circuses as an interested partner and manager. His New York Circus during the 1870's was considered to be of the highest class of arenic entertainment.

Martinho Lowande, Sr., (1839-1927) a four-horse rider and bareback carrying act, was a member of a Brazilian family of riders. He performed in the United States as early as 1871, when he was with Adam Forepaugh, and continued until at least 1904, when he was with the Walter L. Main organization.

Ben Maginley, (1832-1888) clown, began his career as an actor. In 1863, he organized a circus and entered the arena as a clown for the first time. For the next fifteen years, he was associated with various circuses as co-proprietor, equestrian director and performer. Following the 1877 season with P. T. Barnum's Greatest Show on Earth, he returned to the stage.

James C. Maguire, clown, was connected with Bryan's (1869), Forepaugh's (1870), Joel E. Warner's (1872), Rice's (1872-73), Cooper & Bailey (1874), and the Great Metropolitan Olympiad (1877). In 1877 he was shot in the arm and had to have it amputated.

James Donald Melville, (c.1835-1892) bareback rider, was a Scotsman by birth but migrated to Australia with his parents, where he first entered circus life. He made his New York debut at the Bowery Theatre in 1858 and in no time became one of the most famous riders in the world. Featured in all of the leading circuses of the last half of the century, his final ring appearance may have been with the Melville-Hamilton show in 1991. He fathered three other performing Melvilles in Frank, George and Alexander.

John Hayes Murray, (1829-1881) showman, made his professional debut performing as a negro minstrel at Barnum's Museum. Possessing an outstanding physique and great strength, he developed skills as an acrobat and general performer. As such he was connected with various circuses at home and abroad. In 1865 his name appeared in the title of Stone, Rosston & Murray's Circus. He stopped performing in 1871, but continued in management until his death.

John V. ("Pogey") O'Brien, (1836-1889) a man of dubious ethics, conducted shows under various titles: Bryan's, Sheldenberger's, Campbell's, Rothchild's, etc. Throughout his career his reputation was tarnished as one who was dishonest with employees and who carried with his show a compliment of gamblers and thieves. Justice ultimately prevailed, for he died in poverty.

Charles C. Pell, (1818-1889) was agent for Levi J. North when only twenty years of age. In his over thirty years in the business, he was connected with the likes of Rockwell & Co. (1847-48), Mile's Circus Royale (1863), Dan Castello's (1867-69), James M. Nixon's (1870), Lake's Hippo-Olympiad (1871), Barnum's Traveling World's Fair (1872), and Montgomery Queen's (1874-76).

Charles A. Potter, (c. 1845-1818) was program agent with John H. Murray's Great Railroad Circus, 1874-75, and press agent for the show in 1877. He was later connected with Den Stone's Grand Circus and Musical Brigade, Forepaugh's, and the Great Wallace shows. With the latter, 1895-98, he completed his 27th year in the business. After this, he located in Danielson, CT, and continued as advertising agent and reporter for the *Wendham County Transcript.*

Montgomery Queen, purchased an interest in Rosston, Springer & Co., 1872, and took out Montgomery Queen's Circus the following year. He had the show in California, 1877, but at the start of the following year, bankruptcy was announced and the outfit was sold at auction. In 1879, Queen was reported to be connected with a trolley company in Brooklyn, NY.

Dan Rice, (1823-1900) clown and showman, was one of the most noted and controversial of circus performers. He began clowning with old John Robinson's circus, 1839; within a few years he was starring in his own company. Throughout his career he was one of the highest paid performers in the business; yet an erratic disposition and a fondness for the bottle created antagonisms.

Burr Robbins, (1837-1908) showman, entered the circus business in 1858 as a property man for Spalding & Rogers. It was more than ten years later before he took out a circus in his name. He operated the Burr Robbins' Circus until 1888. Robbins had a talent for saving

and investing money. In his waning years his holdings totaled some forty pieces of property, including a ranch in Kansas.

James Robinson, (James Fitzgerald, 1835-1917) bareback rider, learned to ride while with old John Robinson, from whom he took the name. He was touted as the greatest bareback rider of his day and became an international star, a darling in England and on the Continent. Beginning in 1869, a show was on the road under his name. Ultimately, he retired to a farm near Mexico, MO, where he trained horses.

Charles J. Rogers, (1817-1895) rider and proprietor, was the son of English equestrian John Rogers, who came to America in 1816 with the James West company. In 1826 he was an apprentice rider with the old Quick & Mead circus and developed into, as some have said, "the greatest scenic rider that America has ever had." By good fortune, he went into partnership with Dr. Gilbert R. Spalding in 1848. As Spalding & Rogers, the relationship continued until Rogers' retirement in 1865.

Frank H. Rosston, (1827-1874) showman, was employed by Dan Rice at age fifteen and remained with him for seventeen years, part of that time as a co-partner. He was ringmaster and co-proprietor with Stone, Rosston & Co., 1864-66, and equestrian director and co-proprietor with Springer, Rosston & Henderson, 1871. He had the concert privileges with Montgomery Queen's Circus, 1873.

Peter Sells, (1845-1904) showman and agent, was one of the four Sells brothers. He was the advertiser , router and, later, the railroad contractor for the show. Following brother Ephraim's retirement in 1896, the Sells Bros.' circus was combined with the Forepaugh circus, owned by James A. Bailey to form Forepaugh-Sells, managed by Lewis Sells. Peter was general agent for this 50 or 60 car show.

Simon H. Semon, (?-1910) contracting agent, the son of agent Harry W. Semon, he was in the business for forty years with some of the premier circuses of his era: Adam Forepaugh's (12 years, concluding in 1891), John Robinson's (1892), Buffalo Bill's (1896), and Forepaugh-Sells' (1904).

Dr. Gilbert R. Spalding, (1812-1880) proprietor, acquired the title of doctor when he was the owner of a drug and paint store, 1840-45, in Albany, NY. He was on the road as Spalding's North American Circus, 1847-48. He went into partnership with Charles J. Rogers after the 1848 season. Over the years, the men had two and sometimes three shows out at the same time, traveling by boat, rail, and land. Spalding's last venture in the circus business occurred in 1874-75 when he was co-proprietor with John O'Brien and Ben Maginley of Melville, Maginley & Cooke's Continental Circus and Thespian Co. He retired to his home in Saugerties, NY, in 1879.

Andrew J. Springer, (?-1886) agent, was connected with various circuses from the late 1860's to the 1880's, including J. M. French's Oriental Circus, James Robinson's, L. B. Lent's, Warner & Henderson's, Batcheller & Doris', and S. H. Barrett's. He had an interest in Rosston, Springer & Henderson's Great Mastodon Caravan, Circus and Menagerie in 1871-72.

John Stetson, pedestrian, gave exhibitions in the circus ring. Later, he became publisher of the *Sporting Times,* a Boston weekly. This and many other ventures made him millions. He was married to the beautiful equestrienne, Katie Stokes.

Robert John Danville Stickney, (1871-1941) principal and four-horse rider and horse trainer, was the son of the leaper and pad rider Robert T. Stickney and Kate Robinson, daughter of old John F. Robinson. He was connected with a variety of circuses from the late 1880's through 1920. Eventually, he gave up riding and exhibited his horses, ponies, and dogs at parks and fairs.

Denison W. Stone, (1824-1892) clown and showman, brother of bareback rider Eaton Stone, began his circus career with Ira Cole's Zoological Institute. He became a clown in 1840, having appeared in the pantomime of "Mother Goose." Two years later, he entered into a series of circus managements: Stone & McCollum, Stone & Madigan, Stone & Murray, Den Stone's Circus and Central Park Menagerie, and, by 1878, Stone's Grand Circus and Musical Brigade. Throughout his career, he clowned for most of the major circus organizations.

Isaac VanAmburgh, (1808-1865) wild beast tamer, became connected with menageries around 1829 and made his New York debut at the Richmond Hill Theatre in 1833. That same year he was assistant keeper to a Mr. Roberts with June, Titus & Angevine's menagerie. When Roberts was severely torn in 1837, VanAmburgh became the permanent keeper. He went to Europe in 1838 and remained for seven years. On returning in 1845, VanAmburgh & Co. was established in his name. He retired from active ring participation in the mid-1850's. He frequently used a crow bar to beat his animals into submission; consequently, he is credited with changing the style of performance from displays of docility to blatant challenges between man and beast.

W. T. B. Van Orden, agent, was Spalding's brother-in-law. He was manager with the North American Circus, 1844, and was agent with Spalding & Rogers, 1853-64. Subsequently, he was connected with the Parisian Circus, an aggregation of notables assembled for the Paris Exposition of 1867. There are occasional references made regarding Van Orden, but he remains a man of elusive biography.

Joel E. Warner, (1832-1914) showman, began his career as a magician, 1850. After ending an engagement at the American Museum, New Orleans, under the management of Dan Rice, he joined Spalding & Rogers as assistant agent under Van Orden. In 1871 he started into management for himself and continued off and on. With the merging of Barnum and Bailey, he became a representative for that circus and, as such, claimed responsibility for the importation of Jumbo and "The Wild Man from Borneo." Around 1889, he retired from the business and became prominent in the Central Michigan Agricultural Society and occupied himself with lecturing.

P. Bowles Wooten, showman, was a livery stable owner in Atlanta, GA, when he joined with Andrew Haight in taking out a circus, 1871. He sold his interest at the end of the season. At last report, he was a horse and mule trader in Nashville, TN.

INDEX

192

Rockwell & Co., 46, 134, 185
Rockwell & Stone, 85
Rogers, Charles J., 11, 46, 72, 73, 74,
  75, 88, 186, 187
Rogers, John, 72, 186
Rogers, Nat, 48
Rolland, Caroline, 62
Rolland, William, 63
Rooney, Pat, 157
Rose, Byron V., 154, 173
"Rosedale," 172
Rosina, Mlle., 33
Rosston, Frank, 57, 87, 104, 186
Rosston, Springer & Henderson, 187
Rothchild's Circus, 185
Runnells, Burnell, 49
Russell & Morgan Co., 163, 164
Russell, Piclo, 28
Salvini, 145
San Francisco Minstrels, 25, 95
Sands, Nathans & Co., 178
Sanger, 126
Satterlee & Bell's Circus, 177
Saunders, 71
Schote, Capt., 135
Scudder's Museum, 92
"Sculptor's Dream, The", 167
Seal, David, 145
Seeley, Charles, 135, 167
Sells Bros., 38, 39, 54, 55, 150, 177,
  183, 186
Sells, Allen, 12, 158
Sells, Ephraim, 12
Sells, Lewis, 54, 186
Sells, Peter, 7, 12, 16, 38, 39, 41, 54,
  126, 166, 186
Sells, William, 167
Semon, Harry W., 186
Semon, Simon H., 43, 44, 186

Sharpley, Sam, 93, 96
Sharpley, Sheridan & Mack, 5
Sharpley's Minstrels, 93
Sheldenberger's Circus, 186
Sheridan & Mack, 93
Sheridan, Mack & Day, 121
Sherwood, Charles, 48, 49
Showles, J. J., 168
Showles, Jacob A., 174
Siam (elephant), 66
Sickels, David B., 107, 119
Siegrist Brothers, 49
Siegrist, Francois, 48
Sig. Sautelle's Circus, 181
Simpson, 78
Sinn, William E., 114
Sivals, Charles, 55
Smith, Asa, 73
Smith, Avery, 12, 25, 85, 87, 104, 139,
  147, 159, 176
Smith, S. S., 116
Smith, Sol, 83
Sneden, 167
Snook, 167
Snow Brothers, 142
Snow, Ben, 142
Snyder's Hotel, 72
Southern Hotel, 95
Spalding, Dr. Gilbert R., 3, 7, 11, 13, 28,
  46, 88, 104, 116, 122, 147, 187-188
Spalding & Bidwell, 3, 168, 181
Spalding & Rogers, 3, 47, 86, 88, 122,
  131, 138, 147, 177, 186, 188
Spalding's North American Circus, 187,
  188
Spencer, Sandy, 25, 141
Springer, Andrew J., 28, 187
Springer, Rosston & Henderson, 186

www.ingramcontent.com/pod-product-compliance
Lightning Source LLC
LaVergne TN
LVHW011325080426
835513LV00006B/192